T0339542

Angels
without
Borders

Trends and Policies
Shaping Angel Investment Worldwide

Angels without Borders

Trends and Policies
Shaping Angel Investment Worldwide

Editors

John May
New Vantage Group, USA

Manhong Mannie Liu
Chinese Academy of Sciences, China

World Scientific

NEW JERSEY · LONDON · SINGAPORE · BEIJING · SHANGHAI · HONG KONG · TAIPEI · CHENNAI · TOKYO

Published by

World Scientific Publishing Co. Pte. Ltd.

5 Toh Tuck Link, Singapore 596224

USA office: 27 Warren Street, Suite 401-402, Hackensack, NJ 07601

UK office: 57 Shelton Street, Covent Garden, London WC2H 9HE

British Library Cataloguing-in-Publication Data
A catalogue record for this book is available from the British Library.

ANGELS WITHOUT BORDERS
Trends and Policies Shaping Angel Investment Worldwide

ISBN 978-981-4733-05-2
ISBN 978-981-4725-14-9 (pbk)

In-house Editor: Li Hongyan

Printed in Singapore

Dedicated to

KEAN SPENCER MAY–MOSES

TESLA ELISE MONTGOMERY

the true angels to their grandparents

Contents

Preface   *ix*

About Editors   *xi*

Angel Investing: Trends and Issues   **1**

1. Overview of Angel Investing Worldwide   3
   The Editors
2. Sources of Capital for Start-ups   7
   Bill Payne
3. Women Angel Investors   25
   Peggy Wallace and Rebecca Conti
4. Angel Impact Investing   33
   Wayne Silby and Jenna Nicholas
5. Crowdfunding and Angel Investing   43
   Charles Sidman

Angel Investing: Countries and Regions   **59**

6. Israel   61
   D. Todd Dollinger and Steve Rhodes
7. France   75
   Philippe Gluntz
8. South Africa   83
   Craig Mullett
9. Hong Kong   91
   Allen Yeung
10. United States   99
    Marianne Hudson
11. Germany   115
    Dr. Ute Gunther
12. Scotland   123
    Nelson Gray
13. China   139
    Wang Jiani and Chen Su

14. Turkey 151
    Baybars Altuntas
15. Italy 157
    Eng. Paolo Anselmo and Luigi Amati
16. Australia 163
    Jordan Green
17. Belgium 177
    Reginald Vossen and Claire Munck
18. Spain 187
    Juan Roure and Amparo De San Jose
19. United Arab Emirates 195
    Heather Henyon
20. United Kingdom 203
    Jenny Tooth
21. India 215
    Ashish Dave and Mohit Agarwal
22. Netherlands 225
    René A.G. Reijtenbagh
23. Singapore 233
    Poh-Kam Wong
24. Canada 243
    Ross Finlay and Blake Witkin
25. Portugal 249
    João Trigo Da Roza and Francisco Banha
26. New Zealand 255
    Franceska Banga and David Lewis
27. Russia 263
    Ivan Protopopov and Konstantin Fokin
28. Colombia 271
    Juan Pablo Rodriguez Neira
29. Austria 277
    Bernard Litzka
30. Finland 281
    Jan D. Oker-Blom
31. Switzerland 285
    Brigitte Baumann
32. Over the Horizon 293
    The Editors

Preface

On a hot summer day several years ago, John and Mannie were invited to give a talk at the University of Virginia on angel investing. Driving together on the beautiful, green Route 29 they started entertaining the idea of writing a book together on the business angel movement around the world.

After many email brainstorming sessions and telephone discussions with John in Washington, DC and Mannie in Beijing, they sharpened their focus on the role of investment policies and programs that supported angel investing. Angel investing is booming all over the world, but in very different ways from country to country, and sometimes from region to region within countries.

Angel investment is early–stage private investment that has high risks. Both venture capital and angel capital is investing in start–up companies. However, angels invest their own after–tax money, while venture capitalists are usually investing other people's money. In addition, compared with venture capitalists, policymakers should know that angel investors also have the following characteristics:

1. In terms of investment stage: angel investing is a bit earlier than the VCs.
2. In terms of investment amount: angel investments are a bit smaller than the VCs.
3. In terms of investment cost: angel investing takes a lower valuation than the VCs.
4. In terms of investment decisionmaking: angel investors are generally a bit faster than the VCs.
5. In terms of risk: angels take more risk than the VCs.

Angel investors whom we have met in our travels around the world, play an extremely important role in their country's entrepreneurial economy and innovation. Since angel investors invest in early stage and seed stage ventures, they usually face much higher risks. Angel investors are indispensable players in a country's start–up ecosystem. At the same time, angel investing by definition is a high–risk activity. Therefore, the angel investment ecosystem usually needs some support from the public sector. To encourage angel investment and other early stage investments, some governments have set up favorable policies to promote angel investments. One of the exceptional contributions of this book is that it allows readers to compare the policies of various nations.

Angels Without Borders has two parts. In Part One, experienced angel investors canvass their investment principles and practices, and they discuss trends shaping the angel investment movement, such as crowdfunding, impact investing and angel investing by and for women.

In Part Two, angel investment leaders and experts from 26 countries and regions—including both developed and developing economies—examine how policies and programs are supporting angel investing activities within their nations. These chapters are meant as field guides, the personal views of seasoned investors and experts. As such, they are not intended to be exhaustive catalogues of information. Rather, they are meant to note key actors and developments, and provide perspective. We have arranged them randomly according to regions to avoid, as much as possible, connotations of ranking or partiality on our behalf.

We hope this book will benefit angel investors, policymakers and, of course, entrepreneurs (without whom angels would not exist)! More importantly, the book will connect angels from countries all over the world with each other, so they will have an opportunity to share experiences and learn from each others' efforts to promote angel investing.

John May

Manhong Mannie Liu

ABOUT THE EDITORS

JOHN MAY is the Managing Partner of the New Vantage Group, which has organized five angel investing organizations in the Washington, D.C. area since 1999, placing funds into more than 75 companies. He is the co–author of two books on angel investing, *Every Business Needs an Angel* and *State of the Art: An Executive Briefing on Cutting-Edge Practices in American Angel Investing*. May is Chair–Emeritus of the Angel Capital Association and Co–chairman of the Global Business Angel Network. He is a lead instructor for the "Power of Angel Investing" seminar produced by the Angel Resource Institute and supported by the Ewing Marion Kauffman Foundation, a Batten Fellow at the Darden Graduate School of Business Administration at the University of Virginia and a Managing Director of Seraphim, a UK–based venture capital fund. May served on the board of directors of the Mid–Atlantic Venture Association, the trade association for the venture capital industry in the Mid-Atlantic region. May began his work in angel investing when he co–founded the Investors' Circle, a network of over 200 investors who use private capital to fund businesses that address social and environmental issues. May also co–founded The Dinner Club, an investment group of 60 Washington, D.C. angels who collectively invest in regional early stage ventures. *Washingtonian Magazine* named May one of its 100 Tech Titans of DC. At the Angel Capital Association Summit in San Francisco, CA on May 6, 2010, May was awarded the 2010 Hans Severiens Award for the contributions to the angel investing industry.

MANHONG MANNIE LIU is Chairman of National Venture Capital Research Committee at The Chinese Society for Management Modernization; Director, Venture Capital Research Group at the Chinese Academy of Sciences, Research Center on Fictitious Economy and Data Science (FEDS); Professor, Renmin University of China; Board Member, China Venture Capital Research Institute; Editor in Chief, *China Venture Capital Journal*; Vice Dean, Beijing EDUI Technology Research Institute; Founder and Honorary Chair of China Business Angels Association; Vice Chair, Ecological Development Union

International; Board member, World Business Angels Association; and Board Director, Chief Group Hong Kong. Professor Liu has several publications on angel investing, her book *Angel Investment and Private Capital*, (2003, in Chinese) is considered the first book in this field in China. Professor Liu received her Ph.D. from Cornell University in 1994, prior to her joining the faculty at Renmin University, she has also worked as research faculty at Harvard University. Her most recent publications include: "Angel Investment in China: Theory and Practice," (in Chinese) Feb. 2015; *Renewable Energy in China: Towards a Green Economy* (3 volumes), (Hardcover, English) Enrich Professional Publishing, Oct. 2013; *China Venture Capital: 20 years of History* (Chinese), China Development Publishing, Nov. 2011; *Green Economy and its Implementation in China* (English) Enrich Professional Publishing, Singapore, May 2011; *Venture Capital* (Chinese) University of International Business and Economics Press, May 2011; *New China Business Strategies: Chinese and American Companies As Global Partners* (Hardcover, English), co–authored with John Miligan-Whyte, Specialist Press International, Aug 2009; *Start-ups Financing Guidance: Angel Investment* (Chinese) Economic Management Publishing, Dec. 2009. Profesor Liu is considered one of the pioneers in China's venture capital research field. Her book *Venture Capital: Innovation and Finance* (in Chinese, Renmin University Press, 1998) was one of the books to introduce the concept of venture capital to China, and it served as a guide for many Chinese first–generation venture capitalists.

ASSOCIATE EDITORS

KRISTA TUOMI is a professor in the International Economic Policy program at the School of International Service, American University, Washington DC. Her recent research has focused on best practices in the start-up investment climate, particularly on policies related to angel investing and seed financing.

JOSEPH O'KEEFE is senior advisor to the president and CEO of the Overseas Private Investment Corporation, the development finance institution of the U.S. government. Previously, he was the head of corporate relations for the International Finance Corporation of the World Bank Group.

Part I

Angel Investing

Trends and Issues

Overview of
Angel Investing Worldwide

Angels Without Borders is a geographical narrative at heart. It covers angel investing activities in a diverse array of economies—small and large, developing and advanced, and those with high-tech and traditional sectors. Angel investing is not "going global"; it is there already. It simply has not garnered the recognition it deserves.

Angel investors are now crossing other boundaries—financial, economic, cultural, and technological—that are just as important as political boundaries. They are doing so rapidly, and with an enthusiasm and willingness to experiment. However, they are finding that, to successfully invest across borders, they need to understand better the economic policies, tax requirements (or incentives) and characteristics of other countries and regions.

Angels rarely operate within in a single sphere of investing. They must possess a knowledge of finance, management, market analysis, law, politics, and often science, technology and logistics. Many either have been entrepreneurs or have developed a deep understanding of entrepreneurship. Angels, by necessity, are connectors, people who envision how disparate elements of talent, technology and capital can be combined for success. In many cases, their contribution is a life-saver for start-ups passing through the "Valley of Death" stage.[1]

What is so conspicuously different now is that angels are no longer making such connections in an ad hoc way for their own accounts. They want to change what is sometimes called the "ecosystem" of risk capital into a much larger, more efficient and more systematic

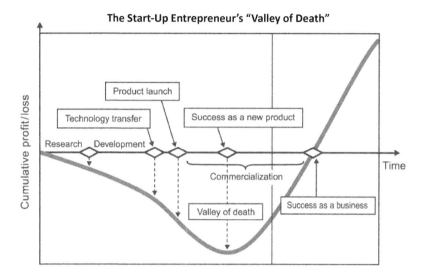

The Start-Up Entrepreneur's "Valley of Death"

approach, one that informs cultural attitudes about entrepreneurship, identifies promising talent and ideas as early as possible, and creates formal platforms (e.g., clubs, incubators, and accelerators) to make their activities more viable.

To do so, they have had to do more than network with each other, they have had to engage policymakers, politicians, economists, and bureaucrats as never before. Rather than merely assessing the diversity of their own portfolios and their multiples at exit, they have had to design and conduct original research into the profiles and investment strategies of peers. Ironically, even as they have been crossing others' borders, they have had to consider creating some of their own, such as minimum investment commitments for angel club membership or regulatory frameworks for crowdfunding.

Policymakers and the media are increasingly paying more attention to angel investors, but it is important to recall just how recently this attention has come and why. As of the early 2000s, for example, angel investors were providing as much as half the equity financing for start-ups in some countries, but were virtually invisible in research literature. Angel investors have always been more private than their counterparts, venture capitalists. In many cases, they might invest in small deals that were never publicly revealed. Dramatic differences in the evolution entrepreneurship across countries and regions also hindered public awareness and understanding. Similar types of investment activities were often put in different bureaucratic categories or given different names from place to place.

Several forces converged in recent years to bring angel investors to the forefront. The dot.com boom of the late 1990s followed by the bust of the mid-2000s created two cohorts of visionaries with an appetite for entrepreneurial risk: those who had succeeded beyond all expectations and suddenly had capital to invest in more ventures and up-and-comers; and those who had not been so fortunate but had ideas and had seen the angel investment process work well. Of critical importance was the fact that e-commerce ventures had succeeded not just in the United States but other advanced economies as well. The rapid adoption and almost frictionless growth of such ventures created jobs, captured imaginations, and enabled synergies across numerous sectors. Telephones, digital computer networks, and banks for example, had all existed in parallel sectors for decades. However, it was not until the internet and dot.com revolution that a small specialty e-store could sell goods to a buyer using a smartphone on the other side of the planet.

The global economic crisis that reverberated throughout advanced economies beginning around 2007 created other dynamics favorable to the rise of angel investing. In scores of nations, political parties and policymakers alike began to realize that job creation by legacy sectors and financing hrough traditional channels such as SME facilities, venture capital, private equity funds, and investment banks was no longer sufficient. Unemployment rates proved stubbornly high. The pace of start-ups, a key source of additional jobs, was too slow. And there were too few investors prepared to repeatedly back high-risk, early-stage start-ups. Angels came to be viewed as less of a novelty and more of a necessity. The result has been a profusion of public policy experiments with incentives, incubators, accelerators, strategic alliances with schools and industries, as well as public-private partnerships for due diligence and co-investment.

Through the early 2000s, angel investing was largely a domestic activity. Over the past decade, however, angel investors have started to think and act more globally in three respects. E-commerce, of course, necessitated more familiarity with foreign tax laws and commercial regulations than ever before. Second, a growing body of research began to reveal that some nations, e.g., Israel, Scotland, the United States, were consistently outperforming others in commercializing innovative ideas and providing capital to start-ups. Even if the degree of success enjoyed by Silicon Valley might never be replicated, ever more nations believed that moving their economies toward that model was a sound long-term strategy. Indeed, several authors later in the book discuss how their nations or regions have taken schemes or laws from other nations in whole cloth. Third, haltingly at first and then with more momentum, transnational initiatives such as the European Business Angels Network (founded in 1999) and the Business Angel Network of Southeast Asia (2001) began to coalesce to promote their activities, formalize cross-pollination of ideas and encourage deal flow.

As much as the first decade and a half of this century has proven exciting for angel investing, some of its most exciting prospects are ahead. Technological changes, such as crowdfunding platforms, are not only creating new opportunities for innovative ideas and start-ups, they are inculcating an entrepreneurial culture that is broader and less tied to sectors traditionally favored by angels. More profound is the growing awareness that the capital, tools, and networks of angel investors can be used for societal and environmental change under the banner of impact investing. The not-so-secret secret about angel investors is that a large proportion of them, perhaps most, invest for reasons that have little to do with big payoffs. By definition, angel investors already have wealth. The reward that they often seek is intangible: a mentor-mentee relationship, a chance to give back to their community, the satisfaction in seeing a friend or relative succeed, or the chance to participate in a cause larger than the success of a firm.

Enjoy this book. Rarely in the history of modern finance have so many factors converged to create a transformation that will empower so many people. That story is captured here.

Endnotes

[1] Osawa, Yoshitaka and Kumiko Miyazaki, "An Empirical Analysis of the Valley of Death," Asian Journal of Technology Innovation (2006).

Sources of Capital for Start-Ups

Bill Payne

Financing start-up ventures is only one piece of the entrepreneurial puzzle and surely not as important as the quality of the management team or perhaps other aspects of venture creation. However, raising money is critical to success for many of the high-growth new companies that fuel job and wealth creation around the world. Angel investing is one source of financing for entrepreneurs. But understanding the importance of angel capital requires an appreciation of the entire capital food chain for start-up ventures. These sources are covered below, essentially in the order that entrepreneurs seek certain types of capital, from idea stage to the stage of rapid revenue growth.

CAPITAL SOURCES FOR ENTREPRENEURS

In spite of what the press might lead us to believe, only a tiny fraction of entrepreneurs are funded by venture capitalists in a coffee shop based

---

BILL PAYNE is an angel investor, board member, and advisor to entrepreneurs. In 1971, he co-founded Solid State Dielectrics, Inc. and 12 years later sold the company to Du Pont. He has invested in more than 60 start-up companies and helped found four angel groups. He authored an eBook entitled, *The Definitive Guide to Raising Money from Angels*. From 1995 to 2007, he was Entrepreneur-in-Residence with the Ewing Marion Kauffman Foundation. In 2009, he was awarded the prestigious Hans Severiens Memorial Award for Outstanding Contribution to Angel Investing. He was also named New Zealand Arch Angel for 2010 by the Angel Association of New Zealand.

on a business plan written on a paper napkin. Most entrepreneurs fund start-ups with savings or wages from their employers (working in their free time) while tinkering with ideas about their new venture. They pivot often, trying one idea after another, molding the beginnings of a product plan. This idea stage may take a weekend or several years, but during this stage, the entrepreneur uses personal resources to fund the business. Entrepreneurs typically invest a few hundred to hundreds of thousands of dollars in their new enterprises.

FRIENDS, FAMILY (AND FOOLS?)

Seeking capital from friends and family ("FF" capital) generally starts early, as a business idea is evolving, and quite often after an entrepreneur has exhausted personal resources. Friends and family generally invest based on their assessment of the person, not necessarily after an exhaustive review of the product idea or business plan. FF capital is considered "dumb money," that is, the investment is capital only, and it contributes no business savvy to the new enterprise. FF capital can be a gift or loan to the entrepreneur or the company, or capital to purchase a small fraction of the ownership of the company. One popular form of lending from FF to entrepreneurs is convertible debt, i.e., debt that converts to equity when subsequent financing is secured from angel investors or venture capitalists. The conversion pricing may be structured with a discount to the price of the subsequent round to compensate for the additional risk assumed by the FF lender. For many entrepreneurs, self-funding or FF capital may be sufficient to fund the company to positive cash flow (company-generated cash from earnings produced by revenues of the product). As an example, many mobile applications have been brought to market by software developers, generating millions of dollars in revenues and earnings with very little investment. Perhaps the developer writes code in free time while working at an unrelated job. In fact, very few entrepreneurs need or are qualified to seek capital from some of the other sources discussed below. Friends and family invest a few dollars to a few tens of thousands of dollars in new companies.

GOVERNMENT SOURCES OF CAPITAL

Entrepreneurs often benefit from local, regional and national government funding sources. These may be research grants, development contracts or economic development resources. While these may purchase a product or technology, they are often low-interest loans or even grants to start-up entrepreneurs. Government grants are available in some regions to fund the commercialization costs of product development and sometimes construction of production facilities. However, seldom do government resources exceed $500,000 per start-up.

CROWDFUNDING

Historically, entrepreneurs starting or operating private companies in developed countries were restricted to raising capital from sophisticated or accredited (wealthy) investors. More recently, however, some jurisdictions have authorized them to raise money from smaller investors, often through websites. Crowdfunding is now legal in some countries. Further, regulations vary significantly by region. Where legal, crowdfunding is typically used by entrepreneurs at the very earliest stage of company development. Some consider crowd equity funding to be blurring the distinction between friends and family investors and angel investors. It is expected that the round size for crowd equity sources, where legal, will range from a few thousand to $1 million, with very few above $1 million.

ANGEL INVESTMENT

Unlike venture capitalists, angels invest their personal assets in start-up ventures. Angel investment is considered an "active" asset class, meaning that investors take a role in growing the company, serving as directors, mentors and advisors to the start-up entrepreneur. Angels seldom, however, become employees in the start-up. Prior to funding, most angels require some customer validation of the start-up's products, preferably by purchasing products or perhaps testing of prototypes. Entrepreneurs should not seek angel capital until their company's product is ready for sale. Ninety percent of angel investments per round per company range from $100,000 to $1 million.

VENTURE CAPITAL

Venture capitalists (VCs) raise money from large institutional investors (such as university endowments) and then invest those funds in start-up companies. While some VCs invest at the same early stage as angels, most VCs invest in later stage companies, that is, companies with revenues and perhaps even profits. VCs also expect to take an active role in the governance of portfolio companies (usually as directors) and can provide useful introductions to customers, partners and subsequent investors in start-up ventures. The range of investment size for VCs is quite large, from $100,000 to $100 million or more.

SUPER ANGELS

Super angels are typically wealthy entrepreneurs who have exited companies and seek to invest in start-ups. Each often has a large "rolodex" of contacts among investors, potential customers and partners. Many aim to invest in a large number of start-ups to reduce the risk of the asset class. It is not uncommon for super angels to raise a small VC fund, sometimes called mini-funds: smaller, nimble that can make decisions rapidly. Super angels often invest in the same size of rounds and in companies at the same stage of development as do angels.

BANKS

Banks typically expect borrowers to provide collateral and a healthy income stream (or both) to assure loan repayment. Collateral is an asset that can provide security for a loan. Banks are generally not risk-takers, and their interest rates are far below the returns expected by start-up investors. Consequently, banks are seldom "investors" in early stage companies. Once a company is established and has a track record of generating cash flow, banks are often a source of working capital and equipment loans for these more mature companies.

PUBLIC CAPITAL

Mature start-ups must go through a rigid and rigorous approval process to sell shares through an initial public offering. Their shares can then be bought and sold on public markets, such as those in New York, London and other major cities. "Going public" enables such companies to raise large amounts of capital for rapid growth.

TWO WORLDS: SILICON VALLEY AND EVERYWHERE ELSE

Most of the information available to entrepreneurs on raising capital is generated by the media in Silicon Valley. Unfortunately, neither the press nor start-up entrepreneurs realize that Silicon Valley is a unique environment, with practices that may or may not be used other places. Consider a few examples:

- The valuation of start-ups is generally higher in the competitive environment of Silicon Valley than elsewhere. Consequently, for a given investment, investors in Silicon Valley purchase a smaller fraction of start-ups than do investors elsewhere.
- It is common for Silicon Valley investors to fund start-up ventures with convertible debt (loans that later convert into equity ownership), while many investors elsewhere insist on purchasing equity from the outset.
- Deal terms often differ. For example, "redemption rights," enabling investors to insist on repayment at a later date, are not common in Silicon Valley but are often used elsewhere.

It is important for entrepreneurs, investors and others in the start-up ecosystem to understand that local practice dictates the terms and conditions of start-up investment. Basing investment expectations on activities in Silicon Valley as documented in the media is often inappropriate. Often, deal terms in Auckland, Edinburgh and San Diego are more similar to one another than to those in Silicon Valley.

ANGEL INVESTORS

Who are these angels? Wealthy business persons have been providing start-up capital for entrepreneurs for millennia. The term "angel investor" is analogous to Broadway angels, who historically funded new theatrical productions. "Angel investor" was first coined by Professor Bill Wetzel at the University of New Hampshire in 1978. Angels are typically experienced business persons, often entrepreneurs who have exited their own companies or retired corporate executives. Angels are active mentors, directors and advisors, but seldom full-time employees. Angels tend to invest in start-ups operating in business sectors familiar to them. Most angels invest locally, within an hour's drive of their residences. Evaluating local deals before investment and then engaging with local portfolio companies after funding is better suited to the lifestyle of these part-time investors.

Angel investing in start-up companies has been limited to accredited or sophisticated investors in many jurisdictions. While the definitions of eligible investors vary somewhat from country to country, investing in private companies without restricted disclosure generally requires investors to have substantial net worth (>US$1 million or more) or significant income ($200,000 per annum, or more) and often require a significant amount of business and investing experience. The assumption made by regulators is that to be eligible to invest in private companies, angels must have enough business and investing experience to evaluate a deal and sufficient resources to be unaffected financially if their investment is lost.

Historically, most angels acted independently. Angel groups began to emerge in most regions of the world after 2000, giving investors the option of joining a local group and investing alongside other angels. Angels choose to join groups for several reasons: to see more deals; to evaluate deals with other investors with sector expertise; to learn from peers with more experience; to find additional investors for larger rounds of investment; and to invest with others under identical and attractive deal terms. While only a small fraction of all angels have chosen to join groups, the number of groups in the US has grown from less than 10 in the early 1990s to about 400. Angel group formation in Europe has grown at a similar rate.

There are several models for angel groups, but none seem to be dominating the marketplace. Angel networks are groups of wealthy investors who join forces to manage deal flow and process deals together and then individually invest, small or larger amounts of cash, depending on their interest and means. Seldom do all members of a network invest in a deal. Members of angel funds pool capital in advance and then screen and scrub deals together. When due diligence indicates a deal is probably fundable, the deal is presented to the fund membership for a majority (or super majority) vote on investment. In general, all investment by members of angel networks and angel funds is defined by a single term sheet (abbreviated deal description). The operations of these angel groups are funded through dues charged to members, sponsorships by professional organizations, and fees to entrepreneurs. Management of groups can be by hired or supplied by the members themselves, often as volunteers.

Many business angel networks (BANS) in Europe operate a bit differently than those elsewhere. Deal flow managers (for-profit or not-for-profit organizations) screen deals and coach entrepreneurs, and then invite local angels to attend pitching sessions. Entrepreneurs and investors may be charged fees. Once entrepreneurs make their presentation, entrepreneurs and investors work independently of the deal flow manager to close a deal. Angels conduct due diligence in small groups and make investment offers to entrepreneurs. In many cases, there is little or no coordination among investors on deals.

RETURNS TO ANGELS IN GROUPS

Prior to 2007, pundits speculated that angels should expect annualized returns of 20 to 25 percent on a large portfolio but that returns were skewed because about half of angel-funded companies went out of business with no return to investors. Little reliable data was available. In November 2007, Wiltbank and Boeker published a study of returns to angel investors in groups, reporting 1,137 exits from 539 angels made over the previous decade.[1] The study found:

- Angels enjoyed an internal rate of return of about 27 percent per annum, 2.6 times their invested capital.
- However, as anticipated earlier, 52 percent of funded companies failed to return invested capital.
- Seven percent of companies yielded a 10x return or more, representing 75 percent of the total return on invested capital.
- The average time to exit was 3.5 years, but this was a misleading statistic. Early exits almost were failures, with very high-multiple exits generally achieved only after 5 years or more.

Returns to angels were shown to be commensurate with risk. That is, investment in very high-risk, seed and start-up stage companies will likely result in returns greater than 20 percent per year. However, the skewed distribution of returns suggests a strategy of smaller investments in a larger number of companies, perhaps 25 companies or more over the lifetime of the investor, to increase the likelihood of enjoying returns of 20 percent per annum or more. A portfolio strategy of investing smaller amounts in a larger number of companies is a critical success factor for angels. A Monte Carlo scenario of the data from the Wiltbank study revealed the following:

Investments	Anticipated Return
6	50 percent chance of return of capital
12	75 percent confidence level of 2.6x return
48	95 percent confidence level of 2.6x return

Angels who make only six investments over their lifetimes, have only a 50-50 chance of eventually getting their capital returned, while making 12 investments improves the odds to 75 percent that angels will see the returns of the Wiltbank study (2.6x invested capital). The Wiltbank and Boeker study also provides insights into how angels manage deal flow and engage with funded companies. Better practices in due diligence, co-investment and interactions with portfolio companies after investment inform both the returns data and conclusions of this study.

What about the returns on time invested in portfolio companies? Angels spend significant time evaluating investments before funding and then considerably more time mentoring and advising entrepreneurs and monitoring investments after closing deals. They are motivated for various reasons: giving back to the community; following the example their mentors; helping with local economic development; or a desire to continue using their business skills. Working with entrepreneurs is altruistic—angel investors do not expect a return on invested time.

THE ANGEL INVESTING PROCESS

Locating entrepreneurs with fundable companies can be a challenge for solo angels. Networking with other angels and professional service providers, while difficult and time-consuming, can provide referenced deals. Entrepreneurship centers and university technology transfer offices can also source deals to angels. Generally, solo angels carefully build a reputation within their communities. As a result, deals then find those angels. Solo angels, similar to most wealthy people, operate quietly, out of the public view. Most solo angels prefer anonymity while they sustain a modest, quality deal flow.

Most angel groups invite entrepreneurs to apply for funding via websites, encouraging deal flow while individual members maintain their privacy. Angel group websites provide the criteria of the deals that members seek and the process that entrepreneurs must use to achieve funding. Most angel groups make it easy for local entrepreneurs to find them. They expect entrepreneurs to apply for funding or at least provide an executive summary of their plans through the group website. Upon completion of the application by entrepreneurs, the website converts this questionnaire into a standardized one-page executive summary for an initial pre-screening by the group. Members or staff review the application to confirm that the applicant meets the criteria for investment of the group. Applicants who meet the criteria and elicit interest among the group are then invited to present their proposals to the group, or a subset of the group, along with staff. Several entrepreneurs might be invited to give a presentation to a screening meeting—typically 15-minutes in length with a Powerpoint presentation, followed by a question-and-answer session. Members who are interested can then initiate the due diligence process.

Due diligence is a detailed, thorough process of confirming the soundness of a proposal according to numerous factors that could affect investment performance. Assessing customer validation, for example, is a critical component. Investors want confirmation that customers or potential customers are interested in purchasing the product. Background checks of the legal records of the entrepreneur, management team and sometimes advisors and co-investors, are conducted. Competing products are evaluated. Angel investors confirm that the entrepreneurs have a solid hold on the intellectual property owned by the company or used in its products. Sales channels and business partnerships are gauged. All aspects of the business are evaluated to verify the investment quality of the applicant. Most angel groups designate a team of four to six members, sometimes including staff, to conduct due diligence for the group and report regularly to members who are interested in a deal. The team can expect to spend 50-100 hours collectively in validating an investment prospect. Since these angels are part-time investors, entrepreneurs should expect this due diligence process to require one to two months.

A term sheet is negotiated at the outset of due diligence. Term sheets are abbreviated investment terms covering all aspects of the funding agreements, such as the amount of capital to be raised, the percentage of ownership to be acquired by the investors, the rights reserved for investors and anticipated closing date. Term sheets are generally two to six pages in length. Company or investor-selected attorneys then create much more detailed, definitive agreements necessary to close the funding round. These documents are normally at least 50 pages.

Once a term sheet has been negotiated, the due diligence team has completed its activities and an investment presentation is often scheduled for the entire angel group. It is common for both the entrepreneur and the lead member of the due diligence team to make presentations on the opportunity. Members who missed the initial screening meeting may be getting their first exposure to the company. Also, the due diligence team may have made suggestions to the entrepreneur that resulted in a significant revision of the business plan. As a result, the investment meeting can provide all members of the angel group with a fresh look at the investment proposal.

If the pitch is successful, the entrepreneur and angel group may sign the documents necessary to commit funding for the company. In many cases, however, the amount of funding raised from a single angel group may be less than the amouont required to achieve the desired milestones. If so, the lead investor from the local angel group often will introduce the entrepreneur to leaders of neighboring angel organizations in an effort to raise additional funds through syndication.

MORE THAN MONEY, ANGELS INVEST TIME

While less publicized than the angel investing process, the engagement by angels with portfolio companies after funding is perhaps the most important value angel investors bring to their funded entrepreneurs. Typically, this engagement involves two overlapping roles: mentor and director. Entrepreneurs can benefit from one or perhaps two of the investors engaging with the company in mentoring or director roles. The selection of this investor or investors from among the 10 to 25 investors in the company is based on an agreement between the investors and the entrepreneur, and is often detailed in the term sheet.

Mentors work directly with entrepreneur and/or team members to help grow the company. Rather than advising or directing the entrepreneur, the mentor typically uses the Socratic method of posing key questions that will provide the entrepreneur with a number of reasonable growth scenarios to consider, based on the mentor's direct experience. The development of a long-term personal relationship between the mentor/ investor and the entrepreneur can be a very rewarding experience for both. Investors often require, via the term sheet, a seat on the board of directors. While directors can mentor the entrepreneurs and the management team, they also have other roles and responsibilities. Directors have the fiduciary responsibility to represent the company and all its shareholders. Boards of directors are usually very supportive of the entrepreneur. There are, however, times when the best interest of the entrepreneur may differ from those of the company and shareholders. The investor-director is often responsible for making sure the company is providing investors with adequate updates on progress. Directors can be very useful in connecting the company with major customers and partners, helping to complete subsequent funding rounds, building a quality management team and helping the company prepare to execute a successful exit for investors.

ASSOCIATIONS OF ANGEL GROUPS

In the late 1990s, organizations of angel groups began to form, first at the national level and later within smaller regions and among countries sharing common interests. These associations aimed to provide a forum for angel leaders to network, share best practices, educate members on the angel investing process and provide information to the public sector on angel investing. The European Business Angel Network (EBAN), followed soon thereafter by the Angel Capital Association (ACA) in the United States, are two such highly influential organizations. Each represents 200 or more angel groups and as many as 10,000 investors. Large national and international organizations have subsequently been organized elsewhere around the world.

Formal meetings of regional, national and international organizations of angel group leaders provide an ideal opportunity to leaders of new organizations to learn the practices and operations of more mature groups, and they enable new groups to move more rapidly up the learning curve. These meetings regularly offer formal education and training for newer angels on processing deals, term sheets and the post-investment relationship between investors and entrepreneurs.

While networking, education and sharing best practices have proven fruitful and rewarding outcomes for these organizations, two additional benefits have emerged: deal syndication, and public policy advocacy. The syndication of individual deals among multiple angel groups to raise larger rounds of funding requires a willingness to share due diligence and invest using a single term sheet. Critical to the success of this shared interest is familiarity and trust among angel leaders in different organizations. Larger organizations of angel groups have facilitated the networking necessary to build trust as well as the sharing of better practices of syndication. The influence of these larger angel organizations on public policy has also grown. Angel investors are now widely recognized as critical sources of capital to start-ups that create a significant proportion of new jobs. Thus, expanding angel investment at the local, regional, national and international level has become a common goal for many in the public sector. Providing these public agencies with information necessary to make informed decisions on tax policies, grant-making and programs to encourage entrepreneurs and investors has become an important role of these angel organizations over the past decade.

National, regional and international organizations of angel groups have varying levels of importance. Clearly, for island nations, such as Australia, New Zealand and Japan, a strong national organization can have significant local influence. Just as clearly, the importance of the European Union dictates that an organization of national angel organizations from multiple countries (EBAN) is necessary to address economic development and angel issues in the EU.

The need to syndicate deals among multiple groups has spawned informal regional organizations of angel groups. In several areas of the United States (the Northeast; the Northwest; the Southwest; and states such as Ohio, Texas and Wisconsin), angel groups participate in regular teleconferences and organized meetings to discuss syndicating deals requiring larger amounts of capital. Angel groups across New Zealand routinely compare investment opportunities, share due diligence and then co-invest in a majority of the deals funded there.

Cross-border angel investment is still localized. Angels in Seattle, for example, commonly invest in Canadian deals in and around

Vancouver, and vice versa. But most such investments are due to the proximity of the deals to the investors and not the attractiveness of the investment climate in another jurisdiction. Indeed, differences in tax laws and other regulations often discourage or preclude cross-border investing by angels. Most investment by angels in foreign companies is, in fact, regional and often facilitated by regional organizations of angel groups.

Broad participation in a worldwide organization of angels groups has not yet occurred. However, the need for larger and larger angel rounds and the interest of some angels in funding companies in very narrow business sectors may eventually foster such participation. Some angels enjoy investing in far-off companies and others scour the world for interesting companies in their particular sector. But they currently represent a tiny fraction of angel deals. A "united nations" of angel organizations may arise, but broad interest in such an organization has not yet surfaced.

TRENDS: ONLINE ANGEL GROUPS

The rapid expansion of internet access has fostered the creation of online angel groups, such as AngelList and Gust.com. Solo angels and qualified organizations of investors (including angels) sign up as members, often after some screening to qualify them. Entrepreneurs are encouraged to submit abbreviated business plans along with video pitches, PowerPoint presentations and other supplemental materials to a website. Investors are then provided access to the proposals and the dance begins. In some instances, entrepreneurs are provided direct access to investors who have previously shown interest in the region or sector. Angels can usually find other investors interested in the same deal and cooperate on due diligence and investment terms. In 2013, AngelList began inviting active and/or celebrity angels to syndicate deals, i.e., indicate an interest in leading deals and actively encouraging members of AngelList to invest alongside them. More recently, AngelList and other crowdfunding platforms have encouraged co-investment with angel groups, especially those local to a deal. While the ultimate impact of online groups is still unclear, they already represent an important new source of capital for entrepreneurs. Their success could have a significant impact on angel investing.

TRENDS: SIDECAR FUNDS FOR ANGEL NETWORKS

Angel networks—groups screening and scrubbing deals together with members making individual investment decisions—have found that organizing angel funds to invest alongside the network can bring important benefits to investors and entrepreneurs. Network members are encouraged to invest in the fund. In some cases, the fund invests only in deals also funded by the network; in other cases, the fund managers have the flexibility to investor more broadly.

Sidecar funds have several benefits. Working alongside a network, they can help raise more money for deals requiring a substantial amount of funding. They invest in a greater number of deals than do most members of networks, which enables fund members to rather quickly assemble a more diversified portfolio than they could operating solo. They can engage wealthy investors that might not have the time to contribute to angel networks. And qualified service providers (attorneys, accountants, bankers, etc.), who may feel a conflict of interest in joining angel networks, may feel much less inhibited to invest in sidecar funds. In a similar manner, angel funds encourage members to invest alongside the fund in deals that are particularly attractive to the members. This offers members the option of increasing their commitment to attractive deals while increasing the investment leverage of the angel funds.

AN EMPHASIS ON EXITS

Angel investment is an asset class, that is, investors expect to harvest their investment in a portfolio of companies over a reasonable period of time, earning a significant return at exit, perhaps as much as 25 percent per annum, as noted in the study above. These exits are a critical component, without which investors will, at some point, simply decline additional investment in entrepreneurs. About half of angel investments do not return their capital, resulting in a shut-down of the company. Successful investments are usually harvested via the acquisition of the funded company by a larger public company for cash or perhaps for stock in the acquiring public company. There are additional means of harvest, such as an initial public offering, a buy-back of shares by the entrepreneur or company, etc., but a merger or acquisition is by far the most common and attractive exit for angels today.

New angels groups focus their energy on managing deal flow and making investments. In the past, angels found that later-stage investors (venture capitalists or strategic corporate investors) often took the lead in facilitating an exit. However, in recent years, angels have found that the length of time to exit is simply too long if venture capitalists or other investors drive the exit, and that delay negatively affects returns. Many angel groups now find themselves with large portfolios of funded companies with very few exit options. As a result, members are spending energy and funds keeping companies from going out of business rather than seeking new portfolio companies. In some cases, this has caused attrition in membership or a reluctance of newcomers to join. Consequently, many angel groups have become much more proactive in working with the board of directors of portfolio companies to facilitate exits. This process generally involves creating alignment among stakeholders, preparing the company for exit, identifying potential buyers and executing a sale of the company. In the early years, the groups focused on processing deal flow.

VC TRENDS AND THEIR IMPACT ON ANGEL INVESTORS

Since the internet invesment bubble burst in 2000, traditional VC funds have increased in size—raising more money and consequently increasing the typical size of each investments. Large investments are usually made in later stage companies. The number of seed and start-up investments is currently increasing, but the percentage of VC investment in early stage investments is smaller than in the late 1990s. For many reasons, the returns of VC funds have decreased and their institutional investors have been reluctant to invest in new funds. Consequently, the number of VC firms has decreased. During this period, the volume of angel investment has grown and stabilized at about $20 billion per year in the US and at relatively high numbers elsewhere in the world.

Angels have found it more difficult to find follow-on VC financing for attractive deals than in the past. Consequently, angels all over the world have been forced to increase their fractions of invested capital in portfolio companies by leading follow-on investment rounds. Many angels have chosen to look for companies that can grow to a sustainable stage and then exit with less capital, without the need for

VC financing. Conversely, if a deal clearly requires significant capital to achieve positive cash flow, angels are reluctant to invest without first identifying possible follow-on investors. Angels now look for deals with the stated objective of an "early exit" within the first five years after funding and without raising huge amounts of money. The impact of this change in perspective by sophisticated angels has been a reluctance to invest in capital-intensive deals, such as clean energy and biotech companies. The public, including angels, sees the benefits that clean energy and biotechnology can bring to our society, but angels do not have a reasonable expectation of returns on investment with timely exits from such deals.

THE POTENTIAL IMPACTS OF CROWD EQUITY FUNDING

As of the writing of this book, the impact of legal crowd equity financing on angel and VC investing is unknown. However, some tentative observations and key questions are identifiable:

- Will US regulators make the prospects of crowd equity funding simply unappealing through a combination of limits on investments and onerous regulations?
- Once legalized in the US, will crowd equity funding prompt many smaller investors to enter this asset class and constitute a major source of capital for start-up ventures?
- The range in the size of rounds of most crowdfunding is likely to be a few hundred dollars to perhaps as much as $1 million. If so, crowd equity financing will compete with friends and family, angel investors and super angels, but not with VC investments. It is conceivable that angel investing might be the area of the ecosystem most impacted by crowdfunding.

Many angel investors and VCs might be hesitant to invest in companies that have previously raised crowd equity funding. Neither class of professional investors (angels or VCs) prefers to invest with a large number of less sophisticated investors. The investment expectations of crowdsources will be varied and unknown. Will litigation result from failed crowdsourced investments? Can crowdsources impede the direction that subsequent investors aspire to take funded companies? Many companies might raise crowdfunding and not need additional capital to become self-sustaining with internally generated cash flow. Will they grow or become smaller (lifestyle) businesses? If they rely only on crowdfunding will they be able to provide exits for crowd investors? Is crowd equity financing a fad? Will crowd investors, after a decade or more, simply stop if their returns are poor or nonexistent?

ACCELERATORS AND INCUBATORS: ARE THEY WORKING?

Business incubators have been assisting entrepreneurs with some degree of effectiveness for decades. Incubators usually offer start-up entrepreneurs office space at reduced rent, office services, professional services, advisory services and the advantages of starting and growing a start-up surrounded by peers. Business incubators seldom offer start-up capital to founders, but may exchange rent and services for a small share of ownership. Many incubators have adopted a policy that requires tenants to exit the incubation facilities within two to three years. Successful start-ups graduate and move into conventional real estate offices and factories. While many incubator graduates are successful in raising angel capital, these companies do not represent a large fraction of total angel funded companies.

More recently, business accelerators have emerged as important sources of support for start-up entrepreneurs. Accelerators provide short-term support for start-ups, often as little as three months in duration. While accelerators provide business and office services, their primary focus is mentoring, e.g., introducing start-up companies to experienced entrepreneurs who can help guide them. Many accelerators also offer entrepreneurs some start-up capital, usually ranging from a few thousand dollars to as much as $100,000. An important feature of most accelerators is "demo day," a graduation ceremony in which accelerator start-ups pitch investors for funding. Many angels investors see these occasions as a good opportunity to meet exciting start-ups. However, accelerators also represent a small fraction of angel deal flow.

SECONDARY MARKETS

In recent years, secondary markets for the purchase and sale of equity securities of small private companies have emerged. On the surface, these markets sound like interesting opportunities for friends and family, angels and VCs to sell their stakes to other private investors and enjoy some profits from their time and money. Secondary markets have become important exit routes for investors in some well-known Silicon Valley start-ups. Unfortunately, it is very difficult to create a market for small, unknown start-up companies of the type typically funded by angels in the rest of the world. Consequently, secondary markets have limited relevance for most start-up investors.

Endnotes

[1] Wiltbank, Robert and Boeker, Warren. "Returns to Angel Investors in Groups" (November 1, 2007).

Women Angel Investors

Peggy Wallace and Rebecca Conti

GOLDEN SEEDS EMPOWERING WOMEN

The Ewing Marion Kauffman Foundation cites the shortage of women angels and entrepreneurs as a "missed opportunity for women, for the entrepreneurial community and for US competitiveness as a whole."[1] According to the Center for Venture Research (CVR), in 2004 there were only 11,250 female angel investors in the United States, five percent of the total.[2] Only 3.2 percent of ventures that received angel capital were women-led.[3] As evident in the chart below that summarizes research from the CVR, today one out of every five angel investors in the US is female and one out of every five angel-funded companies are women-led. Golden Seeds has played a role in creating an environment where women have the knowledge, skills and access to deals needed to be angel investors. The rise of female angels, in turn, has played a significant role in the growth in funding of female entrepreneurs.

Golden Seeds founder Stephanie Newby had noticed the obvious absence of female peers in her corporate career on Wall Street. She believed that the quickest way for women to reach leadership positions

---

PEGGY WALLACE is the Managing Partner and Portfolio Manager of the Golden Seeds Fund LP, which has invested more than $70 million in 65 women-led comanies since 2005. REBECCA CONTI is a Senior Analyst of Mergers and Aquistions at Covanta Energy. Previously, she was a Golden Seeds analyst.

was to invest in start-ups led by women. Newby created a template and vision for Golden Seeds in the mid-1990s that came to fruition with the market launch of Golden Seeds in 2005. The group is headquartered in New York City with active chapters today in New York, Boston, Silicon Valley and Texas. Golden Seeds has become a leading force in focusing on women's leadership, gender diversity, entrepreneurship and job creation. It aims to create an environment in which:

- women-led companies are seriously considered for venture funding;
- gender diversity in management, widely known to produce better financial results, is enabled;
- women are active investors in start-ups;
- women entrepreneurs and investors have the opportunity to create wealth for themselves and others; and,
- the economy benefits in many ways from these vibrant activities.

Newby left Wall Street in the late 1990s and, after taking some time with her family, volunteered at a venture fund where she learned the fundamentals of venture capital investing. There, she discovered the angel market and subsequently joined the New York Angels. Newby began attending events up and down the Eastern seaboard to identify potential women entrepreneurs and investors. She worked with groups promoting women's entrepreneurial development such as Springboard, and quickly determined that women entrepreneurs needed to have more women investors who could relate to them as business leaders. That was when she focused on establishing Golden Seeds as an angel group consisting of male and female investors backing women-led companies. She quickly enlisted a number of female leaders whom she had worked with or known on Wall Street, and who readily recognized the importance of this initiative. At the time, there were no investment groups dedicated to investing in companies with women in the C-suite.

From the outset, Golden Seeds was established to welcome male investors and about 20 percent of Golden Seeds' current members are men. The ultimate goal of Golden Seeds is to invest in gender diversity. The organization does skew more female, as the number of women investors outside of the organization is still so unbalanced. Golden Seeds also took a stance on the definition of women-led companies that has proven to be prescient. It has always defined women-led companies as companies with a woman in a C-level position, preferably CEO. But if the woman is a co-founder, other C-level positions are considered. Golden Seeds confirms that at least one woman has power and influence in the company and that she holds significant equity. Golden Seeds realized that many companies have female co-founders and therefore looks at the relative equity positon held by the female

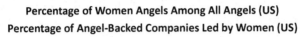

Percentage of Women Angels Among All Angels (US)
Percentage of Angel-Backed Companies Led by Women (US)

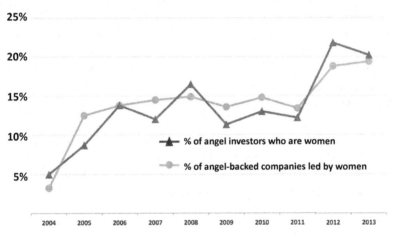

co-founder. Does she have the same equity or more than the male founders? Golden Seeds seeks to help women entrepreneurs create wealth through the businesses they build. There are many programs in the United States that focus on "women-owned" companies and require women to own 51 percent of the equity of their business. These programs tend to support the creation of service and supply companies that often fund their companies internally or through debt. Golden Seeds focuses on high-growth enterprises that are attractive to angels and venture capitalists, where investment via equity is needed for many years before such enterprises become creditworthy.

Golden Seeds was created with a strong foundation of processes, which has been a hallmark of its progress and success. Because there were not many female angels to recruit in its earliest days, Golden Seeds created a core curriculum to educate individuals on how to invest in and look for sound, differentiated business models with the potential for high returns. The venture capital industry was then 98 percent male (and still is about 96 percent male[4]) so there were not many opportunities to engage female venture capitalists. Golden Seeds actively sought accredited women and men who had succeeded and prospered at the highest levels of corporations, law, medicine, and academia to become members and invest in early stage start-ups. Members were largely found through referral networks that continue to expand with each new member who joins.

Golden Seeds also developed a curriculum to educate members to effectively serve as board members and advisors to investee companies. Today, Golden Seeds holds about 35 board seats within its organization. Angel investing is a high-risk asset class, and Golden Seeds has always been careful to encourage investors to be educated on the asset class and understand the need for diversified portfolios. Over the years, the curriculum has grown to four course modules and is now widely used throughout the industry to teach organizations and individuals the fundamentals of angel investing. The courses have also proven to be a highly effective way for new members to meet other members and develop their own networks within the Golden Seeds' community.

When Golden Seeds was started, most angel groups tended to invest locally and in technology businesses, with some groups focused on the life sciences. Golden Seeds' niche was women entrepreneurs, so it began receiving funding requests from all over the United States very early on. The Boston Chapter was formed early in Golden Seeds' history because New England was a region where women angels had been early market participants. The nationwide focus of Golden Seeds set it apart from other angel groups and attracted many investors who wanted to see wider geographic deal flow. Golden Seeds observed the types of companies that women were presenting and saw a concentration in the technology, life sciences and consumer sectors. It actively sought members with backgrounds in these three areas to create the expertise to evaluate these investments. Golden Seeds was one of very few angel groups that built a focus on life sciences and is now one of the largest life science angel groups in the United States. Golden Seeds' sector and geographic diversity have been differentiating factors that have also proven attractive to many potential investors.

In order to bring more capital to women-led companies, Golden Seeds raised two funds. The first was a small sidecar fund raised in 2008. In 2012, the firm raised an investment committee fund with eight fund partners, six of whom are females. While the percentage of female angel investors is growing, the percentage of female venture capital decisionmakers is practically flat. In fact, of venture capital fund managers at funds with over $200 million nationwide, only 4 percent are female.[5] Thus, Golden Seeds now operates a hybrid model of angel group and funds which it sees as critical to what remains a fairly capital-starved sector. The inclusion of funds in the Golden Seeds model has allowed more capital to be invested during each round and reduce the time entrepreneurs are on the road fundraising. Golden Seeds has always syndicated widely with angel groups across the US, as well as with an ever increasing number of venture funds.

Today, there are several groups that have contributed to the positive trends of investment in female entrepreneurs. A few notables include Astia Angels, 37 Angels, Belle Capital USA, Pipeline Fellowship, and Springboard Enterprises, among others. These groups are not investing time and money in women-led companies simply to create equality. They are doing so because it has been extensively proven that gender diversity among management produces greater returns. According to a study done by Emory University, female-run early stage companies are 15 percent more likely to be profitable than male-run businesses, even though they are 40 percent less likely to be funded.[6] Research by Dow Jones supports these findings. Companies have a greater chance of going public, operating profitably or being sold for more money than they have raised when they have female founders, board members, C-level execs or VPs.[7] McKinsey & Company echoes this concept in their study "Women Matter: Gender Diversity, a Corporate Performance Driver" which found that companies with gender-diverse leadership teams have a 10 percent higher average return on equity, 48 percent increased average EBIT, and 1.7x higher stock price growth between 2005 and 2007.[8] The gender diversity case for investment is further substantiated in a 2014 study conducted by Catalyst, which examined Fortune 500 companies with at least three female directors. Such companies saw a 66 percent average increase in return on invested capital, a 42 percent average increase in sales, and a 53 percent average increase in return on equity.[9] Golden Seeds embraced the data available in 2004, and each year more data emerges supporting the investment thesis.

In 2005, Golden Seeds received only 53 qualified applicants for funding and ended the year with 12 members and two investments. This number steadily grew, and in 2013 the group received 340 qualified applicants. Now numbering over 300 members, the nationwide group has received over 2,000 applicants and as of July 2014 had invested $69 million in 62 companies. Almost 10 years from its inception, over two times more women-led companies are seeking angel capital than when Golden Seeds was founded. Golden Seeds members bring far-reaching experience, skills, networks, stature and capital to propel the economy through Golden Seeds investments. They actively participate in screening companies, conducting due diligence and mentoring entrepreneurs.

There is clear evidence that gender diversity leads to greater success. Golden Seeds continues to develop initiatives to promote diverse investing and management teams. Golden Seeds holds monthly office hours in each of its four regions. Through these sessions, Golden Seeds members have provided advice to hundreds of female entrepreneurs throughout the country. Furthermore, Golden Seeds has made it easier for other female angel investors to formalize their activities into groups by providing on-going consulting advice and basic legal and process documents. These initiatives have led to the first Golden Seeds "empowered" angel groups being founded in Australia, Scale Ventures. Golden Seeds is hopeful that initiatives developed by Golden Seeds and peer groups will continue to shape the market into a gender diverse place.

Endnotes

[1] "Women and Angel Investing: An Untapped Pool of Equity for Entrepreneurs," Ewing Marion Kauffman Foundation (2006).
[2] Sohl, Jeffrey. "The Angel Investor Market." Center for Venture Research (2004- 2013). University of New Hampshire.
[3] Klein, Karen. "Rise of Female Angel Investors Fuels Women-Run Companies" (2014). *BloombergBusinessweek*.
[4] Primack, Dan. "Venture Capital's Stunning Lack of Female Decisionmakers." *Fortune* (2014).
[5] Ibid.
[6] Jones, Kevin. "Getting Real with the Gender Lens | SOCAP." SOCAP.

(2013). Emory University.

[7] "Women at the Wheel: Do Female Executives Drive Start-Up Success?" Women in VC Study Research Team (2012). Dow Jones VentureSource.

[8] "Women Matter: Gender Diversity, a Corporate Performance Driver." McKinsey & Company (2007).

[9] Carter, Nancy, Lois Joy, Harvey Wagner, and Sriram Narayanan. "The Bottom Line: Corporate Performance and Women's Representation on Boards" (2007) *Catalyst*.

Angel Impact Investing

Wayne Silby and Jenna Nicholas

OVERVIEW

Impact investors actively place capital in businesses and projects that seek to generate financial returns while also achieving measurable impacts on some of the world's most pressing social and environmental challenges. Angel impact investors support companies that, due to their early stage of development, would not usually receive institutional support. They can also provide great value to potential co-investors through their analysis of early stage impact deals. Analysis of such deals is challenging because it can be difficult to differentiate between companies that may be truly catalytic and have high prospects of impact and growth, and those that may not. Interest in impact investing is growing for the second generation in high-net worth families who are thinking about how to use family assets in a meaningful and innovative way. Impact investing is also a way for millennials to incorporate their values into investing. Furthermore, many students at top business schools are greatly attracted to the social impact club and are keen to pursue impact investing careers. This nascent field is thus playing an increasingly important role in the global landscape of investing.

WAYNE SILBY is the founding chairman of Calvert Social Funds and co-founder of the Social Venture Network, a group of socially oriented enterpreneurs and investors. JENNA NICHOLAS is co-founder and CEO of Phoenix Global Impact, a social enterprise consulting firm.

SPECTRUM OF IMPACT INVESTMENTS

There is a range of perspectives in angel impact investing. Some expect high financial returns, whereas others are willing to accept lower returns in expectation of higher social impact. Philanthropic investors, such as high-net worth individuals and foundations, are more likely to make investments with expectations of lower returns. There is an increasing amount of creativity in these investments and new products are continually being created by social entrepreneurs to cater to these investors. This type of capital has proven extremely important, as it enables companies that would not otherwise receive support to benefit from a head start. For example, the microfinance industry would not have been able to develop had it not been for early investors and concessionary capital. There are also investors on the other side of the spectrum, with very high expectations of return. These investors will only invest in companies with good prospects of reaping such returns.

CALVERT SPECIAL EQUITIES

An early example of impact investing is Calvert Special Equity, an initiative embedded within the Calvert Mutual Funds, which Wayne Silby co-founded with John Guffey.[1] Calvert Special Equities has long been an investor in entrepreneurial companies and funds that generate sustainable solutions to pressing environmental and social problems. Since its 1992 launch, the Special Equities Program has invested approximately $70 million of venture capital into companies and funds across a range of sectors, including clean energy, microfinance, education, bio-pharmaceuticals, diagnostics, and sustainable agriculture. Some investee companies of Calvert Special Equities, such as the natural pest control firm Marrone Bio Innovations,[2] have been incredibly successful and have been able to reach initial public offerings. Others have not been as successful. It can be difficult during the early stages of a company to assesss the likelihood of success.

Another Calvert Special Equities investment, Lumni,[3] has the potential to greatly change education through reshaping the provision of student loans. In several countries of Latin America less than one third of students attend college. In a region where private universities are prohibitively expensive, Lumni, in collaboration with the Multilateral Investment Fund (MIF) of the Inter-American Development Bank

Group, designs, structures and manages funds that provide merit-based financing with repayment schemes based on a fixed percentage of future income. It is a market-driven, scalable solution to higher education financing.

Calvert Special Equities also invests in impact funds such as SJF Ventures.[4] SJF Ventures provides equity financing in amounts ranging from $1 million to $10 million, solo or in syndicate, to companies in the resource efficiency, sustainability and technology-enhanced services sectors. SJF Ventures achieved upper single digit returns with its first fund, putting it in a great position for its second fund.

INVESTORS' CIRCLE

A number of groups have formed to help support angel investors interested in early stage social enterprises. For example John May and Wayne Silby co-founded Investors' Circle,[5] the oldest and largest early stage impact investing network. Together with hundreds of angels, venture capitalists, foundations and family offices, it has propelled $172 million in initial investment and $4 billion in follow-on investment into 271 enterprises dedicated to improving the environment, education, health and community. The capital that Investors' Circle members have provided to the education sector has been particularly valuable, as it has provided an opportunity for the newly wealthy to explore different investment opportunities in a friendly environment.

PATIENT CAPITAL COLLABORATIVE

One initiative that arose through Investors' Circle is the Patient Capital Collaborative of SustainVC,[6] led by Tom Balderston and Schuyler Lance. SustainVC makes investments in early and expansion stage companies that provide social and environmental benefits. They target "triple bottom line" companies primarily in sectors such as food and organics, health and wellness, energy and the environment, education and media, and community and international development.

CALVERT DEALS THROUGH INVESTORS' CIRCLE

Calvert Special Equities has invested in two companies through Investors' Circle, Bioceptive and Kickboard. Bioceptive is a women's health company currently developing a patent-pending intrauterine device that vastly simplifies the insertion procedure while significantly reducing the adverse effects associated with current techniques.[7] Kickboard works with schools to go one level deeper than a traditional gradebook in terms of using data to achieve results.[8] Whether a school-wide behavior or incentive program is based around the use of stars, charts, merits or scholar dollars, Kickboard can streamline and automate the program for improved consistency.

GRAY GHOST VENTURES

The Calvert Special Equities investment in Kickboard was made as a co-investment with Gray Ghost Ventures.[9] Led by Bob Pattillo, Gray Ghost Ventures is a microfinance and social venture capital firm dedicated to providing market-based capital solutions to entrepreneurs who address the needs of low-income communities in emerging markets. Their approach is to target those who are still in the proof-of-concept stage by providing early, small amounts of capital. For example, Gray Ghost Ventures invested in d.light design,[10] a fast-growing international consumer products company serving the poor who lack access to reliable electricity. The mission of d.light is to enable households without reliable electricity to attain the same quality of life as those with access to electricity. That entails replacing kerosene lanterns with clean, safe, and bright light powered by solar energy. Another example is M-Kopa,[11] a mobile technology company based in Nairobi, Kenya. Since 2010 they have helped Kenyans acquire solar power products by offering innovative payment plans and a distribution model tailored to the needs of their customers.

VILLAGE CAPITAL

Gray Ghost Ventures also provided the initial seed investment for Village Capital,[12] a group supporting mission-driven entrepreneurs around the world. Their programs harness peer-to-peer support to develop and invest in business concepts. Groups such as Village Capital have been instrumental in supporting early stage social entrepreneurs. They play a powerful role in connecting impact angel investors to viable early stage social enterprises. At a recent Village Capital's Venture Forum in Louisville, social entrepreneurs from across the country gathered to take full advantage of the support network of other entrepreneurs, investors and mentors. These programs also connect to local entrepreneurial ecosystems and angel investors. For example, a local angel investor, Benton Keith was one of the hosts who helped to put together the Louisville event.[13] The engagement between local and external investors helped ensure knowledge transfer through personal introductions and ultimately the sharing of risk, responsibility and due diligence. The entrepreneurs also take part in an accelerator program that connects them to mentors and investors. At the end of the program, Village Capital allows entrepreneurs vote among themselves for a winner rather than rely on external judges.

Village Capital has accelerators around the world. At the accelerator in China, for example, the company One Earth Designs[14] produced SolSource, a high-performance parabolic concentrator that harnesses solar energy for outdoor cooking. Inspired by the need to address the pervasive indoor pollution from household stoves in rural China, SolSource was the first of a growing range of products in One Earth Designs' mission to bring innovative, clean energy to people around the world. The Calvert Special Equities team made a trip to Qinghai province, China and provided early stage capital to One Earth Designs.

CHINA

Angel impact investing plays a particularly important role in countries such as China where there is no well-established ecosystem for entrepreneurs and investors. Over the past 30 years, China's increasing wealth has created a new class of entrepreneurs and investors. A number of them now look for ways to give back to society. Programs such as Village Capital, in conjunction with public-private partnerships such as ECSEL[15] and the Schoenfeld Foundation, help to support this emerging ecosystem. An example of an impact angel investor in China is Wang Bing of the Ai You Foundation. Wang Bing is a tech investor who has spent time in the United States learning about impact investing. Taking this knowledge and experience back to China, he has made a number of investments in early stage social enterprises.

One investment made by Calvert Special Equities in China is the Shangrila Farm cooperative, which makes organic products that range from gourmet coffee to natural cosmetics. They donate a portion of profits to their nonprofit partner, the Yunnan Mountain Heritage Foundation, to support poverty alleviation, cultural preservation and community service in the mountainous Yunnan province. They also provide income generation by buying at fair trade prices and offer training to local farmers.

TONIIC

Another example of an impact network that supports angel investors is Toniic.[16] Toniic was co-founded by Charly and Lisa Kleissner,[17] both pioneers in impact investing. It helps investors connect to one another, and to causes they care most deeply about. Toniic has regular calls where members share deals they are considering. An annual retreat in Big Sur at the Kleissner home is a perk for all involved. Stephanie Cohn Rupp, the CEO of Toniic, suggests that it is often easier for philanthropists to become impact angel investors than for people who come from a more traditional venture capital background. This is because there are not that many deals in the impact investing space that meet the expectations of typical venture capitalists. According to Stephanie, one of Toniic's greatest strengths is its sense of community. People feel as though they are part of a group of like-minded individuals whom they can share and grow with. This is particularly important for people who are new to impact investing. They find strength in a community of people who can help them to navigate the impact investing field.

ASPEN NETWORK OF DEVELOPMENT ENTREPRENEURS

One of the greatest needs for impact angel investors is access to strong deal flow. The Aspen Network of Development Entrepreneurs (ANDE),[18] a global network of organizations that promotes entrepreneurship in developing countries, addresses this need. Services and programming efforts focus on providing financial support for small and growing businesses and entrepreneurs whose organizations are too large for microfinance loans and too small for traditional bank loans. The Calvert Foundation is an active member of ANDE.

SOCIAL VENTURE NETWORK

Another community supporting angel impact investors is the Social Venture Network,[19] which was co-founded by Wayne Silby and Josh

Mailman in 1987. Mailman is an active investor in the most game-changing for-profit and non-profit enterprises he can find. He believes that it is important to redefine finance as an essential vehicle to promote positive societal change. He is also the Managing Director of Serious Change L.P., a $70 million impact investment vehicle started in 2006.

IMPACTASSETS

For new angel impact investors there can be various challenges in identifying the best legal entity to use to invest in social enterprises. ImpactAssets enables philanthropists and individual investors to engage in impact investing by delivering products (including a donor advised fund and impact investment notes) and providing educational resources to support individuals and advisors looking to engage in impact investing.[20] ImpactAssets currently administers over $100 million in assets, building toward a long-term goal of $1 billion in assets.

SOCAP CONFERENCE

For the past six years, the Social Capital Markets (SOCAP) conference has been the preeminent impact investing conference.[21] With over 1,500 attendees, the conference is over-subscribed and has grown greatly over the years. SOCAP connects leading global innovators (investors, foundations, institutions and social entrepreneurs) to build a market at the intersection of "money and meaning." Gatherings such as SOCAP have been extremely helpful for new impact angel investors who seek like-minded investors and leading social enterprises.

EVENTS

Recognizing the importance of convening, the Calvert Special Equities team has been organizing impact salons in Washington, DC. It can be a challenging process when people are first starting out to navigate the impact investing industry and therefore any support that can be provided is helpful. An impact salon road show has been suggested to engage with investors across the country that could benefit from participating in communities of learning and sharing deal flow. A number of years ago, Wayne Silby bought the URL www. investingpledge.org. The idea was similar to the Giving Pledge, whereby high-net worth individuals pledge to give 50 percent of their capital to philanthropic causes. The Investing Pledge would involve high-net worth individuals pledging to commit a small percentage of their capital towards impact investing.

CROWDFUNDING

Crowdfunding platforms for angel investors provide direct access to social entrepreneurs. The recent Jumpstart Our Business Startups Act (JOBS Act) has further facilitated crowdfunding. The JOBS Act is intended to encourage funding of small American businesses by easing various securities regulations. With bipartisan support, it was signed into law by President Barack Obama in 2012. An example of a crowdfunding platform is Crowdfunder,[22] co-founded by Chance Barnett, which helps investors take equity stakes in companies through syndicated deals. Other examples are Fundrise,[23] which is a crowdfunding real estate platform, and Solar Mosaic,[24] which connects investors to high quality solar projects. Their mission is to open up clean energy investing and fundamentally change the way energy is financed. Crowdfunding is still in infancy. However, an increasing number of social investors are attracted to it, and it holds great promise for assisting investors with deal flow. One of the particularly promising dimensions is the ability of crowdfunding platforms to syndicate deals for investors online.

METRICS AND ASSESSMENT

One of the most needed toolkits for angel impact investors is metrics. Impact investing metrics is a much-debated issue, as it is far more difficult to measure social impact than financial returns. The Global Impact Investing Network[25] has developed the Impact Reporting Investment Standards[26] to help investors assess the social impact of potential investees. These metrics enable investors to benchmark investees against other companies in the same sector. Another helpful mechanism for angel impact investors is the B Corp[27] certification for sustainable businesses. Certified B Corporations are leading a global movement to redefine success in business. Over 600 businesses have already joined the B Corps community, which encourages all companies to compete not just to be the best *in* the world, but to be the best *for* the world.

CONCLUSION

Conducting due diligence on deals to determine the strengths and weaknesses of various investment opportunities can be very challenging. Furthermore, it is essential that there be a follow-up process after investment. Being an angel investor in impact investing is a labor of love and requires much hard work. Having the support of like-minded investors as various options are considered is a very valuable component to effective decisionmaking. Pioneers in the impact angel investing are paving the way for future generations.

Endnotes

[1] The Special Equities team includes Wayne Silby, Daryn Dodson, Jeremy Sookhoo and Jenna Nicholas, http://specialequities.net.
[2] http://www.marronebioinnovations.com.
[3] http://www.lumni.net/foreducationalinstitutions.
[4] http://www.sjfventures.com.
[5] http://www.investorscircle.net.
[6] http://ww.sustainvc.com.
[7] http://www.bioceptive.com.
[8] http://www.kickboardforteachers.com.
[9] http://www.grayghostventures.com.
[10] http://www.dlightdesign.com.
[11] http://www.m-kopa.com.
[12] http://www.vilcap.com .
[13] http://www.radiclecapital.com.
[14] http://www.oneearthdesigns.com.
[15] Electronic Components for European Leadership (ECSEL), http://www.ecsel-ju.eu/web/index.php.
[16] http://www.toniic.com.
[17] http://www.klfelicitasfoundation.org/index.php/about.
[18] http://en.wikipedia.org/wiki/Aspen_Network_of_Development_Entrepreneurs.
[19] http://www.svn.org.
[20] http://www.impactassets.org.
[21] http://socialcapitalmarkets.net.
[22] http://www.crowdfunder.com.
[23] https://fundrise.com.
[24] https://joinmosaic.com.
[25] http://www.thegiin.org/cgi-bin/iowa/home/index.html.
[26] http://iris.thegiin.org.
[27] http://www.bcorporation.net.

Crowdfunding and Angel Investing

Charles Sidman

OVERVIEW

Crowdfunding comprises a varied and often misunderstood collection of business and project financing mechanisms that is explosively increasing in scope and importance worldwide each year. Indeed, its diversity can be its most confusing feature, leading even current practitioners as well as interested or potentially affected individuals and groups to mistaken conclusions and expectations.

Crowdfunding is significant for, and should be understood and participated in by, the accredited angel investor community for three major reasons. First, in its securities-based forms, crowdfunding investors (although often new to the game and non-accredited in their financial status) are by definition business angels. They write checks to individual enterprises with personal funds, and have all the same issues and objectives as their more experienced and wealthier accredited angel colleagues. Crowdfunding may serve as a training ground and qualification channel for future accredited angel investors.

CHARLES SIDMAN founded and manages the internationally active ECS Capital Partners fund and, more recently, the non-accredited group, Crowdfunding Investment Angels. A charter member of the Angel Capital Association, he was previously a professor at the Medical, Business and Honors Colleges of the University of Cincinnati, and is past president of the Crowdfunding Professional Association.

Second, as a set of funding sources and mechanisms, crowdfunding increasingly complements as well as competes with traditional network-based accredited angel investment. Importantly, early support from crowdfunding can allow companies to further develop and market test their products, thus providing later angel and venture investors more advanced and substantially de-risked deal flow.

Third, crowdfunding has important social implications. It makes a financially rewarding asset class more democratically accessible, fosters entrepreneurial and community development, and supplements traditional but often dysfunctional social governance mechanisms with more effective and participatory models. In this last sense, crowdfunding enriches the world in which all investors operate.

DEFINITIONS

Crowdfunding is, by definition, a subset of crowdsourcing (the gathering of any resource from many providers). Specifically, it is concerned with raising financial support for projects and enterprises from a large number of usually small contributors (the "crowd"), and is now typically done via the internet and mediating entities called "platforms". With the exception of these technical aspects, crowdfunding is not new. Financing through broad popular contribution has been conducted in a wide array of activities throughout history, including the mounting of the Statue of Liberty (a gift from France) in New York harbor, traditional philanthropic fundraising by nonprofit religious, educational, medical and other institutions, street-side collection of spare change by the Salvation Army or scenic fountains, etc. In each case, people donate to a project or cause that they feel to be worthwhile.

Of a more investment nature, initial public offerings (IPO's) of registered securities, once more frequent and done earlier in company development than is usual today, were traditionally a means of supporting a business through the sale of ownership (or other financial) interests in the offering company. Participation in an IPO was never limited by law to a privileged economic class, but was open to anyone who could walk into a brokerage with the required (often minimal) funds. Public offerings can thus be considered the initial form of securities-based crowdfunding. After the Wall Street crash of 1929 and the ensuing Great Depression, securities laws were introduced that more tightly regulated registered (public) securities, and limited purchase of unregistered (private) securities to only the wealthy. The latter created a formal, although ostensibly protective, legal barrier for the great majority of citizens against participating in a significant and rewarding asset class. Recent loosening of this past 80-plus years of securities law is an important but not total explanation for the present crowdfunding revolution.

There is a spectrum of crowdfunding activities, both within the United States and across other nations. In addition to traditional philanthropy and the corporate IPO's that can be considered pre-internet precursors of today's crowdfunding, the following seven varieties are all legitimate parts of this growing ecosystem of funding mechanisms.

DONATION-BASED CROWDFUNDING

Growing directly out of and continuing in the vein of traditional philanthropy, billions of dollars per year are now donated over the internet (as well as through older means) by ordinary citizens in support of causes or projects that motivate them. Disaster relief, social aid, medical or other research, civic development, support of worthy institutions, etc., are now vastly enabled through use of the internet. The essence of donation-based crowdfunding is that no return other than the recipient's gratitude and the donor's satisfaction are provided in return for the gift. Nevertheless, donation-based crowdfunding can be used in support of for-profit enterprises. Legal regulation is minimal except for the usual prohibitions against misleading public statements, or the support of organizations and causes outlawed by a particular government.

REWARD-BASED CROWDFUNDING

Reward-based crowdfunding resembles the donation form in that it too is a modern continuation of time-honored practice, in this case that of mass marketing a product or service already available or soon to be (i.e. pre-selling) via the internet. In return for the financial contribution (that may be worth more than the actual value of the product, in which case an element of donation crowdfunding is also occurring), the purchaser receives the promised product or service, or another concrete perk (such as a t-shirt, celebrity interaction, etc.) but no financial stake or security interest in the business. Interestingly, the perk provided can represent a commercially valuable right (future pricing, operating territories, etc.), as long as this is structured in a contract but not security form. The ability to widely sell a product that, in some cases, has not even been fully designed or produced can be of enormous benefit to a young enterprise. The market exposure and customer development resulting can provide tremendous product validation, supporter and brand development, and in some cases recursive testing and re-design, all of which enable and de-risk later investment and corporate development.

A classic example demonstrating the possible impact of reward-based crowdfunding on traditional angel investment is the Occulus Rift story. There, an initial $2 million in reward-based crowdfunding (for the pre-purchase of innovative and yet-to-be-produced virtual reality goggles) led directly to an infusion of more than $75 million in venture capital, followed shortly by a $2 billion acquisition by Facebook. The initial reward crowdfunding campaign, which was conducted on Kickstarter, allowed the company to entirely bypass angel investments. Since no corporate security is being sold in reward-based crowdfunding (similarly to the donation form), the only regulations involved are those of general commercial truthfulness and delivery on commitments.

PEER-TO-PEER LENDING

The third type of crowdfunding considered here, namely peer-to-peer lending, shares with all other forms the essential function of raising capital from a broad range of providers, again largely through the use of the internet and mediating platforms. About a decade old, and named for its original arrangement of facilitating the lending of money from a large number of lenders to their borrowing peers, the practice has broadened in that much of the capital provided via peer-to-peer lending platforms today actually comes from institutions who find this an attractive market in which to invest.

In addition to the technical innovation of using the internet for broad reach and participation (like the first two forms of crowdfunding discussed above), two distinct features of peer-to-peer lending are as follows. First, individuals can now participate as lenders directly and profitably in consumer credit (thus competing, for better or worse, with commercial institutions). Second, this form of lending is regulated by both national law and state banking authorities, and thus is not uniformly available nationwide. Peer-to-peer lending is already a multi-billion dollar per year industry, and is frequently used by entrepreneurs to supplement personal, friend, and family financial resources in the early years of growing their businesses. It is also seen as attractive by lending institutions that are more restricted by banking regulations when lending directly.

INTRASTATE CROWDFUNDING

Even under the more restrictive national securities regulations instituted during the Great Depression, latitude was left for states to fashion their own rules for securities offerings taking place entirely within their jurisdictions (i.e., when both offerer and buyers are legitimate residents of the state in question). Thus, for the past roughly 80 years, the federal prohibition against ordinary (i.e. not just wealthier and "accredited") individuals investing in unregistered (private) securities did not necessarily apply at the state level.

After the 2012 passage of the federal Jumpstart Our Business Startups (JOBS) Act, an unexpectedly lengthy process of administrative rulemaking delayed implementation of certain types of crowdfunding (discussed below) and heightened interest in long-existing intrastate exemptions. Thus, more than half of the states by mid-2015 had enacted, clarified or were considering intrastate crowdfunding exemptions. Although these intrastate exemptions to federal registration requirements allow all individuals—i.e. the crowd, and not just accredited persons—to invest in private securities (either equity or debt) offered by firms within their states, continuing federal restrictions on interstate investments in unregistered securities limit the size and impact of intrastate crowdfunding largely to local enterprise and community development rather than the seeking of "swing-for-the-fences" financial returns. Still, on the basis of local pride and community self-help, intrastate crowdfunding is passionately supported by many.

JOBS ACT TITLE II: GENERAL SOLICITATION

An element of the JOBS Act that was simultaneously revolutionary as well as catch-up in nature was its elimination of the previous 80-plus year ban on "general solicitation," defined as the public solicitation, announcement or even mention of an existing or proximate offer to sell, and opportunity to buy, private (i.e., unregistered) securities. It was revolutionary that publication of non-registered security offers would be allowed, but also a somewhat belated legitimization and regularization of what on-line portals for accredited investors had been doing for several years. The actual purchase of securities that have been generally solicited under Title II of the JOBS Act is absolutely restricted to accredited purchasers, and the newly permissible general awareness of such offers is balanced by a requirement for more stringent proof that purchasers are in fact accredited. "Quiet," or so-called "Rule 506b" (i.e. not generally solicited), private offerings can still be sold to investors who simply self-certify that they are accredited (as determined by net worth or income thresholds). However, "generally solicited," now termed "Rule 506c" offerings, can only be sold to investors whose accredited status has been verified by hard data or external professionals.

Since its beginning in September, 2013, the scale of generally solicited 506c offerings has already reached multi-billions of dollars per year, and indeed has enlarged the pool of accredited investors aware of and participating in private securities offerings. General solicitation represents a novel and currently most active form of crowdfunding, even though its participating crowd is limited to the small percentage of the population that is better-off. Indeed, general solicitation under Title II of the JOBS Act is often referred to as "crowdfunding for the wealthy".

JOBS ACT TITLE III: SECURITIES-BASED CROWDFUNDING FOR ALL

The most potentially ground-breaking component of the JOBS Act, and the last to become active (at least a year away as of early 2015), is Title III's eagerly awaited opening of access to small (up to $1 million per year) private security offerings (both debt and equity) to all individuals, regardless of (although still proportionate to) their financial means. These are the opportunities that angel investors typically concentrate on and support, as they are not yet ready for the deeper pocketbooks and more conservative tastes of most venture capitalists. Legislators and regulators have sought to balance open participation and investor protection. While reversing the 80-plus year ban on universal access to these early-stage private security offerings, they hope to avoid a repetition of the financial hardships undergone by many from investment bubbles before and after the Great Depression.

The rules emerging include what experienced accredited angels generally consider to be best investment practices, but that are now mandated in heretofore unregulated private transactions. Given the somewhat unwieldy marriage of public oversight and regulation with private security culture and practice, it remains to be seen whether the final rules for JOBS Act Title III crowdfunding will allow a vigorous entrepreneurial fundraising market open to all nationally and comparable to what accredited angel investors have previously enjoyed privately, or to the contrary, whether the procedures and limitations mandated for investor protection will stifle the intended outcomes. Some of the issues still being debated, and that may yet be re-legislated even before the first regulations are implemented, concern dollar limits on issuer fund raises, issuer reporting and investor protection, as well as industry processes and liabilities.

JOBS ACT TITLE IV: REGULATION A+ "STREAMLINED IPO'S"

A final significant and innovative crowdfunding mechanism contained in the 2012 JOBS Act is Title IV's facilitation (under an enhanced Regulation A, termed colloquially "Reg A+") of IPO's up to $20 million or $50 million, under two sets of regulations. At its lower end, Reg A+ IPO's may compete with the Rule 506 private offerings that have long been the bread and butter of angel investing, but now with the advantages of being generally solicitable, providing immediately transferable securities, and being available without question to both accredited and non-accredited (i.e. all) investors. Regulation A+ is also intended to reverse the longstanding trend of public offerings occurring later in company development and at higher valuations. If successful, IPO's may return to their original place as the initial major form of securities-based crowdfunding, allowing entrepreneurs and growing companies to again raise capital from the masses. Regulation A+ became operative in mid-2015.

WHAT IT ALL MEANS—THE POSITIVES

The first major positive outcome of all forms of crowdfunding considered together is that they vastly enlarge the pool of early stage investors aware of and able to support (financially and otherwise) the entrepreneurial economy. These new participants are necessarily regarded as angel investors since they provide funds from their own accounts on an individual basis. Of the seven forms of crowdfunding summarized above, all but one (general solicitation of private offerings under Title II of the JOBS Act) are available to non-accredited investors. Non-accredited outnumber accredited investors in the US by more than 10-to-1, and they control significant pools of funds including retirement assets. Moreover, removing arbitrary and wealth-based legal barriers to economic opportunity is profoundly democratic. As will be discussed further below, many of the new and non-accredited participants in crowdfunding will lose rather than make money. Some, however, will achieve profitable outcomes, which in combination with the education and experience gained thereby, may qualify them to take their place as new members of the accredited investor community.

A second important benefit of crowdfunding, as seen from the perspective of the accredited angel and venture capital communities that have traditionally financed the entrepreneurial endeavor, is that the additional resources, enhanced market testing and supporter development of crowdfunding clearly lead in many cases to more mature and de-risked opportunities for professional investors' consideration. Opposition to, or disdain for, crowdfunding by traditional investors may thus be compared to "cutting off one's nose to spite one's face." Accredited angels should work with and participate in crowdfunding because the latter will, on balance, benefit their interests and activities.

The third major benefit of crowdfunding is the important social lubrication that it allows. By furnishing additional channels for the development, testing and financing of innovative products, services, projects, etc., crowdfunding may provide much-needed relief from what many regard as the restrictions and even paralysis of hyper-politicized and often dysfunctional governments, monopolistic institutions, rigid investment practices, etc. In this sense, and making no apology for the standards and practices developed by the professional angel community, many entrepreneurs consider the well-established accredited angel community to be part of the problem requiring the crowdfunding solution. Be that as it may, evolution teaches us that a greater diversity of participating candidates leads to a healthier ecosystem, by allowing enhanced opportunity for fitness selection.

Finally, the variety of international crowdfunding approaches and models constitutes a worldwide laboratory that all can participate in and learn from. The Australian Small Scale Offerings Board (ASSOB), which is most comparable to JOBS Act Title III securities-based crowdfunding in the above list of forms, has an almost 10-year track record of impressive issuer survival (proving that crowdfunded enterprises are not necessarily inferior and destined for early failure), as well as no known cases of demonstrated investor fraud. By contrast, some American authorities are so concerned about the faintest possibility of investor fraud that they seem willing to "kill the golden goose" in order to prevent this. Similarly, the United Kingdom's equity crowdfunding platform, Seedrs, is another hugely successful industry pioneer, in part because this model aggregates all individual investors in a single fund raise into one special purpose vehicle that Seedrs then manages and represents. Such aggregation provides significantly simpler negotiation and subsequent investor relations for the issuing company, as well as an experienced and larger voice on behalf of individual investors. Such a structure is specifically precluded in the United States by Title III of the 2012 American JOBS Act, however, due to fear and distrust of large and powerful investment institutions such as hedge funds. On the other hand, the list of investor protections written into Title III of the 2012 JOBS Act, and incorporated into proposed regulations, constitutes a (laudable to this observer) checklist of best practices that experienced angel investors usually specify in deal documents, even if they are not always observed in practice. Theory aside, practical experimentation will be an irreplaceable guide going forward, and all countries and models can contribute in this regard.

CONCERNS

Notwithstanding the numerous benefits of crowdfunding, a number of cautions should be noted. Indeed, these concerns are a major reason why crowdfunding models are taking on such varied forms in different jurisdictions and the pace of implementation has been so frustratingly slow from the perspective of enthusiasts. A balanced perspective is important. Several of the crowdfunding forms discussed above represent significant changes in how business and finance have been done for almost a century, ways that would not have endured so long if they were not perceived as having value. Indeed, legal institutions and cultural norms have both inertia and momentum that, like a large ship, take significant time and energy to change or redirect. "Rome was not built in a day."

A first caution to note—and the easiest to solve since it requires only education—is that the diversity of crowdfunding forms and models can be its own worst enemy. So many established practices and institutions are being affected that it is easy to focus too narrowly and confuse a specific form of crowdfunding with the whole. Of the seven varieties in the crowdfunding spectrum delineated at the start of this chapter, at least four (donation and rewards as non-securities-based forms, peer-to-peer consumer lending, and general solicitation to accredited investors) have each become multi-billion dollar per year enterprises. Even if one's particular ox is being gored, it would be inaccurate to say that the impact of crowdfunding is dubious. Some experienced investors still feel (or hope) that crowdfunding for equity will yet prove irrelevant, but it is manifestly here to stay for accredited investors via general solicitation, and for non-accredited investors even today under intrastate exemptions. Facilitated IPO's under JOBS Act Title IV have begun and are a form of equity crowdfunding open to all. If one still wishes to be sceptical about the impact of equity crowdfunding, one would have to narrowly identify that sector of crowdfunding allowing non-accredited investors national access to unregistered securities, the goal of long-delayed Title III of the 2012 JOBS Act. It is not likely that this will be delayed forever, under either the 2012 JOBS Act or possible replacements and modifications. Equity-based crowdfunding for all is thus here to stay. Yet one cannot take the merits or activity of any one form of crowdfunding to justify or reflect those of other forms or the field as a whole.

Comparisons between crowdfunding and accredited angel or venture capitalist activities are questionable for three reasons. First, much of the support coming through the various forms of crowdfunding represents traditional investors merely incorporating newer technologies and approaches into what they have always done (ex. general solicitation of private securities to both older groups.) Second, some crowdfunding represents financing that was not previously considered under the umbrella of angel or VC investing (ex. the non-securities based forms, peer-to-peer lending, and the reinvigorated IPO's of JOBS Act Title IV.) Finally, much of crowdfunding is activity by entities rather than individual angels or funds (ex. much of peer-to-peer, general solicitation and facilitated IPO's.) Although crowdfunding activity in its entirety is greater as of 2015 than the totals of either accredited angels or venture capitalists, claims that it should be regarded as more significant than these other spheres are dubious.

The scope and scale of crowdfunding do not preclude the possibility of unwelcome outcomes. Issuer fraud resulting in harm to investors is a top concern of all. However, given the more than ample (to this observer) safeguards written into the current statute and regulations, the inherent plenitude of individuals observing (and probing, discussing, etc.) each deal, and the excellent records in this regard of the long-established ASSOB and newer Seedrs, deal-based fraud will remain an ever-important concern but not a likely common scenario.

That said, another practice that could be considered in the vein of systematic fraud is the all-too-common and sometimes simply outlandish over-hype of crowdfunding's prospects or impact by parties standing to benefit from funding activity per se rather than successful entrepreneurial and investor outcomes. Some political figures, starry-eyed enthusiasts, and selling intermediaries and professional service providers have an inherent conflict of interest, but regularly cloak themselves in a mantle of concern for entrepreneurs and investors. All major forms of crowdfunding differ from traditional angel practice in the essential (and in some cases even mandated) participation of intermediary third parties (who naturally must be compensated for their services), in addition to the issuers and investors. In this regard, crowdfunding should be compared to pooled investment funds managed by professionals. There, longstanding practice is for the professional managers to earn their primary compensation as a proportion of the gains (so called "carried interest") created for their investors. Interests are thus more closely aligned between fund managers and their investors and investees than is the case between crowdfunding intermediaries and their customers, since crowdfunding intermediaries typically take their cut on the front end and no longer have "skin in the game." It is important to note that some jurisdictions allow crowdfunding intermediaries to invest or be awarded a share of ownership, and thus have interests more aligned over the long term with the companies whose fund raises they manage and the investors involved. The current statute and proposed regulations governing JOBS Act Title III securities-based crowdfunding in the US explicitly disallow such participation and long-term alignment of interests.

In addition to the ongoing reevaluation of the definition of accredited investors, required by the Dodd-Frank Act and generally regarded as unwarranted and unwelcome by the angel community, crowdfunding has opened the door to more intrusive government scrutiny and regulation of who can invest and how. This is ironic since the overriding spirit and intent of crowdfunding has always been to broaden participation in the entrepreneurial ecosystem, not restrict it further. As a base case, anyone in the public could for many years buy whatever publicly offered or traded securities they wished, and there were no government limitations on the sale of private securities to accredited investors after simple self-certification as such.

Several forms of crowdfunding, however, now carry government-imposed and intrusive-in-practice limitations, ostensibly so that a putatively wise government can protect non-accredited investors from themselves. Thus, generally solicited (JOBS Act Title II, or 506c) private securities can be sold only to accredited investors, and self-certification as such is no longer sufficient. Quantitative written proof of financial qualification (easier for income testing; difficult or worse for net worth in many cases) now must be furnished to issuers themselves, or through certain professional third parties. Such proofs are considered by many accredited angels to involve such weighty issues of privacy, confidentiality, etc., that many simply will not participate in generally solicited 506c deals as a result. Also, while everyone will eventually be able to purchase private securities under JOBS Act Title III, as well as IPO's done under JOBS Act Title IV (Reg A+), the amount that any non-accredited investor can purchase is limited to a government-established proportion of an investor's income or net worth. Respected parties exist who feel that these restrictions on private security sales to inexperienced non-accredited investors should be extended to protect accredited investors from themselves as well. Such required proofs of qualification and limitations on individual decisionmaking constitute to this writer a damaging and undesirable extension of the role and reach of government.

The greatest concern pertaining to security-based (especially equity) crowdfunding is the virtual certainty of massive investor losses, on balance, by the majority of newly enfranchised non-accredited and newly attracted accredited investors who can or will soon be able to participate. It is the proverbial "elephant in the room". Almost everyone knows that early-stage investing is high-risk, even though (and because) it can earn high returns. Peer-to-peer lending is inherently lower risk with lower return as compared to equity investing. Under the rubric of equity, both general solicitation to an expanded participating pool of accredited investors, and reinvigorated IPO's to the masses, are extensions of practices with long-accepted social understandings, even though many newer accredited angels and individual public market investors will not do well in either. These facts and expectations are not emphasized by many enthusiasts and industry representatives who stand to make money on each transaction regardless of the outcome for investors, a situation that may result in growing pressure for fiduciary standards and accountability by industry professionals.
Non-accredited investors in equity crowdfunding (Title III of the JOBS Act, or the equivalent) are likely to have the worst overall outcomes of all. Not only will many not have the personality, information, time and financial resources usually required to accumulate the experience and portfolio of a successful angel, but the limitations imposed for their own financial well-being may, ironically, mediate against their financial success. Perhaps the greatest of these is that on total amounts of investment allowed per year. Experienced investors know that, when a company is doing well (or poorly) and raises an additional round, well-considered follow-on investments can make or break one's investment outcome. In many cases, non-accredited angels who first invest under JOBS Act Title III (or its equivalent) will be unable to maintain their position when a company conducts a subsequent raise under Title III or another mechanism open only to accredited investors. Other handicaps also attach in particular to this investor class.

Why do the expected overall poor investment outcomes for non-accredited equity investors matter? Can anything be done to mitigate them? From a systemic perspective, a growing population of individuals with poor investment outcomes will neither sustainably support entrepreneurs nor provide the profits necessary for the mediating industry. Political pressures against and further regulation of (ostensibly protecting) the overall investing enterprise, both crowdfunding and otherwise, could also increase as a result. In response to these concerns, the best available answers would seem to be education, mentoring and collaboration. These activities, to which national and international angel associations are deeply devoted, should be extended as rapidly as possible to all investors in the entrepreneurial economy, not only current accredited participants. As one example, Crowdfunding Investment (CFI) Angels is an independent virtual network for crowdfunding investors (and especially those newly enfranchised and non-accredited), analogous to traditional groups of collaborating accredited investors that make up various national angel organizations. CFI Angels has been accepted as an affiliate member of the American Angel Capital Association (ACA), and will work to bring the knowledge and best practices developed by the ACA and its organizational peers to the population of new and non-accredited angels now able to participate for the first time in entrepreneurial finance via crowdfunding. Some of these will ultimately qualify as and join the accredited angel community.

CONCLUSION

Crowdfunding's proverbial cat is now out of the bag. It is both unlikely to, and should never, be replaced. In 2015, all crowdfunding mechanisms together are expected to provide as much capital for start-up and growing businesses as the accredited angel and venture communities have each furnished yearly for several decades now. Entrepreneurs worldwide are learning that support for their growing enterprises can be obtained in an increasing myriad of ways, to great practical advantage. As importantly, the range of those who provide capital is expanding from only the wealthiest to anyone and everyone interested, which is democratically only right and proper. Established players such as accredited angels, venture capitalists, banks, etc., must increasingly recognize, collaborate and compete anew for their places in this rapidly evolving ecosystem, and some long-accepted past freedoms and practices are being subjected to new oversight and compromise. As a bottom line conclusion, the rapidly increasing scale and diversity of financing mechanisms and sources collectively known as crowdfunding will continue to make the entrepreneurial ecosystem in general, and the world of angel investing specifically, more exciting, challenging, healthier and more vigorous, benefiting all.

Part II

Angel Investing

Profiles of Countries and Regions

Israel

D. Todd Dollinger and Steve Rhodes

START-UP NATION

Israel is a young country, a mere 67 years old. Just a few of the significant challenges facing Israel since its declaration of independence have included: absorbing waves of immigrants, most of whom arrived as penniless refugees; defending against hostile neighbors in a volatile region; and feeding a rapidly growing population despite harsh agricultural conditions. These same challenges have been Israel's source of inspiration. Israel's former president, Shimon Peres, wrote in his foreword to Dan Senor and Saul Singer's best-selling book, *Start-Up Nation*, "Israel bred creativity proportionate not to the size of our country, but to the dangers we faced."[1] With none of the oil that made many of its neighbors immensely wealthy, Israel built a strong, thriving economy from human capital. If there is one story reporters consistently fail to adequately cover (despite extensive coverage),

---

TODD DOLLINGER is the Chairman and CEO of The Trendlines Group, chairman of Trendlines Medical, and a director and chairman of the board of a number of public and private companies. In 1993, he and Steve Rhodes founded Trendlines as a business development consultancy. Trendlines now invests through its two government-franchised business incubators, Trendlines Medical and Trendlines Agtech, and through Trendlines Labs, its in-house invention incubator. STEVE RHODES is the Chairman and CEO of The Trendlines Group, chairman of Trendlines Agtech, and a director and chairman of the board of a number of public and private companies.

it is that Israel has the "greatest concentration of innovation and entrepreneurship in the world today."[2] With a population just over eight million, Israel ranks:[3]

- First in total expenditure on civilian R&D as a percent of GDP
- First in quality of scientific research
- Second in venture capital availability, with some 70 active venture capital funds, including 14 international funds with permanent offices, plus numerous foreign venture and private equity funds that have active representatives in Israel
- Third, after the US and China, in the number of companies listed on NASDAQ, as well as more than 60 Israeli companies traded on European exchanges)
- Fourth in utility patents per citizen

Yet another testimony to Israel's world-class entrepreneurial stature comes from the 2012 report of the Startup Ecosystem Report 2012, in which Tel Aviv ranks second globally because it has the "second highest output index of start-ups with a healthy funnel of start-ups across the developmental life cycle, a highly developed funding ecosystem, a strong entrepreneurial culture, a vibrant support ecosystem and a plentiful supply of talent."

As was the case in Europe, Israel's economy in its first decades was largely socialist. It was only in the 1980s—and even more so in the 1990s—that privatization, decentralization and broad economic liberalization developed momentum and transformed Israel's economy into one of the most open in the world. As a young country founded as a socialist state, Israel does not have a long history of personal wealth accumulation. Further, despite the fact that personal wealth is increasing in Israel (and the gap between wealthy and poor is growing), the number of high net-worth individuals that constitute the pool of potential angel investors is limited both by high taxes and a small population.

The angel investing scene in Israel today is difficult to characterize and quantify. It is highly fragmented with angel clubs forming and dissolving all the time. The Bible tells us that Jacob wrestled with an angel in order to receive God's blessing. Today, Israel's entrepreneurs are wrestling with the fact that organized angel investing is still very much in its formative period in Israel. More than one Israeli entrepreneur has felt that seeking funding directly from God was a better alternative than wrestling with angels. The historical difficulty of gaining access to angel investors in Israel and the painful funding gap that this has created for start-ups have been partly resolved in two ways. Israeli start-ups have been proactive in pursuing angel investment outside of Israel. In addition, the Israeli government has stepped up to the plate with public-private early stage funding initiatives.

INCUBATORS, ISRAELI-STYLE

One of the key drivers of Israel's start-up ecosystem, the Technological Incubators Program (TIP), was launched in 1991 by the Office of the Chief Scientist (OCS) of the Ministry of the Economy (formerly, Ministry of Trade and Commerce). In its early years, the Technological Incubators Program had a largely social objective, namely capitalizing on the talents of scientists and engineers immigrating to Israel from the former Soviet Union. Technology incubators were established throughout the country in cooperation with local and regional economic development organizations. The incubators provided a framework within which the inventions of immigrant engineers and scientists and others could progress towards commercialization.

As a result of privatization, which took place from 2002 to 2007, all government-licensed incubators are now owned and operated by Israeli and foreign investment firms, and multinational corporations seeking to tap into Israeli innovation. Israeli government-licensed incubator owners compete for eight-year licenses that entitle them to apply for TIP grants when they form new companies. With access to a rich deal flow of innovative ideas, incubators' investment committees select investment opportunities and seek approval for TIP funding. Each incubator portfolio company receives seed investment of up to $700,000 over a two-year period, of which 85 percent is a contingency grant provided by the OCS and repayable in the event of success, as a royalty on the company's revenues or at exit. The 15 percent balance is from incubator owners. To some extent, Israeli incubators fill the angel investor void while also housing the companies in the incubators' facilities and providing substantial additional support.

Each year, 75 to 85 new ventures are established within TIP. In addition to funds, incubator owners provide: offices; administrative, financial and legal services; business and professional guidance; and exposure to an extensive network of strategic partners and follow-on investors. (The authors' company, The Trendlines Group, invests through two government-franchised incubators.) During our portfolio companies' first two years, portfolio companies' high-risk profiles are reduced by: achieving technology proof-of-concept or working prototypes, filing patents to protect intellectual property, preparing a well-considered business plan, mapping regulatory compliance pathways, and initiating discussions with potential strategic partners or customers.

Israeli incubator portfolio companies have proven attractive to angel investors. Considerable effort is expended in growing networks of investors in Israel and abroad. Angel investors are often the next-round investors, following the founding investment made by the incubators themselves. There are currently 19 government-licensed technology incubators. Some have multiple sectors of interest, eight are focused primarily on medical technologies, seven focus on information and communication technologies, including security and new media, and three on cleantech. Trendlines Agtech, owned by Trendlines, has a unique area of expertise in food and agriculture technologies, specifically those related to solving global food and water crises.

An industrial technology incubator has been established in Haifa in order to support the commercialization of lower-tech ventures. There are now also two government-licensed biotechnology incubators. Their portfolio companies are funded for three years instead of two. A competitive process for establishing the country's second biotech incubator took place in 2013 and was won by FutuRx, a company owned jointly by Orbimed, Johnson & Johnson, and Takeda of Japan. Alliances of venture capital and strategic partners operating incubators are increasingly common in Israel.

MEASURING SUCCESS

As of 2008, approximately 38 percent of the 1,175 incubator companies formed since 1991 continued beyond their first two years. Since the establishment of the TIP in 1991, every $1 that the Israeli government provided has attracted more than $5 in private investment. This has driven growth in the high-tech sector, created high-quality jobs, and increased tax revenues while returning capital and interest to the government. A growing number of companies that began in incubators have matured into vibrant enterprises that employ dozens or, in some cases, hundreds of people, and have taken their place on the world stage. Some examples are: Protalix Biotherapeutics, which develops and commercializes recombinant therapeutic proteins expressed through its proprietary plant cell-based expression system, ProCellEx®; Mazor Robotics, which is a world leader in robotic solutions for spinal surgery; and Aeronautics, which produces cutting-edge unmanned aviation and surface vehicles. The TIP model has been so successful that it is now being adopted by private entities that provide seed-stage investments to their portfolio companies and seek an innovation pipeline. Some examples of private incubators are: KARAT, founded by the Israel Electric Corporation to support energy-related start-ups;[4] Haifa-based NESTech; Microdel, which focuses on low-tech initiatives; and Rainbow Medical, which seeds medical start-up companies based on the inventions of its founder, Yossi Gross.

START-UP ACCELERATORS

Inspired by the American start-up accelerator programs Techstars and Y Combinator, there are a growing number of start-up accelerators in Israel that provide a place to work, mentoring by experienced business advisors, and access to investor networks. All of the accelerator programs in Israel, for example, culminate in a demo day, where leading angel and VC investors provide feedback, conduct follow-on meetings, and provide valuable connections to other investors. In contrast to Israeli government-licensed incubators that commit to their portfolio companies for a minimum of two to three years, accelerators offer short-lived programs of a few months. They tend to be focused on software, mobile, and new media ventures that have less-demanding development and go-to-market cycles than, for example, medical, agritech or other advanced technology ventures.

Some of the Israeli accelerators provide seed funding and take equity. For example, the Elevator is a program that runs for three months in Israel followed by one month in New York or Berlin. In exchange for workspace, mentoring, a package of services, and a seed investment of $20,000, the program takes up to 10 percent in founder shares. In their last two cycles, 90 percent of the portfolio companies raised follow-on investments. DreamIT Ventures Israel is an accelerator that focuses on software-related ventures that can be developed into products within three months. Five Israel-based teams are selected each year. They start with one month in Israel followed by three months in New York. In addition to a seed investment of up to $30,000, DreamIT Ventures provides extensive mentoring as well as access to angel and venture investors—for which they take 8 percent equity. Another example is Upwest Labs, which was founded in Silicon Valley by leading Silicon Valley-based Israeli entrepreneurs as a Y Combinator-like accelerator specifically for Israeli start-ups. In addition, multinational giants offering start-up acceleration in Israel include Microsoft, Google, and Samsung, among others. There also are a number of academia-based accelerators and programs that have an excellent reputation for generating good quality start-up deal flow. A leading example is the Zell Entrepreneurship Program. Sponsored by Chicago businessman Sam Zell, this program is in its 12th year at the Interdisciplinary College in Herzliya. It allows outstanding undergraduate students in their third year to do advanced entrepreneurial studies in anticipation of working in entrepreneurial companies or starting their own.

INVESTOR EVENTS AND COMPETITIONS

One of the important components of the Israeli entrepreneurial ecosystem is investor events where early-stage innovative ventures can pitch to and network with an audience of potential investors. A good example of such an event is AgriVest, an annual event organized by Trendlines Agtech, Israel's only agritech-focused incubator. An independent committee of industry experts, government officials, agritech investors, and patent firms select leading Israeli agritech start-ups to pitch to an audience of local and international investors and strategic partners.

Perhaps the best known of the innovation competitions is the BizTEC Entrepreneurship Challenge. Organized by the Technion-Israel Institute of Technology, it is open to students from all Israeli academic institutions as a showcase for technology-based ventures.

Approximately 25 semifinalists participate in a two-month mentoring course, after which eight finalists compete for four category prizes and one first place prize. Each of the finalist teams is eligible for a chance to represent Israel in an all-expenses-paid trip to Intel Challenge Europe.

An interesting combination of a competition with an acceleration opportunity is MassChallenge Israel. An Israel-based panel identifies high-potential start-ups in Israel to participate in the MassChallenge accelerator in Boston. During the four-month accelerator period the Israeli start-ups have access to mentors, several hundred entrepreneurs, education, training, networking events, free office space, and a chance to win some of the $1 million in cash prizes. In addition, many of Israel's leading annual business conferences draw large international audiences and use this as a platform to showcase Israel innovation through start-up competitions. A case in point is the Israel Mobile Summit, which is sponsored by some of the many multinationals that have established a presence in Israel, such as Qualcomm, Yahoo, Google, IBM and Intel.

ANGEL INVESTMENT ACTIVITY TODAY

While Israel does not have a meaningful tradition of organized angel investing, the trend is slowly gaining momentum. We do not expect to see much traction in the short term as angels are more demanding on valuations, preferences, governance, and board positions than other financing options available to entrepreneurs. The list of angel investing success stories is growing, however. LabPixies, acquired by Google, returned $25 million to the angel investors who put in less than $2 million over four years. Playtika was bought by Harrah's Entertainment for $85 million after only one year of operation and $1 million in angel investment. Face.com raised more than $6 million during its four years of operation, but its original angel investors did well when Facebook bought the company for $100 million. There is a growing cadre of Israeli serial entrepreneurs with multiple exits to their credit who are now active angel investors. A notable example is Yossi Vardi, one of the original investors in the first major instant messaging service, ICQ, which was sold to AOL. Vardi has gone on to invest in more than 50 tech companies in software, energy, internet, mobile, and cleantech. Another ICQ co-founder, Yair Goldfinger, is an active angel investor who brings "smart money" to companies he supports and has had several exits from his start-ups.

Although there are numerous ad hoc angel investment groups that form and re-form in Israel, two of the more active and well-known ones that focus on knowledge-based companies are The Tel Aviv Angel Group and AfterDox. The Tel Aviv Angel Group is composed of high net worth industry leaders from around the world who co-invest in Israeli technology companies. The members of the Tel Aviv Angel Group are involved with the group's portfolio companies. They have partnered with Google in LaunchPad, which is a source of investment deal flow for them. AfterDox, which describes itself as a "smart angels" investment group, is comprised of 50 present and former top executives, mostly from Amdocs. AfterDox was established in mid-2007 and takes part in start-ups' first rounds. It has 11 portfolio companies to date. Another large angel group is the Hagshama Fund. Run by Israeli business leaders and comprised of 8,000 members, Hagshama states that they employ professional due diligence to mitigate risk. Individual investments generally start at roughly $30,000. Although the fund focuses on local and overseas real estate opportunities, it has made investments in industrial, technological and software companies, including an investment in Microdel, a private start-up incubator.

Much as foreign institutional investors have been frequent investors in Israeli VC funds, there is great interest in Israeli start-up companies from overseas angels, largely from the US Some US-based angel groups have been very active investors in Israeli companies. One, Tevel Global, formerly Tevel Angel Club, is dedicated solely to Israeli technology companies. Combining local and international investors, Tevel began in New York in 2007. Tevel and its members have invested in more than 30 companies. One of its first investments was in Virtual Ports, a Trendlines Medical portfolio company.

Whereas classic angel investing is characterized by an individual investing his/her personal funds in pre-seed and seed investment rounds, there are a growing number of "super angel" or "micro VC" funds in Israel that specialize in these early stages of investing but are, typically, investing other peoples' money.

Some examples:

- Inimiti, which is managed by a team of experienced entrepreneurs, with a focus on software and new media. They have, to date, invested in five start-ups.
- Rhodium, founded by Israeli serial entrepreneur and investor, Daniel Recanati, invests in internet, new media and mobile. Self-described as somewhere between a super angel and a VC, it has invested in approximately 15 ventures to date.
- Wadi Ventures, which describes itself as a "European-backed micro-seed venture capital fund supporting Israel's disruptive Internet startups." Founded in August 2012, they offer funding, mentorship, and exposure to European markets.
- Startup Factory, a group that provides seed funding and joins the group of founders to assist in business strategy and follow-on investment. For this financial and non-financial assistance, they take "founder's shares."

CROWDFUNDING

Though very new, crowdfunding in Israel has proven itself an important way to match angels with start-ups seeking capital. OurCrowd is one of the most successful crowdfunding organizations in the world and is, for now, focused almost exclusively on Israeli companies. OurCrowd was founded by Jonathan Medved, an important figure in Israel's high-tech sector with an impressive track record both as an entrepreneur and venture capitalist. OurCrowd allows accredited investors to take advantage of venture-like due diligence and venture-like investment terms while making investments as small as $10,000. OurCrowd also invests in each of the ventures that it presents to investors. OurCrowd principals are developing investment channels as an associated element of their platform. With the channels, they will provide back-office support of the crowdfunding process. However, they will not perform due diligence or invest in the channel partners' companies. In just a few years, OurCrowd has placed more than $110 million in some 69 companies, becoming the single-most active investor in Israel.[5]

PITCHING TO FOREIGN ANGELS

We have noted that there is a robust relationship between Israeli start-ups and foreign angels in general, and American angels in particular.

Trendlines, for example, regularly organizes multi-city US road shows for its portfolio companies to pitch to angel investors. Many US innovation competitions (such as MassChallenge mentioned above) actively recruit Israeli start-up companies to participate. For their own economic development purposes, American state and county level economic development organizations often work with Israeli organizations and governmental entities to organize investment roadshows to introduce Israeli start-ups to angel investors and service providers in their regions.

GOVERNMENT SUPPORT FOR EARLY-STAGE COMPANIES

Over the past 20 years, successive Israeli governments have generally been proactive in their programs and policies to seed the growth of the knowledge-based sector of the economy. TIP is a classic example of a highly successful public-private partnership that has become one of the primary generators of innovative start-up companies. Another example was how the Israeli government, in 1993, jump-started the venture capital industry by allocating $100 million for the Yozma Fund. Ten funds were established together with strategic partners, with the government taking a minority position and the fund owners having a five-year option to buy out the government. By 1997 all of the funds were privatized and nine out of the 15 companies that had taken direct investments went public or were acquired. Today, Israel's venture capital industry has approximately 60 active funds, of which 14 are international VCs with offices in Israel. The capital available for investment by Israeli VC funds at the beginning of 2013 was approximately $2.1 billion. Since 2010, Israel has attracted more venture capital investment per capita than any other country in the world and, in absolute numbers, has more venture capital available than any country other than the US

While quite late to the game (from an international perspective), Israel sought to develop an activist approach to strengthening the angel investing sector. The so-called "Angels' Law" was enacted in 2011 as part of the government's ongoing efforts to maintain the prominent global position of Israel's high-tech sector, which accounts for 40 percent of Israel's exports. The law was intended to mitigate the high risk of investment in companies in the R&D stage. Under the Angels'

Law, angel investments in qualifying Israeli high-tech start-ups were to be tax deductible over three years starting from the year in which the investment was made, with the maximum allowable amount of approximately $1.4 million. At least 75 percent of the invested funds were to be earmarked for R&D expenses. The law proved defective in design and, as of this writing, a committee of Israel's Knesset is reviewing the legislation.

A number of programs are operated by the Office of the Chief Scientist:

- Tnufa: Grants of up to 85 percent of approved expenses are available up to approximately $65,000 per project. These are meant to cover pre-seed activities such as building prototypes, filing patents and developing a business plan.
- R&D Fund: This supports innovative R&D programs for knowledge-based companies, from early-stage through large, mature companies. Grants are from 20 percent to 60 percent of total approved R&D expenditures of the approved projects, with the grants being repaid through royalties if the product is commercially successful. Approximately $400 million is allocated annually for approved projects.
- Binational funds: Israel has bilateral agreements to support joint industrial R&D projects with a long list of countries, including the US, Canada, South Korea and Singapore, as well as Germany, France and many other European countries. Under these agreements, an Israeli company partners with a foreign company to conduct joint R&D, with each government covering 25 percent of the approved budget and the remaining 50 percent covered by the companies themselves. Many early-stage companies in Israel have leveraged these binational funds to create innovative products. Typically, one of the responsibilities of the non-Israel partner is to bring the product to market.

Although government grants can be critical for funding early-stage companies, it should be noted that there is a price to be paid if the Israeli company is acquired by a foreign acquirer that shutters all or part of the Israeli company's activities in Israel. In such scenarios, Office of the Chief Scientist grants may need to be repaid with a 3x multiple (if some R&D continues in Israel) or a 6x multiple (if all technology assets are transferred). However, these are the maximum transfer fees amounts, and they can be substantially reduced under certain circumstances.

THE PROGNOSIS

TIP will continue to be an important source of innovative, early stage ventures in Israel. It is worth noting that every Israeli government since the program's inception in 1991, no matter what its political orientation or the economic climate, has continued to fund the program. The success of the incubators is such that Israel has been acknowledged as the world leader in public-private partnership in incubator funding and success. Another indicator of the government's long-term commitment to the program is the fact that franchises are granted for eight-year terms.

In light of the success of OurCrowd and the momentum of crowdfunding in general, it seems reasonable to expect more crowdfunding entities to be created in Israel. While OurCrowd's success could be the rising tide that raises other ships, their current dominance may make it difficult for competitors to gain traction. OurCrowd has taken a position as one of the most successful crowdfunding platforms in the world, but the fact that it works only with accredited investors may leave an entry point for others.

Regarding the regulatory climate, the Angels' Law, though defective and now being corrected, is a welcome first step in regulators' attempts to create an environment that encourages the high risks of investment in early-stage companies.

The Tel Aviv Stock Exchange (TASE) is an additional option for early-stage companies going public through IPOs or reverse mergers. Less in vogue than it was prior to the 2008 market crash, only a very small number of pre-revenue companies are listing annually. The TASE is highly regulated with similar regulatory burdens for small and large companies. Companies that are dual-listed—i.e., listed on the TASE and a foreign exchange—can choose to follow the rules of the "easier" exchange. Some Israeli companies have listed on US exchanges to reduce their regulatory and reporting burdens. Foreign, that is to say American, angel investment in Israel is an important part of the Israeli seed and early stage funding ecosystem. All accounts suggest growth in foreign direct investment in Israel, even in the youngest of companies.

Angel investing in Israel remains in a state of infancy and is maturing at a slow pace. Organized Israeli angel groups continue to assemble and disband. Some would say that the very nature of the Israeli personality renders the phrase "organized Israeli investment group" an oxymoron.

Endnotes

[1] Senor, Dan and Saul Singer, *Start-up Nation*, 2008, p. xii.

[2] Ibid, p. xvi.

[3] From The Israeli Economy: Fundamentals, Characteristics and Historic Overview, State of Israel Ministry of Finance, International Affairs Department, 2012.

[4] KARAT was developed by Trendlines under contract to the IEC.

[5] OurCrowd invested $1 million in Trendlines and has additionally invested in a Trendlines portfolio companies.

France

Philippe Gluntz

A BRIEF HISTORY OF ANGEL ACTIVITIES

Prior to 2000 there were maybe only a few hundred angel investors in France, most of whom invested alone and were accessible to a small number firms, most of which were internet-based. After the bursting of the internet bubble and the slow recovery, a "mutualized" approach developed: the angel network. This made it easier for angels to source and screen investment opportunities, perform more professional due diligence, and eventually syndicate their investments with other network members.

In 2001, five recently created networks and five commercial structures dealing with early stage investments decided to form a national association, a totally private initiative, called France Angels. It had several goals: to make angel investing more visible to entrepreneurs, private investors and public authorities; to promote angel investing throughout the nation; to increase the number of angels; and to provide professional training and support to network managers and

---

PHILIPPE GLUNTZ is the Chairman and Board Member of several NTIC and Logistic companies, and is heavily involved in the venture capital market, on top of his academic teaching. He is the President of BAE (Confederation of European Business Angels Associations) and works closely with France Angels, the French federation of business angels networks and early stage funds.

new angels. Some public assistance was obtained including grants and support from local governments. Early initiatives included a seminal Angel Congress in 2001, sponsored and hosted by the French Senate; a School of Business Angels, development of a Center of Resources; a training program for network managers; and a network charter and code of conduct. This helped foster membership growth which reached 4,300 angels by 2013. These angels, collectively, belong to more than 85 angel networks and 40 angel funds.

ANGEL NETWORK TYPES

The basic form of angel network in France is a nonprofit association of 30 to 150 angels of diverse entrepreneurial and sectorial experience, who usually are located in the same geographical area. The nonprofit is led either by a group of volunteer angels or by a salaried manager, if such an arrangement is financially sustainable. However, a variety of network types exist: regional (the dominant form with 65 networks across the country); sector-focused (e.g., health care, cleantech, ICT, forestry, robotics, etc), or university alumni-based. Most of technical and business schools across France now have an alumni network or plan to set up one in the near future.

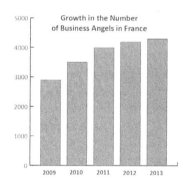

Growth in the Number of Business Angels in France

The growth in regional networks has helped increase co-investment and sharing of best practices, and has had a positive impact on local entrepreneurship ecosystems. Most are based in dynamic areas such as the Paris region, the Lyon region, and the region along the Mediterranean Sea. An interesting network was set up 10 years ago, the Femmes Business Angels, which is only open to female investors. Their membership has grown consistently and reached 100 by 2013. They invest in every kind of start-up, whether led by male or female entrepreneurs.

More than five large angel networks also exist, each having more than 150 members and sometimes several chapters. These are becoming very professional in their processes, and belong to the top tier of European networks. They include: Paris Business Angels; Investessor (West Paris Region); BADGE (the Alumni of leading Engineering and Business Schools and Universities); Arts & Métiers Business Angels (Alumni of Technical Engineering Schools); Grenoble Angels; and Savoie Angels. These networks have all set up one or two sidecar angel funds called SIBAs in order to increase their financial capacity. Forty SIBAs in total are members of France Angels.

The 4,300 members of France Angels have invested in more than 350 start-ups each year, and are currently supporting and mentoring a portfolio of more than 2,000 start-ups and mid-cap firms. The average first round of early stage investment led by angels is €300,000, of which angels supply 30 percent to 80 percent. An estimated 2,500 to 3,000 angels are not members of France Angels. They are either unaware of the angel networks or prefer to syndicate on a case-by-case basis and / or informally with friends. Moreover a number (up to 50) of "super angels" have recently arisen, mostly internet entrepreneurs focused on internet investments. They tend to set up mini-VC structures (better termed an entrepreneur fund), funded by one or several individuals, families or businesses, and managed by professionals in the VC industry. Their high visibility in the internet arena makes them appear more numerous than they actually are.

ANGELS' ROLE IN THE INNOVATION ECOSYSTEM

French angel networks and SIBAs benefit from very active public and private organizations that support innovative start-ups. Incubators, 61 Technopoles and CEEI (European Innovation Centers) are mostly financed by local governments and the European Regional Development Fund (ERDF). Ninety one of these are members of the national association, RETIS, the French affiliate of the European Business Network (EBN). Angels are generally involved in the selection, training and eventual financing of the start-ups hosted by these organizations. RETIS is a key partner of France Angels. There are also a significant number of accelerators mostly in the web sector. Most act as partners of angels, although some perceive themselves more as competitors, since they have been developing their own funding capability. Their growth is supported by the French government, which recently launched the €300 million "French Tech" initiative to increase the number of accelerators in France. In addition to this, a large network of public agencies (e.g., Initiative France with 230 members) and private regional organizations (e.g., Reseau Entreprendre, with regional locations) provide very early stage "no interest/no guarantee" loans to entrepreneurs that range from €20,000 to €80,000. Some angels are simultaneously members of one of these structures, and/or coach selected entrepreneurs in their fundraising process. They act as a source of tangible deal flows for angels networks.

Angels are also very involved in the national and regional clusters (71 in France), which are supported both by public agencies, as well as large corporations in various sectors. Angels provide, generally free of charge, coaching activities and training in fundraising. France Angels is a sponsor and co-leader of the national competition hosted by the national clusters, where start-ups compete for a "Innovative Company of the Clusters" (EIP) label. The Ministry of Research has also financed and set up New Technology Transfer Acceleration Companies (12 SATTs as of today) to help commercialize research, most of which comes from public universities. Angels help these SATTs by providing business advice to potential entrepreneurs.

Investments of French Angels by Sector (2013)

Consumer goods 7%
Industry & Chemistry 9%
Services & Transport 9%
Energy & Cleantech 11%
Health & Biotech 15%
Software & Smartphones 18%
New Digital Services 30%

A large number of seed funds are primary partners of angels. Seed funds are often created by regional governments with co-financing by the ERDF. Private seed funds are financed by regional banks. Public-private early stage funds are financed through the National Early Stage Fund. Some of these invest at seed stage (45 are members of UNICER, a partner of France Angels), and others are industry-focused and multi-regional. Angels are very often lead investors for these funds, but over time some are turning into competitors for good deal flow. France Angels is also an active associate member of the Association Française Des Investisseurs Pour La Croissance, which represents the French VC Industry. Twenty VCs are also associate members of France

Angels. French Angel members are very involved in local economic development activities in their region, which has historically been an important motivation for them to become an active angel.

CROWDFUNDING PLATFORMS

Crowdfunding will be an important part of the angel ecosystem. A new law, released in July 2014, is very liberal in comparison to crowdfunding laws in the US and Europe. It allows equity crowdfunding platforms to raise funds up to €1 million without the need for a prospectus, provided they have been registered with the Autorité des Marchés Financiers (the French equivalent of the US Securities and Exchange Commission) and provide some limited information about the issuer. There are no requirements for initial capital, investor qualification, or maximum contribution. In 2013, the website "Good Morning Crowdfunding" noted that 14 French platforms had already raised €10 million. Almost 3,000 crowdfunders have invested in 4,000 companies or projects. Angels are currently debating how to position themselves with regard to crowdfunding.

GOVERNMENT POLICIES

Since 2006, the French government has offered a tax deduction for direct investment by private investors in SMEs (firms of up to 250 employees and/or €50 million in revenue). This income tax relief program, called Madelin, after the Minister of Finance who launched, was originally 25 percent, with a cap of €20,000 and a commitment to hold shares for five years. This tax relief has been extended to angel funds (SIBAs), which also benefit from a partial guarantee given by the Public Bank Oseo. However, over the years this tax relief has been reduced by successive governments down to 18 percent, with a cap of €10,000. This cap is combined with other types of tax relief such as family care spending. It is now rather ineffective at inducing private individuals to invest in risky start-ups at the seed level.

This tax relief has been extended in more recent years to investment through professional capital investment (FCPI) managed by certified fund managers, provided that more than 70 percent of the fund is invested in early stage. As with direct investors however, reductions in the percentage value have led to a 40 percent decrease in the amount raised by VCs in the past two years. The relief does not help the sidecar funds either, since after 2010 it would require them to employ at least two salaried people and have a maximum of 50 shareholders, making financial sustainability problematic.

In 2007, a new law, TEPA, created a 50 percent tax relief on the wealth tax (now 75 percent), with a cap of €50,000 (now €45,000). In 2008, this measure enabled 73,200 taxpayers to inject €1,1 billion into SMEs. It requires holding shares for at least five years and is applicable to dedicated FCPI and FIP as well. This program has proved more effective than Madelin due to the larger investment caps, but it is only applicable to individuals paying the wealth tax (about 60 percent of angels). Based on tax data collection research, TEPA tax breaks were used by around 70,000 private investors in 2007-2008, for a total tax saving of €600,000-700,000. Most of this amount, however, was investment in SME family businesses which are part of the same tax break system. As such the support for angels investing in non-related SMEs is probably only a small fraction of this total.

GOVERNMENT SUBSIDIES

Since 2001, the Ministry of Finance and Industry has been hosting and sponsoring an annual congress of up to 500 people, and has provided a substantial subsidy to France Angels. This, together with support from the Public Bank, amounted to €80,000, which was more than 50 percent of France Angel's budget. The subsidy has decreased over the years to an annual level of €15,000 and is provided by the new Public Bank for SMEs, BPI France. For the last 10 years, France Angels has also worked with the Ministry on a competitive bid process that has awarded 43 networks a subsidy of €100,000 over three years to help them grow.

Many subsidies have been allocated to regional networks by local governments. One of the first was from the Paris Region and was based on the number of investment pitches organized by a network (€1,000 per pitch with a cap of €30,000). More generally the amount is about €500 per investment, with a cap of €20,000. This has been complemented in several regions by subsidies provided by local development agencies, chambers of commerce, and city government agencies. These have taken the form of secretarial services and the hosting of teams and meetings. Other subsidies have been proposed for promotion and communication campaigns, with an eye toward increasing market awareness of angels and growing their number.

PUBLIC CO-INVESTMENT FUNDS

Over the years it became clear that increasing the number of angel investors was not enough for start-up development. There was a need for additional funding sources, particular for later rounds of financing where VCs were less and less present. This goal of increasing the financial capability of angels has been taken up first by several regions, and they have been setting up regional co-investment funds, investing pari-passu with angels who remain lead investors. Half of the capital comes from regional budgets and half from the ERDF. Seven regional funds are up and running, mostly focused on seed and early stage phases, with one focused on later stage development. The size of these co-investment funds varies from €10 million to €20 million.

In 2013, a €20 million pilot co-investment fund called Angelsource was set up at the national level. Ninety percent of its funding came from the FNA (National Seed Fund of Funds) and 10 percent came from private investors. It is managed by the professional fund management firm, Isource-Gestion, with significant involvement of angels in the selection and investment committees. Angelsource co-invests pari-passu with a selection of angel network members of France Angels who have a demonstrated track record. This selection process makes it possible for Angelsource to save costs by relying on the angels due diligence.

To summarize, the four initiatives of the French government which act as co-investment opportunities for angels are:

- the new public SATTs created to help commercialize research from mostly regional public universities. In just two years, the SATTs have invested around €48 million into innovation projects;
- BpiFrance, the fusion between Oseo and CDC Enterprises which created the first public organization for investing in and developing companies. In 2013 BPI invested €750 million in

    innovation, bringing its total investment to €10 billion;

- FNA, the early stage investment fund managed by BPI France. This fund is endowed with €600 million and targets investments ranging between €5 million and €30 million; and,
- the new crowdfunding platforms, which the French government is currently assessing as a potential developmental investment opportunity.

Extensive information about French angel investor groups, networks, funds, and public agencies can be found at: www.franceangels.org.

South Africa

Craig Mullett

OVERVIEW

The South African economy has undergone tremendous changes since the first democratic government was elected in 1994. There has been a shift away from resource-dependent sectors towards more value-added sectors. The structural imbalances in the workforce have continued however, with an estimated 35.6 percent unemployment rate (using the expanded definition that includes those who have stopped looking for work).[1]

Creating and growing scalable businesses is needed to make significant enlargements of the workforce, but research indicates that South Africa consistently has shown a below-average trend in early stage entrepreneurial activity relative to countries of similar economic development levels. Currently, jobs in South African opportunity-driven businesses in the early-stage entrepreneurial phase average 6.1 per firm, compared to 2.1 for necessity-driven firms.[2]

CRAIG MULLETT is President of Branison Group, a corporate finance firm, based in Connecticut. He is also an active angel investor with Angel Investor Forum and has advised start-up angel groups in South Africa and Barbados. He was Director of Business Development for Amphenol Corporation, an electronics manufacturer, completing 24 acquisitions around the world. Prior to that, he was the founder of HomeWorths, a direct marketing business.

There has been much debate in South Africa to determine which practices would best assist entrepreneurs to both start and grow small businesses, with an emphasis on how they move from survivalist enterprises and micro-businesses to small and medium enterprises with high growth potential (employing more than 100 people). The 2012 Global Entrepreneurship Monitor report suggests that the requirements to increase the number of early stage entrepreneurs include a fast and simple business registration process, easier access to start-up funding at favorable terms, and venture capitalists/angel investors with an appetite for risk.

The South African economy is not growing fast enough to generate sufficient jobs, and the rate of small business creation is hampered by poor government policies that harm competitiveness. South Africa ranks 54th on the Global Competitiveness Index—in the middle of the pack—yet toward the bottom of the rankings for factors that encourage start-up creation. These include education levels, labor market efficiency, internet bandwidth and the availability of scientists and engineers. In addition, the World Economic Forum ranks access to financing as the most problematic factor for doing business in Sub-Saharan Africa.[3]

The entrepreneurial ecosystem requires several key components to function effectively, with none being as important as the individual entrepreneurs who create and grow businesses. As only two percent of small businesses in South Africa have access to bank financing,[4] it is likely that many start-up entrepreneurs will be prevented from pursuing new business creation without access to the finance provided by angel investors.

HISTORY OF ANGEL INVESTMENT IN SOUTH AFRICA

There is limited research on the scope and composition of the angel investment market throughout all of Sub-Saharan Africa, including South Africa. The only formal research on African angel investment appears to be that of Hearn.[5] His study used the performance of IPO's in the North African market to support the theory that business angels are better investors for entrepreneurial ventures than private equity, due to their active involvement with management in a relationship-based economy. Hearn did not conduct any research on the metrics or composition of the angel investor market. Gilbert and Lingelbach find in their research on finance markets in Botswana that angel investment in early stage ventures is "virtually non-existent,"indicating an equity gap for entrepreneurs.[6]

The research conducted to date in South Africa has been part of broader surveys and analyses of the venture finance market. Herrington and his co-authors refer to angel investors in their work for the Global Entrepreneurship Monitor project.[7] They note that entrepreneurial firms migrate from internal bootstrapping finance to friends and family, followed by angels. The authors suggest that the South African angel investment market may not be as large in comparison to venture capital as the proportion in the US, but this is not quantified. The only angel structure/portal that was referenced was the South African Investment Network, which is an online platform that connects entrepreneurs with angel investors.

The South African Venture Capital Association compiled a survey of venture capital in South Africa in 2010.[8] The survey indicated that venture capital fund managers view South African angel investors as operating differently than those in the US, in that they make larger investments in single deals (reportedly as high as R30 million), and they stay invested from start-up to exit. The data on angels in the survey was collected through a questionnaire sent to venture capital fund managers and stakeholders participating in the main venture capital survey, with limited additional distribution to the personal networks of those surveyed. The authors estimated that angel investors consisted of 5 percent of the total value of venture transactions in South Africa from 2000 to July 2010. The survey results indicated the leading investment sector was technology (37 percent), followed by lifestyle (10 percent), with all other sectors totaling 53 percent.

The age of angel investors was analyzed as follows (based at the time investment was made): ages 31-44 (40 percent), 45-59 (30 percent), over 60 (20 percent), under 31 (10 percent). The average angel investment was R2.74 million, with the primary investment objective being return on investment (75 percent), followed by mentoring (13 percent), friends and family (6 percent) and other (6 percent). The background of the investors was business focused, with 35 percent having an entrepreneurial focus, 24 percent general business, 12 percent investment and 29 percent other.

This research indicates that the South African angel investor model at the time was more similar to private investments by smaller family wealth offices or super-angels, both of which are common funding sources in the US, than the angel group model used in the US and other countries. Investors appeared to be largely middle-aged business people, suggesting that this would be the source of members for any potential angel groups.

ANGEL GROUP STRUCTURES AND ORGANIZATIONS

The angel investor model in South Africa described above was noted as "ad hoc and inefficient",[9] and in response South Africa's first formal angel group, AngelHub, was launched in July 2011. AngelHub was co-founded by an early-stage business development firm (MyTrueSpark), a venture capital firm (PoweredbyVC) and a US-based corporate finance firm (Branison Group). Using best practices from international angel groups, AngelHub was structured along similar lines to for-profit US angel groups. Individual member investors pay an annual fee and commit to investing a minimum of R300,000 (institutional member investors commit to a minimum of R1,000,000) over a period of a few years. Since its launch, the group has held quarterly meetings in Cape Town and Johannesburg, signed up dozens of members and made several investments into start-ups. AngelHub also organizes a regular networking event, The Founders Dinner. The focus of the dinner is to bring founders and prospective founders of high-growth ventures together to talk and share experiences, thereby acting as an informal mentor pool and also as a source of prospective new ventures for angel investors.

AngelHub has helped accelerate the development of South Africa's early stage ecosystem, which now includes start-up incubators and several university early-stage funding programs. AngelHub also partnered with the University of Cape Town Graduate School of Business to run a program termed "Find-Make-Grow-Realize" that enables entrepreneurs to move ideas from concept to business execution stage. Ventures emerging from the program are evaluated for investment readiness and may present to AngelHub investors after completion of the program.

When AngelHub was formed, the founders focused on identifying each of the key components of the angel group ecosystem. Drawing upon the experience of, and insights into, the best practices of angel groups in the US, AngelHub was able to run the group using the latest online software platform and use templates that were combinations of designs of established groups. Fortunately the open and cooperative nature of the global angel investor community—specifically the World Business Angel Association and the Angel Capital Association— allowed for prior learning to be applied in the best way to establish and operate an effective angel group. AngelHub was able to secure sponsorships from the Industrial Development Corporation (a South African government-backed organization) and leading South African advisory firms and banks. This was important to give the group credibility as well as financial flexibility to commence operations with full-time staff in Cape Town. As with angel groups in other nations, AngelHub has maintained a low cost base through the use of interns and by sharing office space.

In September 2013 a new Pan-African platform, Angel Africa List, hosted the first AngelFair in Johannesburg that attracted angel investors and start-ups from South Africa and Sub-Saharan Africa. Local early-stage initiatives such as Silicon Cape and 88mph (in Cape Town) and Seed Engine (in Johannesburg) also connect angels informally to start-ups that need funding. AngelHub has shared its model, which is endorsed by Infodev of the World Bank, with other new African angel groups to assist them in getting established. Expanding the angel group ecosystem from South Africa across Sub-Saharan Africa will bring additional flexibility to the various components with more sector expertise and a cross-border focus.

POLICIES TO PROMOTE BUSINESS ANGEL INVESTING

There are currently no direct tax incentives for angel investors in South Africa, despite several recommendations of changes to the taxation code. A study by ECIAfrica Consulting recommended that tax incentives be considered for angel investors to develop the SME investment market in South Africa.[10] The only incentives for start-up investing are an indirect flow-through tax entity contained in s12J of the Income Tax Act.

The South African Revenue Service (SARS) has stated that one of the main challenges to the economic growth of small and medium-sized businesses is access to equity finance. In this regard amendments were made to s12J (effective from 1 July 2009), which was effected by the Taxation Laws Amendment Act of 20093. This amendment related to a qualified Venture Capital Company (VCC), allowing investors (which are limited to include individuals and listed companies) to claim an income tax deduction in respect of the expenditure incurred in exchange for VCC shares, thus offering up to 40 percent tax relief on the investment. In addition to this tax break, which reduces risk capital to 60 percent of the investment, investors also qualify for tax-free dividends. Two key limits apply, namely an annual deduction limit of R750,000 and a cumulative lifetime deduction limit of R2,250,000. When an investment in a VCC is sold then the proceeds (limited to the initial investment cost) are considered a taxable recoupment in terms of s8(4). Any excess gain above the cost is treated under the normal capital gains tax rules.

Unfortunately the qualification requirements of a VCC are exceedingly complex and if the VCC status is withdrawn, the VCC will become liable for penalties. This penalty is equal to 125 percent of the amount that each qualifying investor has invested in the VCC. Due to these burdens, only a handful of companies have attempted to qualify, and it is uncertain if any investments have ever been made in start-ups as a result of the s12J deduction scheme.[11]

No government subsidy programs currently exist in South Africa for either angel investors or angel investor groups. For entrepreneurs, the South African Department of Trade and Industry (DTI) has funded incubators through the Incubation Support Program (ISP). The ISP aims to ensure that small, micro and medium enterprises can graduate into the mainstream economy through the support provided by the incubators. In addition, DTI also funds the Seda Technology Program (STP), which is a division of the Small Enterprise Development Agency that focuses on technology business incubation, technology transfer services and support to small enterprises. The program offers financial assistance in the form of a non-repayable grant up to a maximum of R600,000 per project.

In South Africa angel investors typically make investments directly into South African start-ups through the purchase of shares (even when facilitated through an angel group). Start-ups typically incorporate as private companies. If companies grow to a sufficient size, they may incorporate as publicly held companies, allowing them to offer their shares for sale to the public, although they need not be listed on any stock exchange for the public to hold an interest in the business. Private companies, on the other hand, may not offer their shares for sale to the general public. Private companies are not required to file their annual financial statements with the Registrar of Companies and must include the word "Proprietary" or "(Pty)" at the end of the registered name immediately before the word "Limited" or "Ltd".

The National African Federated Chamber of Commerce (NAFCOC) has called for the establishment of a Small and Medium Enterprise (SME) Ministry[12] that would focus on policies for encouraging start-ups. This would be consistent with the government's National Development Plan that seeks to accelerate South Africa's economic development. Changing the public policy framework to be more supportive of start-ups and angel investing could have significant benefits for new business creation and employment.

ANGEL INVESTMENT TRENDS

The formation of AngelHub has served as a catalyst for new initiatives in the angel investment market in South Africa. The expansion of AngelHub, as well as the formation of additional formal and informal angel networks, should increase the number of active angel investors in South Africa. This may encourage more Sub-Saharan angel investor activity as well, with the added benefit of cross-border investment and expertise. Once enough successful angel exits have occurred with proven rates of return, it is possible that local and foreign investors may commit dedicated capital to South African angel groups in sidecar funds. Some of these foreign investors may be motivated not just by financial return, but also by the social impact of the jobs created by the new business ventures backed by angel investors. South African start-ups are likely to continue to adopt new technologies and virtual infrastructure to operate in an increasingly lean manner, enabling limited angel investor capital to stretch further. Combining this with Africa's positive overall economic outlook, strong demographic trends and nascent mobile computing business models should allow for exciting investment opportunities into the future for South African angel investors.

Endnotes

[1] *Quarterly Labour Force Survey*, 3rd Quarter 2013, Statistics South Africa.
[2] *Global Entrepreneurship Monitor 2012 South Africa*, Natasha Turton and Mike Herrington.
[3] *The Africa Competitiveness Report*, 2011, World Economic Forum.
[4] "The impact of inaccessibility to bank finance and lack of financial management knowledge to small, medium and micro enterprises in Buffalo City Municipality, South Africa", Tendai Chimucheka & Ellen C. Rungani, African Journal of Business Management, 18 July 2011.
[5] "The Effects of Business Angels, Private Equity and Lead Managers on the Performance of North African IPO Firms", Bruce Allen Hearn, 2010, University of Leicester.
[6] "Toward a Process Model of Venture Capital Emergence: The Case of Botswana", Evan Gilbert and David Lingelbach, 2009, University of Stellenbosch.
[7] "Tracking Entrepreneurship in South Africa : a Global Entrepreneurship Monitor Perspective", Michael Herrington, Jacqui Kew & Penny Kew, 2010, University of Cape Town.
[8] SAVCA Venture Capital Survey, Stephan J. Lamprecht, and Eloise Swart, 2010, Venture Solutions.
[9] "Angel funding: Wings for new ventures", Lise Pretorius, Financial Mail 11 July 2011.
[10] "Study into Tax Incentives for Private Investors in Small Businesses", ECIAfrica Consulting, 2006, FinMark Trust.
[11] "Nothing ventured nothing gained", Lee-Ann Steenkamp, April 2010, Accountancy SA.
[12] "SME ministry can drive a small-business revolution", Joe Hlongwane, CityPress 27 August 2013.

Hong Kong

Allen Yeung

OVERVIEW

After China joined the World Trade Organization in 2001 and gradually opened up to global markets, economic and trade cooperation between mainland China and Hong Kong became more cohesive. Since 2007 the central government has introduced a series of favorable tax arrangements for Hong Kong individuals and companies. These preferential tax rates are even lower than the bilateral tax agreements between China and other countries. Coupled with the adoption of common laws and improved infrastructure, this has attracted more individual and institutional funds to Hong Kong.

There are plenty of investors with deep pockets in Hong Kong, some of them semi-retired or retired industrialists. In the 2013 *Wealth Report* by Knight Frank Research, Hong Kong ranked 8th out of 30 global cities with respect to the number of high net worth individuals. These individuals have extensive knowledge, experience, networks, and capital, all of which can help start-ups. According to the 2007 *Global*

ALLEN YEUNG is the Founding Chairman of the Hong Kong Business Angel Network and the Chief Corporate Development Officer for the Hong Kong Science & Technology Parks Corporation. At the latter, he is responsible for incubating technology and innovative design start-up companies, creating synergies among industry and academic sectors, and providing advanced laboratory support facilities for innovation and technology development.

Entrepreneurship Monitor, eight percent of Hong Kong adults had invested in other companies, and Hong Kong ranked second among high-income countries. About 80 percent of these investments were in companies owned by relatives or friends, however, not in unfamiliar start-ups. In fact, Hong Kong technology start-ups are struggling to obtain investment funding between the seed and venture capital stages.

In Hong Kong there are plenty of potential angel investors and projects that need funding. Connecting the two is the issue. This is a because Hong Kong lacks open, organized business angel networks to provide "smart money." To begin remedying this, the Hong Kong Science & Technology Parks Corporation (HKSTP) invited The Chinese University of Hong Kong, the Hong Kong Polytechnic University, the Hong Kong University of Science & Technology, the University of Hong Kong and the Hong Kong Venture Capital and Private Equity Association to form the Hong Kong Business Angel Network (HKBAN) in 2010. Since its establishment in 2011, it has provided an investment matching platform open to all start-ups nominated by partner organizations. These include:

Incubators:
- Hong Kong Cyberport Management Company Ltd. (Cyberport)
- Hong Kong Design Centre (HKDC)
- Hong Kong Science & Technology Parks Corporation (HKSTP)

Universities:
- Hong Kong Baptist University (HKBU)
- Hong Kong University of Science and Technology (HKUST)
- The City University of Hong Kong (City U)
- The Chinese University of Hong Kong (CUHK)
- The Hong Kong Polytechnic University (HKPU)
- The University of Hong Kong (HKU)

Start-up Networks:
- CoCoon
- The Entrepreneurs Club (E Club)
- The Entrepreneurs' Network (TEN)
- The Indus Entrepreneurs (TiE) H K Limited (TiE)
- Economic & Trade Mission, Consulate General of Israel in HK

- Hong Kong Biotechnology Organization
- Hong Kong ICT Awards Steering Committee
- Hong Kong Information Technology Joint Council Ltd. (HKITJC)
- SOW Asia (SoW)

HKBAN now has 99 angel members and, from its establishment up through April 2015, had enabled 27 companies to raise more than HK$149.24 million ($20 million).

THE ECOSYSTEM

Hong Kong is located in the heart of Asia, with half of the world's population within reach in five hours' flight time, including countries such as India, Indonesia, and Japan. More important, Hong Kong is an international gateway to mainland China. It offers easy access to the Greater Pearl River Delta (GPRD) region, one of the world's major manufacturing bases, which has a population of more than 100 million, advanced R&D capabilities, and strong demand for consumer goods and business services. The "One Country, Two Systems" policy, strong rule of law, and a healthy capital market are key attributes of which Hong Kong is proud.

An ideal geographical location and a robust infrastructure are cornerstones for an entrepreneurship ecosystem. The entrepreneurship ecosystem, like a rainforest that weeds out the weakest and embraces strong players, consists of a set of individual elements such as leadership, talent, culture, capital markets, and open-minded customers. R&D talent is the main driving force for technological advancement. In recent years the quality of tertiary education in Hong Kong has been improving. Universities in Hong Kong are ranked very favorably in many global academic rankings. In 2014, two universities in Hong Kong were ranked in the Top 100 in the *Times Higher Education World University Rankings*. In the reputable "QS Asian University Rankings 2014," the University of Hong Kong, the Hong Kong University of Science and Technology, and The Chinese University of Hong Kong ranked within the Top 10. Other tertiary institutions in Hong Kong also ranked within the Top 50 in the survey, including City University of Hong Kong (11th), the Hong Kong Polytechnic University (27th) and the Hong Kong Baptist University (45th). Universities are feeders to the start-up community. To promote entrepreneurship, six universities in Hong Kong have set up knowledge transfer centers and/or business centers to help new ventures and facilitate commercialization of technology. The quality enhancement of tertiary institutions not only advances R&D, but also acts as a source of innovative young talent.

As an international city, Hong Kong also attracts a great deal of overseas talent. Many knowledgeable and ambitious entrepreneurs and researchers in the Hong Kong Science Park are graduates of Harvard University, Stanford University, Massachusetts Institute of Technology, Peking University, Tsinghua University, and other world-class institutes. The Park has also attracted the headquarters of many multinational corporations, including Philips, TDK, Cree, Fujitsu, Freescale, Texas Instruments, TCL, Huawei, and BGI.

Apart from expertise and capital, an entrepreneurial culture is also vital to the ecosystem. In recent years the Hong Kong start-up scene has been thriving, as evidenced by more than 1,000 registered start-ups. Stakeholders provide co-work spaces, incubators and accelerators, who run different activities for start-ups including pre-incubation programs, business plan competitions, mentoring, and training services. The 20-plus co-work spaces regularly organize activities to encourage knowledge and experience exchange among start-ups, and include organizations such as CoCoon, Good Lab, Hive, Hong Kong Commons, Blue Print and TusPark. Government and government-funded institutions are also active in the ecosystem: for example, the Hong Kong Science and Technology Parks Corporation, the Cyberport, Hong Kong Trade Development Council, Invest Hong Kong, the Hong Kong Federation of Youth Groups and the Hong Kong Productivity Council. There are also a number of publicly funding options, including the Innovation and Technology Fund, SME Funding Schemes and Hong Kong Mortgage Corporation Fund. The many government incentives and growing start-up community help strengthen and develop the entrepreneurship ecosystem.

Local universities organize a number of business plan competitions, such as the One Million Dollar Entrepreneurship Competition (from HKUST), the Young Development Council E-Challenge, the Cyberport Micro-fund, the HSBC Young Entrepreneur Award, and the Hong

Kong Federation of Youth Groups. Joint business plan competitions are also regularly organized between universities from Hong Kong, Macau, Taiwan, and Shenzhen.

Some Hong Kong associations and organizations also provide entrepreneurs with support for their training and act as a platform to share experiences, mentorship, and business opportunities created through global strategic relationships. Examples include Accelerator HK, General Assembly, NEST, StartLab Hong Kong, Start-ups HK, AAMA, TiE, Cyberport and HK Design Centre. The incubation program run by HKSTP is one of the leading programs for nurturing start-ups. Since 1992 it has nurtured more than 350 start-ups. Of these, 280 (79 percent) are still in business, four have grown into public listed companies and sixteen were acquired or merged. From an initial size of two employees, many now have more than 200 employees and revenues of more than $10 million. These companies have also filed over 796 intellectual property applications for patents, trademarks and registered designs. They have successfully secured over HK$1 billion in angel and venture capital investment and won 316 awards in the local, regional and international arena. Some outstanding awards obtained by these incubated companies include: the Grand Prix Award in the 43rd International Exhibitions of Inventions of Geneva (2015), won by Vitargent (International) Biotechnology Limited; the Asia Pacific Region Overall Award of Talent Unleashed Awards 2014, won by Ximplar Limited; and the 2012 National Business Incubation Association (NBIA) Tech Incubatee of the Year Awards, won by iMusicTech Limited.

To further strengthen the local start-up community, HKSTP has recently initiated the TechnoPreneur Partnership Program (TPP) to create a collaboration platform for technology ecosystem stakeholders. Through TPP, HKSTP partners with six local universities and 14 start-up communities including the incubators Blueprint and Nest, as well as the co-working spaces Cocoon and TusPark. The program emphasizes network-building and sharing of support services and resources. Adding to the resources available, Accenture recently launched a fintech acceleration program in Hong Kong, after its success with the model in New York and London. Nest and AIA have also launched a healthcare acceleration program, attracting more global start-ups.

ANGEL GROUP STRUCTURES AND ORGANIZATIONS

There are not many organized angel groups in Hong Kong although some global angel groups have established local chapters. Across all angel groups there are estimated to be about 100 active angel investors, i.e., those who have invested in one or more deals in the past 12 months. There are no public or private sidecar funds. However, an increase in active angel investment is much desired. The afore-mentioned local chapters include Angels Den, the Hong Kong Angel Investment Network (HKAIN) and the British Chamber of Commerce in Hong Kong. Founded in 2007 in the UK, Angels Den is a commercially operated angel group. Its offers low upfront fees plus a success fee when companies get funded. HKAIN is a web-based matching service for angel investors and entrepreneurs. It is owned by Angel Investment Network Ltd, a London based investment company founded in 2004. The British Chamber of Commerce in Hong Kong set up the Business Angel Program in 2007 with sponsorship from Baker Tilly. Its website and associated events give their members—entrepreneurs with new business ventures and SMEs looking for funding to expand—the opportunity to present their business plans to investors.

HKBAN was formally established in 2011 with a mission to foster angel investment in Hong Kong by building an open matching platform. Since its inception, it has hosted five to six investment matching gatherings per year. Each partner organization submits "teasers" from its own network of entrepreneurs. A vetting committee determines if any of the companies reaches the investment threshold. The top six companies then make their pitches to angels, who discuss the pros and cons of the deals and question the entrepreneurs. Thereafter, angels and entrepreneurs are left to structure their own deals.

The Asian Business Angel Forum (ABAF), inaugurated in 2010, is Asia's largest gathering of angel investors and emerging businesses, especially in the innovation and technology industry. ABAF events in Singapore, Shanghai, Kuala Lumpur and Mumbai attract business leaders, angel investors, venture capitalists, policymakers and start-up specialists from across the world to support Asia's top entrepreneurs and angel investors. As a founding member, HKBAN hosted ABAF in May 2014. Over 500 angels and entrepreneurs attended.

GOVERNMENT POLICIES TO PROMOTE ANGEL INVESTING

Governments worldwide try to encourage angel investment in view of its positive social and economic contributions. The most common practice is offering tax incentives. The government of Hong Kong has long ascribed to a laissez faire policy. Since the handover in 1997, however, a more active government industrial policy has been introduced. In the early 2000s, the government showed its commitment to innovation and technology development by creating: the Innovation and Technology Commission; the Applied Science and Technology Research Institute (ASTRI); the Hong Kong Science and Technology Parks Corporation; and Hong Kong Cyberport Management Company Limited.

In Hong Kong there is no policy for the direct promotion of business angel investing. The closest policy would be Enterprise Support Scheme (ESS), a major funding initiative under the Innovation and Technology Fund (ITF), which is designed to encourage the private sector to invest in R&D. Approved projects receive support of up to HK$10 million on a dollar-for-dollar matching basis. Enterprises can raise angel investment funds to match it. The Hong Kong government and other industry organizations also offer various funding schemes and support for local SMEs. There are at least 38 such schemes among the funding categories: research and development, market development, creativity and design, financing, environment management, start-up/incubation, operation enhancement, mainland funding schemes, and training.

The ITF also offers a General Support Program (GSP) for non-R&D projects such as conferences, exhibitions, workshops, promotional events, studies, and youth activities. HKBAN successfully applied for funding support from GSP to host the 2014 Asian Business Angel Forum. Recently, the Hong Kong government approved the launch of a corporate Venture Fund, allocating HK$50 million to HKSTP to co-invest with angels and VC funds into start-ups (ranging from seed to Series A stage). Many traditional funds, including real estate family funds, have shown interest in co-investing.

THE FUTURE OF ANGEL INVESTING IN HONG KONG

As founding Chairman of HKBAN and Chief Corporate Development Officer of HKSTP, I have had the opportunity to witness the angel community, and interest in the angel community, grow in the last two years. Even more exciting, the support system for entrepreneurship has been expanding rapidly in Hong Kong lately, with the creation of more co-working spaces, more start-up events, and accelerators. As the volume and quality of deals improve, the attractiveness of angel investment will undoubtedly increase. Although the government of Hong Kong does not yet having a dedicated policy to promote angel investments, once private investment has taken root it should be quite sustainable.

In March 2013 *Forbes* Magazine ranked Hong Kong the Number One Tech Capital to watch in the world after Silicon Valley and New York, ahead of Washington, Tel Aviv, and London. Many have doubts about whether Hong Kong can truly transform itself into a tech capital. I am confident that Hong Kong has all the ingredients. All it needs is to keep fueling the fire of entrepreneurship and its stakeholders. Furthermore, as with the ACA and EBAN, the development of ABAF can bring angels from Asia together each year to share best practices and develop cross-border investment. This will help young ventures develop in the diverse Asian market.

United States

Marianne Hudson

Angel investing has become "serious finance" in the United States. In 2014 an estimated 300,000 angels invested about \$24.1 billion in more than 70,000 high-growth companies.[1] For the last two decades, angel investors have invested in hundreds of thousands of promising start-ups in a wide variety of sectors, and particularly in technology, healthcare, and mobile & telecom.[2] It comes as a surprise to many that angels have provided roughly the same amount of capital as venture capitalists during these decades—and the bigger surprise is that angels have supported more than ten times the number of companies.[3]

American angels particularly provide the vast majority of funding to innovative start-ups, after founders, friends and family provide first support. These angel investors bring their past experience as entrepreneurs, corporate leaders and top professionals to mentor and guide entrepreneurial teams, and this "intellectual capital" may be even more important to entrepreneurial success than the money.

While angel investors have been a secret weapon for many start-ups, most Americans had never heard of angels until very recently. Angel

MARIANNE HUDSON is Executive Director of the Angel Capital Association, the professional association of active accredited investors in North America. She is an active angel investor through both angel groups and accredited platforms, and regularly speaks and writes about angel investing trends and best practices.

deals are mostly private and generally not in reports available to the public. However, the media and public are increasingly recognizing the contributions of the country's angels, perhaps due to the fact that many of today's brand-name corporations were initially financed by angel investors. Examples include Amazon, Facebook, Google, LinkedIn, Starbucks, and Twitter.

An exciting part of American angel investing is that angels—and great deals—can be found in every state in the country. Many in the global start-up community tend to think Silicon Valley represents all equity investing in the US, but actually investors are spread throughout the country. There is considerable diversity in how angels operate and growing evidence that other parts of the country are just as active as Silicon Valley.[4] Sophisticated angels in the Midwest and other parts of the country are not only active, but are recognized for their excellent innovations and good practices throughout the world.

These innovations make angel investing all the more interesting for investors. American angels currently have a wonderful variety of ways to make their investments, allowing them to customize their investing to their personalities and interests. Angels can be independent or invest through formal organizations. They can invest through special online investing platforms for angels, and in all opportunities they have the choice to invest privately or in publicly advertised deals. This variety and innovation fits the American culture of entrepreneurship.

THE AMERICAN CULTURE OF ENTREPRENEURSHIP AND INVESTING

Any discussion of angel investing in the US starts with the country's focus on entrepreneurship. And while many have trouble spelling the word, most realize that this culture started before America was even a country. As the *Economist* wrote, "[American] entrepreneurialism is so deeply rooted in its history. It was founded and then settled by innovators and risk-takers who were willing to sacrifice old certainties for new opportunities. American schoolchildren are raised on stories about inventors such as Benjamin Franklin and Thomas Edison. Entrepreneurs such as Andrew Carnegie and Henry Ford are celebrated in monuments all over the place."[5]

In truth, the US economy did not become based on entrepreneurship until the late 1970s, but the founding history helped the country convert from an economy of managerial capitalism to one of start-ups, fast growth, and invention.

Today, entrepreneurship is a part of the American fabric. The majority of young people are interested in starting their own businesses. Many have attended entrepreneurship courses and programs at more than 300 universities, supplemented their academic experience with Meetups and immersive programs like Startup Weekend, and then developed their business ideas in start-up accelerators. More and more entrepreneurs are becoming sophisticated in how to develop high growth start-ups and get them financed, and most accept the risks of starting new businesses. That said, the majority of new American entrepreneurs have a great deal to learn, in most angels' estimations.

The story of equity investing is similar. Perhaps the first example of angel investing in an American project was Queen Isabella's financing in 1492 of the journey of Christopher Columbus to what would eventually become the Americas. Wealthy individuals have been investing in new businesses ever since; it just wasn't called "angel" investing most of that time. The name "angel investor" came about in the 1930s when Broadway play producers credited their investors for saving their shows, with the dramatic name only these artists could suggest—investors were "angels from heaven." Investors started using the term in earnest during the 1970s as Silicon Valley began to develop, but angel activity remained quiet and private.

During the early years of Silicon Valley, venture capitalists (VCs) funded top start-ups, along the way developing discipline and professional practices that led to a new investing asset class in the US and eventually the world. Over time, however, VCs raised larger and larger funds which also meant they needed to make bigger investments in order to gain commensurate economic rewards. VCs began investing in later and later stage companies, leaving a gap in financing for start-up companies. Angels began filling the start-up funding gap in the mid-1980s and also picked up many of the good investing practices of VCs. Today the angel community is where VCs were in the 1980s, but is rapidly innovating and developing.

Angel investors are now considered the start-up financiers, while VCs providing expansion capital.

A very important thing to understand about the American entrepreneurial ecosystem is that the country is large and diverse, and so are the practices of entrepreneurship and investing. People from other countries, and the American media, seem to believe that all US entrepreneurs and investors are in Silicon Valley and are all huge risk-takers. This just is not true.

There is interesting activity in all 50 states, and also a wide variety of mindsets, knowledge and resources. Past entrepreneurial failure, for example, may be a badge of honor in Silicon Valley, but it is not in the rest of the country. The focus in many parts of the US is on building comfort in taking risks, particularly for investors, and pairing this awareness with education on how to make good investment decisions and mitigate risks. The economics of deals are often quite different as well, as companies in traditional venture capital regions (Silicon Valley, New York, and Boston) often have valuations that are two or three times larger than those in other regions for similar companies. Bill Payne, a top angel investor, compares angel investing to real estate—it's all about location.[6]

NEW EVOLUTION RAPIDLY CHANGES ANGEL INVESTING

American angel investing appears to have been pretty much the same for most of the country's history—until very recently. For 200 years, it was quiet and private, and done mostly by individuals or informal sets of investors. Some of the basic rules for angel investing changed in 1933, when new investor protections were set by the federal government during the Great Depression.

The practices for investing in new firms were essentially the same for the rest of the 20th century. But just as entrepreneurial innovations and technologies have rapidly changed people's lives, the landscape for early stage investing has changed more in the last few years than it has in centuries. Just look at the evolution. In the last 20 years, these major innovations took place, changing angel investing forever and providing exciting opportunities for both investors and entrepreneurs:

1995   Individual angels started investing together with other angels in formal groups.

2006   Groups started co-investing with other angel groups, backing entrepreneurs with the money they needed for success and helping diversify angel portfolios and sometimes syndicating for multiple rounds when VC money was not available.

2006   Accelerators proliferated to fund and develop interesting start-ups for angels to support. Y Combinator and TechStars led this field, partnering with angels throughout the world.

2007   Top angels raised funds from institutional investors and became "super angels," each funding hundreds of start-ups per year. Well known super angels include Ron Conway, Dave McClure, and Reid Hoffman, among others.

2010   Entrepreneurs began using social media such as LinkedIn to connect to potential investors.

2010   Innovative angels harnessed the power of the Internet to connect investors and start-up deals, developing new ways to "curate" interesting deals for private investment. AngelList started the proliferation of online investing platforms for accredited investors,[7] with syndicates of investors forming and providing new ways for traditional angels to fill out their investment rounds.

2012   Congress passed the Jumpstart Our Business Startups (JOBS) Act,[8] creating whole new paths of financing, including equity crowdfunding and allowing for private offerings to be "generally solicited." It should be noted that the regulations for equity crowdfunding for the general public have not yet been released, so this type of financing was not allowed in the US as of publishing time for this book.

More big changes will undoubtedly come as the market continues to innovate and adjusts to rules and regulations that will help the JOBS Act become a reality.

Today, angels have many options to make angel investments. The large majority of American angels still invest independently, but a growing number do so through formal angel groups and online platforms for accredited investors.

ANGEL GROUPS

The number of angel groups in the US continues to grow, with 470 such organizations across the country as of August, 2015. The number of angel groups has grown almost five times in 15 years.

Angel groups have become an important way for angel investors to more easily connect with entrepreneurs in their communities, work together to evaluate investment opportunities and negotiate terms with entrepreneurial firms, be efficient in mentoring and monitoring portfolio companies through board of director service, diversify their investment portfolios, and share investment knowledge and best practices among members. The fact that groups are fun and a great way to meet interesting people is an important draw for many investors.

Angel groups come in many formats: 70 percent are networks (in which each angel decides individually which deals they invest in), 23 percent are funds (where angels pool their funds upfront and take majority votes on investment opportunities), and the remainder are networks with sidecar funds (essentially a cross between the two). Most tend to lead investments in companies in their communities or regions, but will join syndicates in wider geographic areas. Most also invest in a variety of industry sectors, based on the experience and expertise of their member angels, although a small percentage focus on particular sectors such as life sciences or clean technology. Ten groups focus specifically on investing in women or minority-led companies and their members are mostly (but not all) women.

Angel groups have a wide range of sizes and activity levels, but the following averages from survey data in 2014 are helpful to understanding their scale:[9]

- 68 member investors
- 10.3 deals completed during the year
- $2.46 million in total investment dollars throughout the year
- One year after investment, angel-backed companies create a median of 17.5 jobs.

The 2014 Halo Report analyzes the deals of angel groups, and among its key findings are:[10]

- The median total round size is $800,000, with larger valuations for healthcare sector investments. This shows the importance of syndication among angel groups, with about 80 percent of the investments completed by two or more angel groups and other early-stage investors.
- Median pre-money valuation is $3 million, up from $2.5 million in 2013.
- The most active groups were spread across different parts of the country, with five based in traditionally active VC regions (e.g., California, Boston, and New York), but others in Georgia, Maine, Texas, and Wisconsin.
- Two-thirds of the investments, by both number of deals and dollars, are in three sectors: internet, healthcare, and mobile & telecom.

ONLINE (ACCREDITED) INVESTING PLATFORMS

Angels began using websites to make investments in 2010, when AngelList started. Five years later, there may be as many as 100 of these "accredited platforms," serving investors in a variety of ways. A growing number of investors belong to these platforms, and many of these also belong to angel groups.

Platforms offer a range of different structures, from following famous angel investors who lead deals to conducting due diligence and other services for passive investors to connecting investors to communicate deal evaluation among member accredited investors. In addition, some platforms serve primarily like-minded investors. For instance, some focus on life sciences or energy sectors, and others connect women angels who want to invest in women-led companies.

The platforms are also growing in investment activity. Overall investment information on these specific types of investing platforms are not available at this time, but one can get a sense of their activity. In 2014 AngelList investors supported 243 start-ups with a total $104 million. HealthiosXchange investors have invested a total of $350 million in 40 life-science companies since the platform began, and FundersClub investors have funded 151 companies with $42 million since the platform was founded. Each of these figures appear on the platforms' websites.

ANGEL CAPITAL ASSOCIATION

The professional association for angel investors in the US and North America is the Angel Capital Association. The association also has members from Canada and Mexico. ACA was formed in the early 2000s as angel investors wanted to talk with each other, learn better ways to invest, and develop trust to co-invest with each other. After two years of hosting small meetings, ACA formally launched in 2005. Today ACA is the largest association of its kind in the world, aligning like-minded angels to build their early stage investment skills and share innovative ideas and practices. ACA offers professional development, public policy advocacy and significant benefits and resources to its membership of more than 13,000 accredited investors, who invest individually or through 240 angel groups, accredited platforms and family offices (as of August, 2015).

ACA was originally formed as an association of angel group leaders, but evolved over time to serve active accredited investors from North America using whichever investment vehicles they choose. A growing number of members invest on an individual basis or manage online accredited investor platforms. The association has always been led by and financed by angels and the private sector, through a combination of membership dues, private sponsorships, and events such as the annual ACA Summit, which attracts 700 plus investors from throughout the world every Spring to build their investing knowledge and share ideas.

ACA works with a separate "sister" organization, the Angel Resource Institute (ARI), which conducts research on angel investing (including the Halo Report, mentioned earlier) and deep seminars for angels, investors, and the start-up support community. ARI was originally funded by and spun out of the Ewing Marion Kauffman Foundation, a large philanthropic foundation focused on entrepreneurial research, awareness and education.

AMERICAN PUBLIC POLICY FITS
THE AMERICAN ENTREPRENEURIAL SPIRIT

The American entrepreneurial spirit has a big impact on how government is involved in private sector markets. Unlike the majority of countries included in this book, there are very few federal public policies that directly impact angels and other private equity investors. The American view of appropriate public policy for our field might be described as "make sure the infrastructure and economy are well set so that the private sector to flourish on its own."

On a national basis, this means strong systems to: support university education and research; protect intellectual property; balance investor protection with support for capital formation; ensure effective bankruptcy laws; ensure the free flow of goods and services; allow businesses to incorporate easily; and ensure the tax system leads to strong private investment in the country's businesses, among many others.

The federal government has intervened directly in a few areas in the innovation and small business arena to address larger market gaps. Examples include:

- Creation of the Small Business Administration to aid, counsel, assist and protect the interests of small businesses. Among these is a national network of thousands of Small Business Development Centers that provide education and counseling to new and small businesses near them.
- Establishment of grant and financial support programs for small businesses and non-profit entities that support them. The Small Business Innovation Research program provides grants for innovative research that US government departments need, sometimes leading to new commercial products, and newer programs provide operating capital for start-up accelerators and incubators on a competitive basis.
- Support for underserved populations in the small business/ entrepreneurial economy by increasing the participation of women, minorities, military veterans, and rural residents.
- Special tax breaks to incent more research and development by small firms.

- Financial support of basic and applied research at universities and national laboratories.
- Protection of intellectual property rights for innovations developed at universities.
- Immigration laws the allow researchers, innovators and entrepreneurs to build their companies in the US Americans will continue debating the details of expanding this type of immigration in the coming years.

While there have been occasional initiatives that finance investment in smaller businesses, few are long term or particularly well known. Instead Congress and federal officials have focused on securities regulation and an overall tax system that supports business investment in general.

AMERICAN ANGELS MUST BE 'ACCREDITED INVESTORS'

National securities regulation is chief among the US public policy issues for angel investors. The term "accredited investor" has been mentioned several times, and is a critical concept to understand in American angel investing. Here's why: US securities law provides an exemption from securities registration when all investors in an offering are accredited (i.e., they meet wealth and income thresholds),[11] and in instances when all investors make their own investment decisions and no fees are charged for successfully raising capital.

The regulatory exemption is so important that ACA begins its definition of an angel investor with a requirement that the individual is an accredited investor. Angel groups and online investing platforms also require that all member angel investors are accredited investors. By far the biggest public policy challenge for American angel investors during the past decade has been fighting against campaigns to change the definition of accredited investors. Powerful consumer protection organizations have lobbied Congress and securities regulators to decrease the number of people who meet the accredited investor standards as a means of reducing fraud (fraud, as it turns out, that is not related to angel investing).

To date, angel investors have been successful in minimizing these changes, effectively arguing that angel investing has experienced almost no fraud to investors and also pointing out the importance of angel investors to the health of the economy. Kauffman Foundation research shows that all of the net new jobs in the US over the past 25 years have been created by companies that are five years old or less and that the largest portion of those businesses have been high-growth firms.[12] As angel-backed companies are high-growth, and angels are the source of 90 percent of the equity capital that start-ups receive,[13] many easily understand the important economic contribution angel investors make. That said, the issue is expected to continue over many years.

NATIONAL TAX POLICY

As mentioned earlier, American policymakers have provided fewer policies that directly support angel investing than their counterparts in other countries. However, a small number of favorable federal tax policies have been important to the development of strong equity investing in the US[14] These include:

- A lower tax rate for capital gains than for ordinary income tax: several long-time angels say that this was one of the biggest drivers of increased angel investing when these taxes were set in the mid-1990s. When angels had positive exits, it also allowed them more of their returns to be re-invested in new angel investments.
- Ability to recoup some investment losses: angels can maximize tax deductions for capital losses on investments for deals in which they are part of the first $1 million in financing for qualifying businesses.
- Reduced taxes for successful investments: investors can exclude 50 or more percent of their gains on successful exits in qualified small business stock.[15]

The US does not have tax credits to catalyze angel investments on a national basis. Instead, most of the supportive policies and innovative thinking have by initiated by state governments.

STATES PROVIDE TAX BENEFITS AND OTHER SUPPORT

More than half of American states offer some kind of tax credits for new investments in small businesses located within those states.[16]

Many of the state programs have been around for a short time so the results are not yet available, but the state of Wisconsin found its credits resulted in growth of angel investing by more than 10 times over a few years and also seeded companies that attracted more than four times in venture and other follow-on capital.

Many states have also experimented with a variety of programs. The real action and innovation is happening in states that did not start with natural entrepreneurial communities, but want to catalyze healthier ecosystems and minimize the risks inherent in investing in early stage companies. Krista Tuomi, assistant professor at American University, catalogs many of these programs for the angel community:

- Tax credits: 27 states offer tax credits to angels who invest in small businesses, providing an average state income tax credit of 25 percent. The majority of these states restrict the quantity of credits that can be claimed per investor, business, and/or per investment. Most provide criteria for qualifying companies and investors and provide varying allowances on how long unclaimed credits may be carried to future years, how long investment must be held before the tax credits are claimed, whether credits can be transferred to other tax payers, and how states recapture credit dollars if their program requirements are not met.[17]
- Programs to mobilize angel groups and match them with entrepreneurs: the Wisconsin Angel Network is considered a leader in this type of support, with 15 other states experimenting with variants of the idea.
- Direct government funding of investing and support activities. These include co-investment funds, public seed funds, grants that match approved private investments, and funds of funds. Many states took advantage of a one-time federal program, the State Small Business Credit Initiative, to do this.[18]
- Help entrepreneurs to attract federal dollars. Several states provide matching grants and/or expert mentoring to help small firms win federal grants, such as the Small Business Innovation Research program mentioned earlier.

American states continue to innovate on policies and programs to support entrepreneurs, investors and the professionals who support entrepreneurs. These programs can play an important role in offsetting some of the risk inherent in seed investment.

DATA AND EXPERIENCE BUILD SOPHISTICATION AND EVOLUTION

No American angel investing summary would be complete without at least some of the lessons learned from both data on our field and our considerable experience in investing. Important learnings come from both successes and failures!

Underpinning many of these lessons is data and analysis, such as the study on returns of angel investors in groups, led by Robert Wiltbank and published by the Kauffman Foundation.[19] This study, which reviewed more than 1,100 exited investments (both positive and negative), found an overall return of 2.6 times the invested money in 2.5 years—or a gross internal rate of return of about 27 percent.

More important than the average return for this "portfolio" of 1,100 exits, was the wide, unbalanced distribution of exits, with 52 percent of the exits losing some or all of the investment and seven percent providing nearly all of the return. I.e., the average is a poor indicator of the performance for most of the angels who participated. Nonetheless, there are some good takeaways that can lead to better returns:[20]

- **Look for the home run opportunities.** As Wiltbank says, "The returns are massively skewed. Ten percent of all of deals produce 90 percent of the returns." Sophisticated angels have paid attention to this. A few top angels have told me they started out looking for singles and doubles, thinking they could make most of their returns in those deals. Now they have changed their game—it's all about hitting home runs.
- **Diversify your investments.** Not only does a small percentage of deals deliver the biggest returns, but there a 50-50 chance that each individual investment will be a failure or a success, so you need to make many investments to find a home run.
- **Take your time and be patient but persistent.** The 52 percent of the exits that lost money did so in an average of three years, while the big returns took an average of six years. As you wait for the bigger returns, learn by watching others and enjoy the process and the angels and entrepreneurs you meet.

- **Do due diligence.** Just looking at amount of time in due diligence, angels who did more than the median amount of diligence on a deal (20 hours) did significantly better than those below the median. The overall multiple difference was almost six times—5.9x compare to 1.1x! This is mostly about reducing failures. Said another way, 65 percent of the below-median due diligence angels lost money, compared to 45 percent for the above-median group. Now, there's a reason to roll up your sleeves to check the companies out!
- **Invest in what you know.** Putting your specific industry expertise into your investing is common sense. The study showed that when the investor had expertise in the company's industry, the exit was three time higher than for others (3.7x compared to 1.3x, both in around four years). Use your entrepreneurial experience, too. Wiltbank says that "angel investors are well suited to early-stage investing because many have been entrepreneurs themselves."
- **Stay connected to the entrepreneur after you invest.** Investors who met with company leaders often to mentor, coach, or offer strategic consulting and that monitored the company's progress saw an overall multiple of 3.7x in four years. Conversely, those who took a more passive approach reported an average lower multiple of 1.3X in 3.6 years.

These lessons have been part of American angel investing for several years now. As more Americans gain experience as angel investors, we also see a shift in education and best practices. Perhaps the biggest change is to build expertise that lasts throughout the life of an investment. It is no longer enough to learn how to select the right investment opportunities and negotiate the right terms. Instead, top angels put even more emphasis on the best way to support their portfolio companies after they invest so that these companies grow and more easily get to a successful exit. Angels are now learning the finer points of helping their portfolio companies attract follow-on investments, connect with new customers, and find large corporations to acquire them. Not only does this life-cycle focus increase the chances for great financial returns, but many angels particularly enjoy mentoring entrepreneurs and serving on their boards of directors. Many American angels are constantly learning and gaining expertise as investors and supporters of really interesting companies. The coming years are sure to bring new experience, learning, and innovations.

CONTINUED EVOLUTION AND SHARING ACROSS THE GLOBE

With so many exciting innovations within angel investing and early stage investing in general—both within the US and throughout the world—more changes in angel investing are expected in the coming years. In particular, American angels will need to adjust to equity crowdfunding by unaccredited investors once securities regulations are set (perhaps in 2016). Americans also expect a slow growth in cross-border investment as investors across the globe get to know and trust each other and as trusted internet platforms (that address American securities laws) proliferate. Interesting deals abound, as do new knowledge and best practices for angel investing in many parts of the world.

Endnotes

[1] The Angel Investor Market in 2014, Center for Venture Research, University of New Hampshire, May, 2015.

[2] 2014 Halo Report, Angel Resource Institute, www.angelresourceinstitute.org/research/halo-report.aspx. In 2014, these sectors accounted for 68 percent of all deals in the Halo Report dataset.

[3] Center for Venture Research and PwC MoneyTree Report, www.pwcmoneytree.com

[4] 2014 Halo Report, Angel Resource Institute, www.angelresourceinstitute.org/research/halo-report.aspx. The data shows that the Great Lakes region actually had more angel group total dolar investment than the state of California.

[5] The United States of Entrepreneurs, The Economist, www.economist.com/node/13216037, March, 2009.

[6] Why Location Matters For Startup Valuations, Forbes.com, http://www.forbes.com/sites/mariannehudson/2015/06/05/start-up-valuations-why-location-matters/, June, 2015.

[7] US Securities & Exchange Commission, www.sec.gov/answers/accred.htm

[8] Jumpstart Our Business Startups Act, Wikipedia, https://en.wikipedia.org/wiki/Jumpstart-Our_Business-Startups-Act.

[9] 2014 Survey of ACA Member Angel Groups, Angel Capital Association (March, 2015)

[10] 2014 Halo Report, Angel Resource Institute.

[11] US Securities & Exchange Commission, www.sec.gov/answers/accred.htm.

[12] Firm Formation and Growth Series, studies published by Ewing Marion Kauffman Foundation, 2008-2015.

[13] Why Entrepreneurs Need Angels—and How Angels are Improving," Marianne Hudson, Kauffman Thoughtbook 2005, Ewing Marion Kauffman Foundation.

[14] Tax Tips Every Angel Investor Should Know, Marianne Hudson, Forbes.com, November, 2014.

[15] Qualified Small Business Stock, IRC Section 1202, http://www.journalofaccountancy.com/issues/2013/may/20137453.html .

[16] The Angel Capital Association website provides research reports and details on individual state tax programs beginning at http://www.angelcapitalassociation.org/aca-public-policy-state-policies/.

[17] Angel Tax Credits: What Makes Good Policy? Krista Tuomi and Barbara Boxer, presentation at 2014 Angel Capital Association Summit. Average figures for US states: maximum credit allowed: $2 million; restriction on equity: less than 50%; size/age of start-up at time of investment: less than $5 million gross revenue and less than 7 years old; carryover period: 5 years; and holding period: 3 years.

[18] The State Small Business Credit Initiative is a component of the US Small Business Jobs Act of 2010, and was funded with $1.5 Billion of federal dollars to strengthen state programs that provide financing support to small businesses.

[19] Returns to Angel Investors in Groups, Robert Wiltbank and Warren Boeker, published by Kauffman Foundation (2007), available via http://www.angelcapitalassociation.org/research/. A 2015 study was underway as this book was published.

[20] The following bullets are directly from a previous article by Marianne Hudson in Forbes.com, "How Angels Can Enjoy The Best Returns—Financial and Otherwise," September 2014. The article is based on an interview with Robert Wiltbank. http://www.forbes.com/sites/mariannehudson/2014/09/04/how-angels-can-enjoy-the-best-returns-financial-and-otherwise/.

Germany

Dr. Ute Gunther

Angels are the most important investors for early stage companies in Germany. According to an estimate by Zentrum für Europäische Wirtschaftsentwicklung (ZEW) there are currently between 2,700 and 5,400 active angels in Germany.[1] They annually invest between €300 and €400 million,[2] €190 of which goes to the first round of high-tech companies.[3] Angels are estimated to hold around four investments on average,[4] translating into an average investment per engagement of between €50,000 and €150,000.[5] The ZEW study shows that financing of young technology companies by third party equity is still underdeveloped, with only 4.1 percent accessing angels and 0.9 percent accessing venture capital.[6] The proportion of university spinoffs among these is a high 42 percent.[7] Start-ups that receive funding from third parties are larger, grow faster and are more innovative.[8]

ANGELS NETWORKS

There are currently about 40 angel networks in Germany.[9] Their main role is to screen young innovative companies and match them with angels. The angel networks act as intermediaries, increasing

DR. UTE GUNTHER is the Vice President of Business Angels Europe. Since 2001 she has been on the executive board of Business Angels Network Germany, the umbrella organization of the German Business Angels Networks. Since 1999 she has been on the executive board member of Business Angels Agency Ruhr E.V.

investment activity in high-tech companies. They are very important for German economic growth because they channel capital and know-how into innovative projects. Two main types of angel networks exist in Germany. Some economic development agencies have actively built up regional angels networks, often with their own staff taking management roles. These types of networks are mainly focused on regional start-ups. Many private angel networks are also active in Germany. These normally look for innovative start-ups from all over the country, although some focus on specific areas. German angels, even those who are members of a network, mostly invest on an individual basis or in small syndicates of two to five investors. Some networks have also started sidecar funds, with network members as shareholders. These sidecar funds invest alone or in cooperation with one lead investor from the network.

ANGELS NETZWERK DEUTSCHLAND E.V (BAND)

Angels Netzwerk Deutschland E.V. (BAND) was founded in 1998 to build up the angel culture in Germany. It was initiated by the German government, several large financial institutions, some angels and some academics. Between 2001 and 2004 the market for informal VC gained importance as regional angels networks were established and professional standards were defined. Most of the regional networks (around 40) became members of BAND. After 2004 the angel market developed rapidly and became more professional. Conditions for angel investment improved, and the market became more complex and differentiated. Today BAND is recognized as the umbrella organization for the German angel networks. BAND also has private members including scientists and sponsors. It is supported by the federal Ministry of Economics and Technology.

As the angel umbrella organization, BAND is the spokesperson for the German angel community and represents the interests of young, innovative companies. To build up the angel culture in Germany, BAND organizes the exchange of experiences and promotes cooperation. It promotes the model of a "two-winged" angel who provides both capital and management know-how to innovative start-ups. Angels use their personal network of contacts to support start-ups at the beginning of the funding chain, where the bottleneck is greatest.

BAND offers several services for its members and start-ups, including deal-flow management, angel panels and publications. It also organizes events, workshops, and congresses to strengthen the public awareness of the importance of angels. Deal-flow management is particularly important. Every year BAND gets about 600 funding requests. Start-ups send their request via the form "One Pager," which can be downloaded from the BAND website.[10] After a plausibility check, the One Pager is forwarded to angel network members. These network members screen and match proposals. The angel panel is a quarterly evaluation of the angel market initiated by BAND, Rheinisch-Westfälische Technische Hochschule Aachen (RWTH), the VDI nachrichten, Düsseldorf and the University of Duisburg-Essen. It consists of more than 50 active angels who know the market and invest in start-ups. To ensure balance, participants are sourced from different regions in Germany. The panel answers questions on items such as the number of deals, investment amounts, and which industries are attractive. The results of the panel are published after each survey in the VDI nachrichten and other influential journals. Currently the angel panel is the only Europe-wide system analyzing developments in the angel market.

There are a number of BAND publications. BANDquartal is a quarterly online publication about news and trends in the German angel market. BANDneues publishes ad hoc news about the angel market. It is addressed to press representatives and journalists. Angels Guide: BAND consists of several studies and guides concerning the angel market and the process of investing in young innovative start-ups. One of the newest is "Leitfaden für Angels" (The Guide for Angels), written by experts of the German angel scene who use case studies to provide a practical overview of all aspects of the market. It offers practical articles that help investors further professionalize their activities. Founders looking for angel capital can use it to learn about what angels need in order to invest.

BAND events are growing in popularity. German Angel Day (DBT) started in 2001 and is one of the most important events organized by BAND. With more than 500 participants and 150 exhibitors, it is the largest convention of its kind in Europe. An important part of the DBT are the presentations by innovative capital-seeking companies who are chosen by a screening committee of German angels. BAND proclaimed the year 2010 as the "year of the angels." This was the starting point for the decade of the angels, a large-scale ten year initiative to stimulate and promote awareness of the angel market. Every two years BAND also organizes a Community Summit for designated angels to give voice to the work of the angels and allow individual members to interact with and inspire each other. Another regular event is the annual BANDexpertforum, where angels and experts discuss best practices, the legal situation, trends and current syndications. The discussion topics are chosen by BAND and experts are invited to submit abstracts on these to a selection panel. During the Expertforum, those chosen present for 15 minutes, then open the topic to the floor for a 45-minute debate. Every year BAND also gives a "Golden Nose" prize to the German "Angel of the Year," the angel with the best "instinct" for selecting investments. Only start-ups can recommend "their" angel for the award. BAND further organizes several branch oriented matching events with recent ones being held in medical technology, IT and environmental technology. Last, BAND plays a lobbying role on issues such as investment promotion, tax policy and the promotion of entrepreneurship in Germany. Recently, it successfully prevented burdensome tax changes that would have affected angel investments and helped introduce public programs to support angel investments.

THE GERMAN ANGEL ECOSYSTEM

Early-stage financing is becoming more complex, with a variety of active market participants, including:

- Super angels, who are capable of later stage financing rounds on par with venture capital companies and family offices
- Angels networks, who match capital-seeking companies with angels
- Angel or sidecar funds, affiliated with a particular angel network
- Seed funds, which are organized as public-private partnerships (e.g. High-Tech-Gründerfonds (HTGF) that focus on seed and the pre-seed stage investments.
- Venture capital companies
- Family offices
- Incubators/accelerators, who assist founder teams with business ideas, office space and capital

- Crowdinvesting platforms, which are reflective of the fast growth of crowdfunding in Germany (with €3.4 million collected in the first nine months of 2013). In the period from 2010 to the end of the third quarter 2013, 1,350 projects were funded by crowdinvesting.[11]
- Service companies that advise angels during the investment process.
- Experts and consultants such as lawyers, accountants and management consultants who specialize in early-stage financing.
- Scientists who have a research focus on early-stage financing.

In Germany there is no lack of basic entrepreneurial support structures (such as High-Tech Gründerfonds), but many struggle to finance the entire evolution from product innovation to a successful global company. Angels provide much of the high risk early investment and often rely on venture capital for follow-on financing. For the last few years, however, classic venture capital has been declining, which has both reinforced and complicated the role of angels.[12]

GOVERNMENT SUPPORT

According the Global Entrepreneurship Monitor, Germans do not consider entrepreneurial freedom a desirable alternative to wage employment, leading to a low founder rate.[13] The government has recognized this and is trying to promote an entrepreneurial culture, especially by encouraging spin-offs from federal universities. For example, the Federal Ministry of Economics and Technology's "Exist" program aims to instill the spirit of entrepreneurship in all subject areas on campus.[14] From 1998-2012 it invested €104 million into 72 projects on university campuses.[15] A large number of federal states also offer financial support (50-80 percent of the advisory fee) for start-ups to access professional consulting support related to marketing, competitive analysis and business plans.

PUBLIC GRANTS

Since 2013 the Federal Ministry of Economics and Technology has offered a new funding program for angels and start-ups called Investitionszuschuss Wagniskapital. It has a budget of €150 million until 2016 and is targeted at angels who invest in innovative SMEs that are less than 10 years old. Angels receive grants of 20 percent up to €50,000 per year, to increase their financial power for an investment.[16]

The European Angels Fund (EAF) is an initiative advised by the European Investment Fund (EIF), based in Luxembourg, and it allows for a high degree of freedom in terms of decisionmaking and management of investments. To ensure this, EAF verifies the qualifications and experience of angels before entering long-term contractual relationships with them. All investment decisions are then taken by the angels, and their investments are matched on a pari passu basis. Available amounts range between €250.000 and €5 million. The EAF shares investment-related costs on a pro rata basis[17] while gains are divided in a proportion of 60 percent for the angel and 40 percent for the EAF. The EAF was developed with BAND and is currently only available in Germany, with plans to roll it out to other countries.

Since 2005 High-Tech Gründerfonds (HTGF) has been investing in young companies, focusing on early stage life science, materials science and IT firms. In the first five years, HTGF financed approximately 250 companies from the high-tech sector. Together with industrial partners, HTGF launched "Gründerfonds II" in 2011 with a war chest of €301.5 million. (The involvement of large industrial companies opens up possibilities for co-operation between these companies and HTGF funded start-ups.) HTGF provides initial financing up to €500,000 in the form of subordinated convertible loans, acquiring 15 percent of the nominal share of the company. It also offers the opportunity to access up to €1.5 million of follow-on financing.

Recent figures show that German angels are playing an increasingly important role in providing follow-on financing. In the first seven months of 2012, for example, the investment volume by angels in HTGF significantly exceeded that of domestic and foreign venture capital companies in later financing rounds.[18] (They have invested €62 million to date). Co-investment programs like the "ERP Start Fond," which is provided by KfW Development Bank, have helped angel contributions reach seven digits and compensate for the lack of venture capital.[19] ERP Start Fond provides venture capital to small innovative companies with headquarters in Germany. It requires a private lead investor to invest parallel with KfW, who passively invests up 50 percent of the investment amount under the same terms as the investor.

OUTLOOK FOR THE GERMAN ANGEL MARKET

The creation of Investitionszuschuss Wagniskapital has provided an opportunity to stimulate investment in young innovative companies and increase the number of angels. The German government has also supported EAF and established an advisory board for the digital economy. The government aims to make Germany one of the leading ICT economic locations worldwide. These actions are already bearing results. Angels are growing in importance and this trend will be reinforced after more successful exits, when founders become angels themselves.[20] If these developments continue, the decrease in venture capital in Germany can be compensated by angels. Despite this, Germany needs to "catch up." Mobilization of private equity in Germany is far behind other European and non-European countries. Knowledge about angel market development is still insufficient. To strengthen the angel market it is necessary to analyze what is visible (angels who are organized in networks) and what is invisible (angels who are outside of networks). However, there are undisputed actions that can be taken now. Specialized training programs for investors, potential investors and start-ups should be developed. It is also necessary to introduce tax incentives for angel investments. These would include the ability to reinvest capital gains in start-ups without a tax burden within a certain period and better regulation regarding carry-forwards.

Endnotes

1   Helmut Fryges, Sandra Gottschalk, Georg Licht, Kathrin Müller: High-2 Tech Gründungen und Angels, Page IV, ZEW - Zentrum für Europäische Wirtschaftsforschung.
2   Angels Netzwerk Deutschland e.V. (BAND): "Facts and Background on Angels," 2013.
3   Helmut Fryges, Sandra Gottschalk, Georg Licht, Kathrin Müller: High-Tech Gründungen und Angels, Page IV, ZEW - Zentrum für Europäische Wirtschaftsforschung.
4   Angels Netzwerk Deutschland e.V. (BAND) estimates in 2010 in the presentation "Angels Investments" 3.8 investments per Angel; The German economic newspaper "Handelsblatt" estimates in 2007, 4.5 investments; A study published by

"Technologie-Beteiligungs-Gesellschaft mbH" from 2002, estimates 4.8 investments per Angel.

5 Angels Netzwerk Deutschland e.V. (BAND): "Facts and Background on Angels," 2013, estimates 50,000 Euro per engagement.

6 Helmut Fryges, Sandra Gottschalk, Georg Licht, Kathrin Müller: High-Tech Gründungen und Angels, Page IV, ZEW - Zentrum für Europäische Wirtschaftsforschung.

7 Ibid.

8 Ibid.

9 Angels Netzwerk Deutschland e.V., www.business-angels.de.

10 www.business-angels.de.

11 Ibid.

12 Zillikens, Stefanie (High-Tech Gründerfonds Management GmbH), in BANDquartal 03/2013.

13 Sternberg, Rolf; Vorderwülbecke, Arne; Brixy, Udo: Global Entrepreneurship Monitor - country report 2012, Page 23.

14 Federal ministry of economics and technology: http://www.exist.de/exist-gruendungskultur/index.php.

15 Ibid.

16 Bundesamt für Wirtschaft und Ausfuhrkontrolle (BAFA): http://www.exist.de/exist-gruendungskultur/index.php.

17 European Investment Fund (EIF): http://www.eif.org/what_we_do/equity/eaf/.

18 Zillikens, Stefanie in BANDquartal 03/2013.

19 Ibid.

20 Zillikens, Stefanie in BANDquartal 03/2013.

Scotland

Nelson Gray

INTRODUCTION

The positioning of Scotland within the United Kingdom provides a unique opportunity to study the effects that differing economic development policies have on the development of a local angel community. Scotland largely benefits from the same legal and taxation structures as the rest of the UK, and it shares a common currency and language. As with other parts of the UK, policies have been put in place to promote entrepreneurship and encourage research commercialization. Yet the angel community is more extensive in Scotland than in almost any other region in the UK or Europe. This chapter looks at some of the unique features of the Scottish market that have made this possible.

The important differentiator in policy has been the long term government support for the supply side of early stage funding, particularly angels. Moreover, this support used the private sector for policy delivery and was based on continuing research into how the identified market failures changed over time, allowing policy to be adjusted accordingly.

NELSON GRAY is the Special Projects Director of LINC Scotland, the Scottish Angel Capital Association. A member of angel groups in Scotland and the US, he is also on the Investment Advisory Board to the Angel Co-Investment Fund of the UK.

Scotland, with a population of 5.25 million, makes up one third of the land mass of the island of Great Britain and is one of the four countries that, together with England, Wales and Northern Ireland make up the UK. Its position allows it to benefit from its own distinctive policies for the promotion of entrepreneurship and early stage companies as well as those of the UK central government. The Scottish government's economic strategy is to "focus (our) support on those companies who can make the greatest contribution to the Scottish economy." This includes supporting start-ups with the highest growth potential, especially those based in 12 specified growth sectors.[1]

Scotland has 15 universities that include some of the oldest in the world (e.g. University of St Andrews, founded in 1413). Moreover, it has proportionally more universities in the QS "World University Rankings" Top 100 than any other nation in the world,[2] producing one percent of the world's published research with less than 0.1 percent of the world's population.[3] Of the top ten UK universities ranked by number of spinouts over the past three years, five are Scottish.[4]

The focus on high-tech firms has meant that the Scottish government recognizes importance of equity funding and angels. As a result the Scottish angel community has benefited from a wide range of initiatives:

- Policies designed to encourage entrepreneurship and deal flow for angels.
- Tax incentives to encourage individuals to become angels
- State co-investment funds enabling angels to fund more companies over a longer period
- Training and financial support for entrepreneurs, which improves deal flow quality on the demand side
- On the supply side, training and financial support for the formation of investment groups.

Scotland, in particular, has focused on the last three areas, specifically addressing the issues identified by the European Commission as key for the development of angels: building up capability and addressing demand side "investment readiness" problems. As this is addressed, policy can move onto supporting and co-investing while professional networks emerge.[5]

The ability and willingness of the Scottish Government to implement distinctive and innovative policies to meet local needs have seen angel investment increase from an estimated £1.5m in 1996[6] to £51.2m in 2010[7]. This represents 16 percent of the total angel investing in the UK (from 8 percent of the population), leading the OECD to recognize Scotland as the most active angel market in Europe.[8]

Deal Outcomes for European Angel Networks 2007
Source: EBAN, 2008

Data Source	No. of Deals	Amount Invested	Including Co Investment	Average Amount Per Deal
Scotland	61	20.454	41.304	335.3
Belgium	35	7.000		200.0
Netherlands	75	6.200		83.0
Finland	10	5.000		500.0
Catalonia	11	2.530		210.0
Portugal	10	1.660		166.2
UK (not Scotland)	388	226.303	730.715	327.6
France	214	37.000		173.0
Italy	120	19.500		185.0
Sweden	99	15.000		151.5

In 1698 almost every Scottish landowner who had money to spare is said to have invested in the Darien scheme,[10] an ambitious project to secure an Atlantic-Pacific trading colony on the Isthmus of Panama. Absorbing about a quarter of the money circulating in Scotland at the time, its failure bankrupted many. Whether this was Scotland's first syndicated angel investment or an early form of crowdfunding, it does suggest that Scotland has a long history of being willing to financially back entrepreneurs with global ambition.

More successful modern efforts to encourage private investment can be traced to the establishment of the Local Investment Networking Company (LINC) in the 1980s by the economic development agency Glasgow Opportunities Enterprise Trust. As a private nonprofit trust LINC plays a "soft" infrastructure role in supporting the development of the investment market in Scotland. LINC's "Enterprise Trust"[11] status has been particularly important, enabling it to be seen as a partner by both the public sector and the private investment community, and giving it direct access to European Structural Fund resources. This in turn has allowed for greater independence from direct government control and the ability to implement long-term policies. Now called the Scottish Angel Capital Association, LINC has been the instrumental driver over the past 20 years in creating one of the most vibrant angel communities in the world. It is a trusted resource in everything from matching investors to entrepreneurs, to knowledge transfer and public policy development. It has taken a "hands off" approach to individual angel group operations, allowing the industry to develop naturally while acting as a supporting partner.

THE EARLY YEARS

By 1993 high-net-worth individuals were beginning to take more interest in the marketplace following the launches of the highly tax-advantageous Enterprise Investment Scheme, and the earliest self-organised angel groups, Archangel and Braveheart. Entrepreneurs however, were either unfamiliar with the notion of equity funding or deeply resistant to the idea of "giving away" part of their business and having to accept outside "interference." As such, the majority of LINC's resources were devoted to awareness-raising and the education of both entrepreneurs and their advisors (lawyers, accountants) about the merits of using equity and angel investors. This demand-side role continues today, reflecting the constant need to educate new entrepreneurs and other stakeholders while adapting to changes in the market. Also important was the willingness of the early investment groups Archangel and Braveheart to be visible in the market and engage with LINC in the education process on how "real life" angels operate.

POLICY DEVELOPMENT AND MEDIA AWARENESS

LINC represents the industry to government at the Scottish, UK and European levels, and it was a founding member of Business Angels Europe (BAE), the European Business Angels Association (EBAN) and the World Business Angels Association (WBAA). In 2004, LINC initiated the Angel Leaders' Forum (ALF), a liaison network of the leaders of all the Scottish angel groups, who meet every two months to share ideas and discuss issues of common interest. This forum has become a significant influence in the marketplace and with Scottish Enterprise and the Scottish and UK Governments, and it is regularly consulted by policymakers (including H. M. Treasury and H. M. Revenue & Customs), investment managers, and other stakeholders. LINC's awareness-raising objectives have also been pursued through a strategy of building relationships with the media and providing stories and commentary on policy and topical issues whenever possible. Stories about angel-backed companies are now a routine part of business media coverage.

THE RISE OF ANGEL GROUPS

The worldwide trend toward the formation of angel groups was reinforced in Scotland by the dotcom bust of 2000 and the withdrawal of VCs from the early stage market. The angel community responded with increasing levels of collaboration. This coalesced into permanent, structured groups capable of assisting companies over longer periods and multiple rounds of funding. LINC recognised that this was a natural evolution and that it might be constrained by any attempt to manage the market through a "clearing-house" model, by which LINC acted as a traditional BAN, providing deal flow to its angel members. As such, LINC concentrated on growing and empowering independent and free-standing investment groups to operate with more professionalism. This also enabled companies to benefit from access to multiple sources of capital and reduce the influence of any one investment manager.

This was an important "pivot," which effectively marked the launch of LINC 2.0, which now facilitates around 20 angel groups, including Scotland's first women's angel group, Investing Women, launched in 2013.[12] This is probably the largest number of angel groups per capita of any nation, and yet the groups do not treat each other as competitors; they often share intelligence, deals and co-invest in syndicates. Structuring investing in this way provides key benefits to the Scottish economy. Groups are more visible to entrepreneurs. They reduce risk and provide post-investment support (especially for high-net-worth individuals who lack the time and skills to invest on their own). They make more capable partners for the Scottish Co-

Investment Fund. They provide a wider variety of skills and more consistent investment.[13] Companies receive more cash and have more options,[14] and simultaneous deals and multiple rounds are possible, filling the "equity gap" left by the withdrawal of VCs.

It has been suggested that the particular size and geography of Scotland has significantly contributed to its ability to grow angel groups.[15] The distinct Scottish identity facilitates a focus on local investing and a high degree of trust and sharing both within the angel community and the public sector. Policymakers in other regions need to take local business characteristics into account when devising policies to influence the private sector.

Some commentators have suggested that the increase in the number of groups will lead to less capital being available for new company formation, as the groups concentrate their resources on funding their existing portfolio companies.[16] Indeed in 2012 some 70 percent of all the investments made by LINC group members went to support the growth of existing investments. This is one of the reasons Scottish Enterprise helps LINC fund new groups each year.

TAXATION

Taxation policy is largely controlled and implemented by the central UK government, and as a result Scotland benefits from the same extensive tax incentives available to angel investors in other regions of the UK. The principal tax incentive used to encourage more individuals to become angels is the Enterprise Investment Scheme (EIS), introduced in 1994. An additional incentive, the Seed Enterprise Investment Scheme, was introduced in 2011 to increase funding for the earliest stage companies. These tax incentives each provide up-front income tax deductions of 30 to 50 percent of the amounts invested, relief from capital gains tax (28 percent in the UK) if investments are held for three years, relief from the inheritance tax, and a number of other reliefs.

Research suggests that EIS has been effective in making more funding available for entrepreneurs, with one study showing that 24 percent of investments would not have been made without EIS assistance, and 53 percent of investors would have made fewer investments without tax incentives.[17] The report concluded that, "The EIS scheme is therefore a major instrument to encourage more angel investing." Some academics have commented on the potentially negative effects of tax incentives, particularly where such incentives lead to investment being made purely for tax reasons rather than sound business ones.[18] There is a counterproductive effect of encouraging "amateur" investors into the market who may not only lose their money, but also distort valuations. Perhaps more significantly, they may not have the business acumen necessary to provide appropriate support to entrepreneurs. These dangers are mitigated due to the dominance of angel group structures, which provide an appropriate learning environment for new angels.

POLICY DEVELOPMENT: AN EVOLUTIONARY APPROACH

Public policy in Scotland has been effective in developing angel capacity and competency because an evolutionary approach has been taken. For example, the publicly backed Scottish co-investment funds, East of Scotland Investment Fund (ESI) and the Strathclyde Investment Fund (SIF) had a combined £15m available to invest in SMEs in amounts up to £250,000 through a mix of debt and equity. Approximately 40 percent of the funds were provided via grants under ERDF, with the balance coming from local enterprise agencies and the private sector, and in particular the Royal Bank of Scotland. The provision of ERDF grants meant that these funds had to act as more than "just cash" and instead actively address market failure, in this case the skill and knowledge deficiencies on both the demand and supply side.[19] Fund managers not only invested in deals but acted as champions for SME funding, and they organized and participated in many conferences designed to spread media awareness and best practice. On the supply side, the fund managers actively sought to involve the private sector in their deals as co-investors, facilitating knowledge transfer and stimulating interest. On the demand side, advisers to SMEs in the public and private sector were able to advise their clients about available sources of funds, and entrepreneurs started to come forward with proposals. An essential element was that the fund managers had a close working relationship with the public sector and were given specific responsibilities to promote a development agenda based on the benefits of equity finance.

The positive results of the ESI and SIF provided the impetus for the Scottish Co-Investment Fund (SCF) in 2003. This £72m equity fund aims to catalyse long term change by working with private sector partners to improve capacity and capability in the venture capital market, increasing the supply of early stage equity funding to Scottish SMEs. It "matches" private sector cash, investing from £100,000 to £1 million in deals of up to £2 million. SCF follows the lead of its private sector partners and does not find, investigate or negotiate investment deals on its own. Instead, it forms contractual partnerships with active VC fund managers and angel groups, trusting the partner's judgment. The key public policy element here is that Scottish Enterprise only seeks to intervene in the market where genuine market failure exists, withdrawing after the failure has been addressed and capacity has been built. By doing so it does *not* crowd out the private sector, which would only perpetuate the market failure and the need for government support.

The SCF is one of the few co-investment funds in the world to have been formally evaluated.[20] The evaluation concluded that the fund had increased deal capacity and facilitating the development of angel groups. From the point of view of the angel community, the availability of a predictable co-investment resource has allowed new groups to aim for a "critical mass" portfolio size much quicker than would otherwise have been possible. At the same time, it gives mature groups the capacity to continue making new investments while meeting their commitments to follow on with their existing investees.

PUBLIC POLICY LESSONS

Scotland has developed an effective model of angel investing that overcomes the limitations of its population base and remoteness to venture capital funding. The key lessons of the Scottish experience are:

- Policy should be built upon detailed, quality research and local market analysis.
- Supply-side support is effective and should not be dismissed as "using public money to make rich people richer".
- Developing an effective local investment community is an evolutionary process that requires years of consistent funding.

- Actively managed co investment funds with the wider remit of transferring knowledge will help build self-sustaining private sector capacity. This will allow the public sector to move to a passive co-investing role and reduce costs.
- Having multiple private sector partners widens choice for entrepreneurs and reduces fund management costs.
- Continuing support for both building and maintaining angel groups ensures a supply of capital for start-ups while existing investors concentrate on funding their portfolios.
- Continuing research enables adaptation to market developments.
- Demand-side problems associated with underdeveloped firms need to be addressed at the same time as addressing the supply-side problems of inexperienced investors.

Businesses, potential investors and thus the economy all benefit from the coaching provided by national associations and angels groups. Such intangible benefits must not be overlooked in assessments of economic benefit from angel development and support programs.

CASE STUDY

UK TAX INCENTIVES FOR ANGELS AND ENTREPRENEURS

The majority of taxation policies are developed and implemented across the whole of the UK by the UK central government. Successive governments have enacted legislation to encourage innovation and investment. Presently the principal tax incentives aimed at stimulating angel activity are the Enterprise Investments Scheme (EIS)[21] and the Seed Enterprise Investment Scheme. The EIS was introduced in 1994 to use tax relief to incentivize high net worth investors to invest in high risk early stage companies. Companies can raise up to £5m in any 12-month period using the program, which UK government figures suggest has enabled £9.7 billion of investment since its inception. The EIS provides investors in qualifying companies with relief or exemption from a number of personal taxes:

- Income tax relief: 30 percent income tax relief on a maximum investment of up to £1,000,000.
- Tax-free capital gains: as long as shares are held for at least three years, profits from share sales are free of capital gains tax.
- Capital gains deferral relief: any capital gain made on the

disposal of any asset can be deferred by re-investing the gains into EIS-compliant companies. The deferred gain is due on the profitable sale of the new investment.

- Capital loss relief: a capital loss on the sale or write-off of EIS shares can be offset against income in the year the loss arises or the previous tax year. For a high tax rate payer this equates to 35 percent value of the EIS shares.
- Combining income tax relief with capital gains tax deferral and capital loss relief can give the investor a downside loss protection of 6p percent in the £1 invested.
- Inheritance tax relief: investments in EIS-compliant shares can attract inheritance tax business property relief of 100 percent value of investment on gift or on death. (Inheritance tax relief is otherwise charged at death at a rate of 40 percent on estates over the value of £325,000.)

Along with other restrictions, qualifying companies must be an unquoted SME (assets of not more than £7m and fewer than 50 full-time employees) and the investment can only be made by purchasing new "ordinary" shares. Investors are not allowed to be employees of the investee nor have a substantial interest in the investee company during the investment. They are allowed to purchase up to 30 percent of total equity. Individuals who do not wish to be active investors can invest through an EIS Fund, managed by commercial fund managers.[22]

In 2011, the UK introduced a new tax, the Seed Enterprise Investment Scheme (SEIS)[23], aimed at encouraging seed investment into very early stage companies. SEIS is similar to EIS, but with a higher income tax relief of 50 percent. An individual investor can make up to £100,000 of SEIS investments in any one year, and a company can take up to £150,000 of SEIS investment in its life. Once it has spent 70 percent of the SEIS investment it may then also take EIS investment. SEIS investments benefit from tax-free capital gains, capital loss relief and inheritance tax relief in the same way as EIS, but do not, from 2014, benefit from capital gains deferral relief. In order to qualify for SEIS funding a company must have been trading for less than two years, have gross assets of not more than £200,000, and have fewer than 25 full-time employees. Other restrictions are largely similar to those applying to EIS.

There are a wide range of additional tax incentives aimed at both individual entrepreneurs and companies in the UK. For example, Entrepreneurs Relief[24] reduces the amount of capital gains tax paid by an entrepreneur who owns at least 5 percent of the voting rights in a company. The Patent Box[25] tax relief enables companies to reduce their corporation tax on profits made from patents to 10 percent, while the Research & Development Tax Credits[26] allow SMEs to deduct up to 25 percent of their R&D costs from their corporation tax bills (loss-making companies can receive a cash credit of 11 percent of their R&D costs). There are also a variety of Creative Industries Tax Reliefs[27] for the film, animation and television industries, with a computer games tax relief expected soon.

CASE STUDY

BRAVEHEART: ANGEL GROUP TO VENTURE CAPITAL FUND[28]

Braveheart Ventures Ltd (BVL), was formed in January 1997 by four Scottish businessmen as an informal co-investment vehicle. The company was initially run as a not-for-profit company, which allowed founders to share their knowledge and expertise, pool their funds and increase diversification while reducing risk. BVL initially favored investments in young, unlisted Scottish companies with potential for significant growth, usually through commercialization of their intellectual property. The decision was made to alter the structure of the business in 2003, when Braveheart Investment Group plc (the "Group") was formed and acquired BVL. Financial Services Authority authorisation was granted to BVL in 2004, marking Braveheart's transition from an angel investment group to a regulated investment management business. Funds were raised from private investors and the Bank of Scotland with a view to taking the parent company public. Braveheart Investment Group plc was admitted to AIM (ticker BRH:L) in March 2007 and £6 million was raised at the time of listing. This is the only example known to this author of an angel group being developed to float on a public market.

With founding member Geoffrey Thomson at the helm, the business has since expanded via a combination of acquisition, organic growth and joint-venture, to specialize in venture capital investments and investment services to angels, high net worth individuals, family offices and public sector organizations. Throughout its lifetime the focus of the business has been SMEs, and it has seen numerous exits including six IPOs, two trade sales and two secondary buy-outs. At the time of this writing, the company has some £120m of funds under management and offices in London, Leeds, Belfast, Jersey, Monaco and Dubai.

CASE STUDY
ARCHANGELS INFORMAL INVESTMENT

One of the oldest angel groups in the world, Archangel,[29] was formed in Edinburgh in 1992. The group is comprised of more than 100 investor members who invest around £6 million of their own money each year. They have a diverse industry interest. Since 1992, the group has invested in excess of £90 million into some 80 early stage companies and has achieved an IRR of 20 percent on its exited companies (both positive and negative exits combined). The preferred level of investment is £250,000 to £500,000 but can cover a range from £50,000 to £2 million. Beyond funds, Archangels offers a substantial amount of help, advice and connections to their young companies. The group still operates on the four founding principal established in 1992:

- To put something back into Scotland by investing in young people and companies, particularly those in science and emerging technologies
- To look for investments where they can add value by passing on their own business experience
- To have fun
- To make some money

CASE STUDY
LINC SCOTLAND INVESTOR READY FUND

Lack of "investor readiness" can be a major inhibitor to investment. The LINC Investor Ready fund was an attempt to address the two issues of sustainability and quality of delivery. It gave targeted assistance to companies seeking angel equity funding in Scotland by underwriting the costs of "near deal" work identified by investors as being required to secure completion of an investment. The funding for the fund was from the European Regional Development Fund (ERDF) and Scottish Enterprise. The funding provided to the company was by way of a convertible grant. If the deal proceeded to completion the grant could, at the option of LINC, the fund manager, be converted to equity at the price being paid by the new investors, or repaid to the fund, for further future investment. If the investment did not proceed, the grant was written off.

The maximum grant available was the lesser of £15,000 or 50 percent of eligible costs. Applications were judged on economic development grounds, taking account of impacts on employment as well as the value of private investment facilitated. Assistance was available for a range of costs judged to increase the likelihood of angel or private equity investment in the beneficiary company, e.g. costs of market analysis, financial structuring, technology validation, intellectual property investigation and due diligence.

Of the 62 grants made, 18 were repaid, 25 converted and 19 were written off. The availability of relatively modest assistance, targeted by investors, enabled a significant number of investments to proceed that would otherwise have failed to secure funding. The scheme improved the quality of deal flow and encouraged more angel investors. Some of those assisted have gone on to raise significant amounts of new capital. The scheme was found to be scalable and highly cost-effective, and required minimal public sector support.[30]

Endnotes

[1] http://www.scottish-enterprise.com/about-us/what-we-do/growth-sectors.aspx.
[2] www.newsnetscotland.com/index.php/scottish-news/5813-scotland-tops-global-university-rankings.
[3] "A Framework for Higher Education in Scotland: Higher Education Review Phase 2". Scottish Government. http://www.scotland.gov.uk/Publications/2003/03/16786/20354.
[4] Praxisunico Spinouts UK Survey Annual Report 2013.
[5] The Role of Different Funding Models in Stimulating the Creation of Innovative New Companies. What is the most appropriate model for Europe? A study to assist the European Research Area Board, Technopolis Group, 26 September 2011.
[6] "Loan and Equity Funding to SMEs in Central Scotland," Grant Thornton and Elm Crichton Roberts Ltd (1996).
[7] UK Department of Business, Innovation and Skills Annual report on the Angel market in the United Kingdom: 2009/10. Colin Mason and Richard T Harrison, May 2011.

[8] "Financing High Growth Firms, The Role of Angel Investors," OECD, Paris, Dec 2011.

[9] "From Angel Syndication and the Evolution of Risk Capital in a Small Market Economy: Evidence from Scotland," Geoff Gregsona, Sacha Mannb, Richard Harrisonc, Published online in Wiley Online Library, (wileyonlinelibrary.com) DOI: 10.1002/mde.2595, 2013.

[10] *Darien: The Scottish Dream of Empire*, John Prebble, Published by Birlinn Ltd, Edinburgh, 2000.

[11] Enterprise Trusts were established from the 1980s by government as locally led initiatives across Scotland to support the regeneration of communities through focusing on small businesses, encouraging and supporting entrepreneurial activity. Enterprise trusts are run as a business and generating surpluses but re-investing surpluses in services for the benefit of clients.

[12] http://www.scotsman.com/business/management/first-women-s-scottish-Angel-investor-network-launch-1-3051155.

[13] UK Department of Business, Innovation and Skills Annual Reports on the Angel Market in the United Kingdom: 2008/09 and 2009/10, Colin Mason and Richard T Harrison. England fell from £375m to £266.5m, Scotland increased from £51m to £51.2m.

[14] The size of investments in Scotland is higher than in England, with 56 percent of investments in the £200,000 to £999,000 range compared with 43 percent in England. (UK Department of Business, Innovation and Skills Annual Reports on the Angel Market in the United Kingdom: 2008/09, Colin Mason and Richard T Harrison).

[15] "Angel Syndication and the Evolution of Risk Capital in a Small Market Economy: Evidence from Scotland," Geoff Gregsona, Sacha Mannb, Richard Harrisonc, Published online in Wiley Online Library, (wileyonlinelibrary.com) DOI: 10.1002/mde.2595, 2013.

[16] Sohl, J (2007) "The organization of the informal venture capital market," in H Landström (ed) Handbook of Research on Venture Capital, Edward Elgar, pp 347-368.

[17] "Siding with the Angels, Angel investing - promising outcomes and effective strategies," NESTA, 2009.

[18] Riding, Allan L., "Angels and love money investors: segments of the informal market for risk capital", Venture Capital, Volume 10, Number 4, Pages 355-369, 2008.

[19] "Best practice in the development and implementation of EU Structural Funds," New Horizons in Graz, Best Practice IV Conference, 2006".

[20] "Evaluation of the Scottish Co-Investment Fund, A Report to Scottish Enterprise," May 2008 by Keith Hayton (Hayton Consulting), Graham Thom, Vincent Percy, Chris Boyd and Kathleen Latimer (GEN).

[21] http://www.hmrc.gov.uk/eis/.

[22] http://www.hmrc.gov.uk/eis/part1/1-6.htm.

[23] http://www.hmrc.gov.uk/seedeis/.

[24] http://www.hmrc.gov.uk/helpsheets/hs275.pdf.

[25] http://www.hmrc.gov.uk/ct/forms-rates/claims/patent-box.htm.

[26] http://www.hmrc.gov.uk/ct/forms-rates/claims/randd.htm.

[27] http://www.hmrc.gov.uk/ct/forms-rates/claims/creative-industries.htm.

[28] http://www.braveheartgroup.co.uk.

[29] http://www.archangelsonline.com/.

[30] "Addressing Demand Side Constraints in the Informal Venture Capital Market: The Example of LINC Scotland's 'Trial Marriage' Scheme," Colin M Mason* and Richard T Harrison, 2002.

China

Wang Jiani and Chen Su

Informal angel investors who are neither family nor friends of an entrepreneur, can be an excellent financing channel for start-ups.[1] Over the past 20 years angel investment has been developing in tandem with the exponential growth of science and technology start-ups in the US and Europe. Chinese angel investing emerged at the end of the 20th century with the expansion of the internet and high-tech enterprises. In recent years more and more entrepreneurs, investors and professionals have taken part in angel activity. The standardization and institutionalization of angel investment is also speeding up. Various angel associations, groups and networks have been formed in Beijing, Shanghai, Guangzhou and other cities. Numerous policies promoting angel investment have been enacted, particularly in local governments such as Jiangsu province, Hubei province, Ningbo, Wenzhou, Chengdu, Chongqing and Luoyang.

Despite these positive trends, the Chinese angel market and the policy

---

WANG JIANI is a lecturer at the School of Finance, Capital University of Economics and Business. She has been a postdoctoral fellow at China Venture Capital Research Group in the Research Center of Fictitious Economy and Data Sciences, Chinese Academy of Science. She has coauthored a new book on the Chinese angel investment market with Professor Manhong Liu. She also serves as the executive Secretary of China Academy of Venture Capital, Chinese Society for Management Modernization. CHEN SU is a Ph.D. candidate at the School of Finance, Renmin University of China.

Well-Known Investors	Background	Investment Style
Mr. Jun Lei	Founder and CEO of Xiamo Tech, Managing Director of several leading game and software companies	Angel investor on the side; emphasizes target company's talent pool; participates in post-investment management; tends to invest within his social network.
Mr. Xiaoping Xu	Founder of Zhen Fund; Co-founder of New Oriental	Professional angel; participates less in management; emphasizes talent; has strong track record in investing outside of his social network.
Mr. Liqing Zeng	CEO of Dexun Investment; Co-founder of Tencent	Professional angel; focuses on early-stage investment; invests RMB2-10 million; participates in post-investment management; tends to invest within his social network.
Mr. Kaifu Li	Founder of Innovation Works; former executive of Apple, Google, SGI and Microsoft	"Angel+Incubator" model; provides financial and infrastructure support; concentrates on telecommunications.

environment are still sub-optimal. High net worth individuals in China do not consider angel investment an attractive enough investment option, preferring more "stable" returns. According to a survey of high net worth individuals living in 29 major Chinese cities, 60 percent of respondents invested in real estate, 46 percent in equities, 41 percent in fixed income, 13 percent in private equity, and only 5 percent in unlisted companies.[2]

Chinese angel investors tend to be successful entrepreneurs, investors, bankers and other professionals. Compared with mature markets in Western countries, however, China's angel investment is still at an early stage. Many of those who invest in unlisted companies are not familiar with the concept of angel investment, and do not have contacts with other angels or institutions. Actual Chinese angel investors generally come from two groups: Chinese expatriates who have returned home, and inherited second generation wealth. Although there are fewer individual angels than in the West, super angels and government funds are growing fast and play a more important role in China. However, lack of incentives and exit opportunities mean that the Chinese angel market is not yet living up to its potential.

A BRIEF HISTORY OF ANGEL ACTIVITY IN CHINA

Over the last decade venture capital and private equity far outpaced angel investment in China. Rebalancing this is especially important as the Chinese economy is in a crucial stage of structural transformation, one that requires the support that angels provide to start-ups. Initially early stage investment in China was promoted by the government.[3] According to the Angel Investment Environment Research Report in Z-Park, Chinese angels possibly originated with the 1986 "863 Program," which focused on indigenous innovation in biology, aerospace, and information technology, and the 1988 "Torch Program," which supported high-tech industrial zones, including over 1,000 incubators for high-tech start-ups. After the 2000 technology-fueled entrepreneurship boom some Chinese who had studied and worked in western countries returned to China, starting their own business and making angel investments. Taking advantage of their personal wealth, industrial experience, and network of resources, they helped new entrepreneurs succeed in business. They also motivated successful domestic entrepreneurs to engage in angel investing.

DEVELOPMENT OF THE ANGEL MARKET

Most academic research on the Chinese angel market is qualitative, and there are few statistics available. China's first angel research report, the Chinese Angel Investment Research Report, was published in 2006 by the Beijing Software and Information Services Promotion Center, the Internet Lab and the *New Economy Weekly* magazine.[4] The report showed that China's domestic investment in seed stage companies accounted for 17 percent of total venture capital in 2006, amounting to RMB1.054 billion. Capital was mainly invested in the technology, media and telecommunication industries.

More recently Zero2IPO Research Center (2011, 2012), the China Venture Capital Research Institute (2011), Entrepreneur (2012), Z-park Administrative Committee (2013), and the China Business Angel Association (2013) have analyzed the Chinese angel industry. It seems that Western definition of angel investing is inappropriate in the Chinese context. Angel investing in China was used to define a stage of investment rather than a type of investor. So, the type of angel investor is not limited to an individual. According to a report from Zero2IPO Research Center, there are 1463 angel round deals with investment amounts of $ 0.93 billion. These deals were made by individual angels and private funds as well as government funds. Researchers indicate there are at least 1,000 active individual angels (half in Z-park), 100 angel funds, and 50 clubs, groups and networks in China. It also appears that most angel investors are fairly inactive, with 43.75 percent investing in less than five projects. About half invested less than RMB1 million, for less than 5 percent of total equity. The rest invested above RMB5 million. More than 40 percent of angel investment was in Beijing and Shanghai, and the breakdown of the top sectors was telecommunications (57 percent), clean technology and energy (34 percent), and biological medicine (20 percent).

Most angels are men (89 percent), highly educated (49 percent hold at least a master's degrees), work in the financial sector (69 percent), and have entrepreneurial (57 percent) and executive (54 percent) experience. In terms of their investment strategies, over 80 percent of investors visit project sites and over 90 percent co-invest, mostly with family friends or relatives. All surveyed investors signed some form of investment agreement, including an equity transfer agreement (71 percent), an anti-dilution provision (60 percent), and a valuation adjustment mechanism (54 percent). More than 90 percent of investors participate in post-investment management, in particular board seats (89 percent).

ANGELS' INVESTMENT STYLES

Angels have different professional backgrounds, business skills and characteristics, and as such, their investment styles differ. Those with entrepreneurial experiences are able to help start-ups manage more effectively. Corporate executives, like Li Kaifu, rely more on their financial and network resources to assist start-up growth.

PATTERNS OF ANGEL INVESTING

As noted, Chinese angel investing only really emerged in the 2001-2008 period, before which only scattered investments were made. After 2009 the angel market entered a rapid development phase. There was an increase not only in the number of individual angels, but also in angel groups, institutions, incubators and crowdfunding platforms. Angel groups, which include clubs and nonprofits, provide communication opportunities for angel investors and entrepreneurs, and they often co-invest to reduce investment risk. Professional angel investing institutions concentrate and regulate scattered fundraising. Angel incubators reduce investment risk by providing both financial support and entrepreneur services. Powerful companies and local governments also support entrepreneurship in particular fields through platform-based venture funds, such as the Security Venture Fund from Tencent and the Cloud Fund from Alibaba. Since 2013 angel internet platforms have also proliferated, providing co-investment and crowdfunding services.

There are obviously regional differences in China. Z-Park of Beijing, China's "Silicon Valley," is at the forefront of the country's angel activity. Beijing is home to about 60 percent of China's angels, most of them successful and influential entrepreneurs and executives with high media exposure. Angels are also active in Shanghai, though investors there are more dispersed and focus more on the telecommunications industry. In Ningbo, a city in Zhejiang province, potential "angels" currently prefer to invest in upgrading projects in traditional industry

New Incubators in Z-Park
(partial statistics)

Incubators	Type of Organization	Incubation Mode
Innovation Workshop, Legend Star	private capital	comprehensive incubator for early stage
Garage Coffee, 3w Coffee, Virtue Inno Valley	private capital	open office
Entrepreneur, Founder, and 36Kr.com	private capital	entrepreneurship media
Huilongsen, Ba Aolian Chuang	private capital	technology platform incubator
Microsoft Cloud Accelerator, Nokia Experience and Innovation Center, Shi GuOing Culture Industry Incubator, Cloud Valley	platform company	industry incubator
Ivy Pioneer Park	private nonprofit	talent incubator
AAMA	association	teacher-student engagement

sectors. Shenzhen is one of the most active cities in South China. Most Shenzhen investors are part-time angels, running businesses at the same time. In central and west China the number of local angels is growing through government measures, such as the Wuhan and Chengdu angel guiding fund.

ANGEL GROUP STRUCTURES AND ORGANIZATIONS

Angel groups and institutional investors are a natural evolution based on risk diversification, resource sharing, professional management and other benefits. They can be divided into four categories according to the MIT Entrepreneurship Center. Angel funds are professional institutional investors who invest in start-ups. According to a 2013 research report from the China Business Angel Association (CBAA), there are 80 angel funds, including 52 with institutional investors, 15 with an incubator, and 13 with a government background. A prominent example is the Zhen Fund, established by the famous angel investor Xu Xiaoping in 2006. In 2011, the Zhen Fund and Sequoia Capital each invested $15 million to create a new early stage angel fund.

Member-organized angel clubs are groups of active angel investors who share information and make decisions collectively. One of the most powerful in China, the China Youth Angel Investor Leader Association, was founded in 2013. It advocates the concept of "Cooperation Investment, Win-Win, Openness" and is always encouraging more people to join. A unique activity of this association is its monthly salon, in which members recommend quality projects through roadshows. For-profit matching and investment organizations provide consulting services such as screening, due diligence and other charged services.

Usually there are two types of support. The first provides seed financing and incubation services, such as Innovation Workshop, Innovation Valley. Like the Y Combinator in the US, these institutions filter and invest in early-stage projects, providing them with free bandwidth, business counseling, follow-up financing and other value-added services. The second is a business angel network, such as AngelCrunch, Ctquan. Like AngelList and Kickstarter in the US, these platforms provide matching services. Third-party matching services are nonprofit organizations that act as information intermediaries

Region	Local Government Policies *(partial statistics)*
Hubei Province	20 million RMB to support university students' incubator
Shanxi Province	rent subsidies for incubated entrepreneurs
Xiangtan in Hunan Province	financial support from the High-Tech Development Park for university students with advantageous projects, and for incubated entrepreneurs
Shandong Province	a secured loan of up to RMB100,000 is provided to graduates starting their own businesses or running low-profit programs
Zhengzhou Province	a one-time subsidy of RMB5000 is offered for the initial entrepreneurial graduate
Nanjing in Jiangsu Province	free rent and an award of up to RMB 50,000 for students starting their own business in Jiangning District
Xuzhou in Jiangsu Province	a fund of RMB 30 million to guide the entrepreneurship of university students
Chengdu in Sichuan Province	subsidized training in enterpreneurship for students
Tianjin	subsidized housing for graduates who start businesses

between angels and entrepreneurs. In 2008 for instance, the Shanghai Angel Investment Club was co-sponsored by China Technology Venture Association, the Shanghai Venture Capital Association and the Shanghai Technology Entrepreneurship Foundation for Graduates. It aims at bringing together angels to improve professional skills and the investment ecosystem.

Overall, individual Chinese angels have coalesced into multiple organizational forms that improve matching efficiency, time outlays and due diligence. However the relatively young Chinese angel world still faces talent bottlenecks, legal barriers, and policy constraints. As such, more research is needed on the effectiveness of the various structures.

ENTREPRENEURIAL ECOSYSTEM

With the rapid development of the Chinese economy over the past decade, the motivations of entrepreneurs changed from ensuring survival to capitalizing on opportunities. According to the 2013 China Global Entrepreneurship Monitor Report, China has become one of the most active nations in global entrepreneurship, rising from 11th place in 2002 to 2nd place in 2012. The quality of entrepreneurship is not high, however. There are not many highly educated entrepreneurs and most of them focus on low-technology industries.

Since 2002, entrepreneurship education has become more diversified, with the government and universities working together on a "trinity" of reforms including: the establishment of entrepreneurship experimental colleges, the introduction of entrepreneurship practice programs such as SIYB and KAB, and the emphasis on the importance of entrepreneurship education in official documents.[6] Despite this, there is still an inadequate entrepreneurship education system in universities and the caliber of teachers varies widely.

Innovation and entrepreneurship competitions on campuses are an important form of entrepreneurship education. Tsinghua University held China's earliest student business plan competition in May 1998. During the competition, the university also organized lectures and entrepreneurship forums, which helped spread knowledge about entrepreneurship. Since then, the government, media and private institutions have organized various innovation and entrepreneurship events to establish a platform for project exhibition and information exchange. One of these influential activities is the "Dark Horse Series," which has been held in more than 20 cities around China since 2011. It has attracted almost 5,000 firms and more than 700 investors, and directs about RMB200 million to start-ups in each season. In total, it has supplied RMB1 billion to more than 200 firms.

Technology incubators not only promote start-ups, but also benefit innovation, industrial upgrading, regional growth and employment. According to the 2012 China Torch Statistical Yearbook, the number of technology incubators had risen from 73 in 1995 to 1,034 in 2011. As seen in Table 2, there are also many new incubators in Beijing's Z-park.[7] These provide different services to the government model, such as co-work spaces and coaching, which have boosted creativity across the country.

POLICIES TO PROMOTE ANGEL INVESTING

Although there were no polices specifically directed at angels in the 1990s, there were some targeting entrepreneurship, incubators and the development of SMEs. In recent years policies have been introduced to directly foster the Chinese angel market, focusing on seed funding, risk subsidies, and angel networks. In 1999 the SME Technology Innovation Fund was created, the first central government fund to directly support SMEs. In 2007 the Ministries of Science and Finance jointly established another Technology Innovation Fund to support technology SMEs, using risk subsidies and investment protection. By the end of 2012 this fund had invested more than RMB22 billion and supported more than 40,000 SMEs![8]

In 2012 increasing labor cost and raw material prices put pressure on SMEs. In response the Ministry of Finance implemented its "State Council's Decision on Further Support for SMEs, especially Small and Micro Enterprises Healthy Development." From 2012 to 2016, the central government plans to invest RMB15 billion in a National SMS Development Fund that will leverage various types of social capital to jointly support SME development.

As shown in the chart on page 145, local governments also support innovation and entrepreneurship, mainly through grants, subsidies and funds to help reduce entrepreneurs' costs and investment risk. Some local governments, for example those of Chengdu, Jiangsu, and Ningbo, have policies targeted at angel investors.[9]

Unlike in the US, there are no national rules governing investor certification. However a few local governments have instituted regulations as part of their development packages. For example, the Shenzhen Science and Technology and Information Bureau requires individual investors to be experienced, have personal assets of RMB5 million (institutions require RMB30 million), and be recommended by a related industrial association. Ningbo's Angel Guiding Fund requires individuals to have experience and RMB1 million (institutions require RMB30 million). As of February 2015, Ningbo Government had invested in 58 start-ups, with co-investment capital of RMB52.3 million and total angel investment of RMB240 million.

Recently some local governments have started to create funds to leverage co-investment and foster innovation and entrepreneurship. In 2011 the Wuhan government in Hubei Province established an angel fund that has now reached RMB300 million. In 2012 the Chongqing Science and Technology Commission established the RMB100 million Chongqing Youth Innovation and Entrepreneurship Angel Fund. In the same year the Chengdu government in Sichuan Province established a RMB80 million angel fund. Beijing Software Exchange followed with an RMB80 million fund in 2013.

Funds vary in how they operate. The Z-park angel fund directly participates in equity, while the Chengdu Hi-Tech Zone Management Committee appointed the CDHT Investment Co. Ltd to make investments. These Chengdu funds focus on specific sectors. For example, the fund from Wuhan targets opto-electronics, new generation information technology, new materials, advanced equipment manufacturing, high-tech services, biomedicine, new energy and new energy vehicles, energy efficiency and environmental protection, and modern agriculture. These funds play an important role in attracting talent, encouraging innovation and entrepreneurship, and promoting regional industrial development.

Apart from angel funds, some local governments also provide subsidies and risk allowances. In the Chengdu Hi-Tech Zone, if investment institutions invest more than RMB50 million in a start-up, the government will match these investments with 20 percent of funding up to RMB400,000. The Jiangsu local government provides institutions investing in seed or early-stage technology-based SMEs with a risk allowance of up to 30 percent of their first round investment, while the provincial government requires a local government to provide an additional 20 percent. As a result, if an angel institution experiences a loss in the first three years of an investment, it can get compensation for 50 percent of the loss. It is worth mentioning that Z-park made a new policy to incentivize college teachers to become angels and invest in their students' start-ups. If the teacher invests in his students' company, the investee can apply the subsidy with a maximum amount of half of investment.

CONSTRUCTING THE ANGEL NETWORK

Poor communication and a lack of institutional norms are two of the many issues that are prevalent in the Chinese angel industry. To address these, the government supports self-regulating organization through angel networks. The China Business Angel Association (CBAA) is the only member of World Business Angels Association in China, and the only angel group that is a subsidary to a China central government agency, the China Association of Technology Entrepreneurship of Ministry of Science and Technology. It is also supported by the National Torch Center of Ministry of Science and Technology. Its constituents include: individual investors, entrepreneurs, experts, scholars, policymakers, institutional investors, companies, intermediary institutions, universities, science and technology parks, associations, and other social groups. The CBAA publishes information on its website, holds forums and salons, engages in project matchmaking, and conducts training and certification for entrepreneurs. All in all it acts as a multiple communication platform for sharing information and exchanging resources.

ANGEL TRENDS: THE PROGNOSIS

Over the next five to ten years China will continue to transform, offering more business and investment opportunities while developing the angel market. Ever more entrepreneurs who currently benefit from VCs and angels and succeed will join the angel movement and help other start-ups. Chinese angel behavior is also changing, from being purely profit-seeking to focusing more on helping entrepreneurs though non-controlling stakes in start-ups. Crowdfunding is also becoming more popular in China. The angel ecosystem will be key to its future development. In the last two years, third-party services such as virtual incubation, matching services and co-work spaces have emerged. Although not yet mature, these service are already creating a more professional, efficient and standardized operation environment. Recently many excellent entrepreneurial companies have received help from government funds and risk subsidies. More large-scale financing for SMEs is needed however. Local governments have also been experimenting with supportive policies, but since many of these have been copied from elsewhere, their effectiveness in China has yet to be determined. The public sector is moving in the right direction, however, and that should continue to boost innovation and economic development.

Acknowledgements

The author wishes to greatly thank Newhuadu Business School for help and support, and also to thank the National Natural Science Foundation of China (71303224), and China Post-Doctor Science Foundation Project (2014M550814) for their financial support for the research and writing of this article.

Endnotes

1 D. A. Walker. *Financing the Small Firm, Small Business Economics*, 1989, 1(1): 285-296.
2 *The White Paper on Chinese High Net Worth Individuals' Consumption Demand.*
3 M.H. Liu. *Theory and Practices of Angel Investment* [M] Economy and Management Press, 2009 (in Chinese).
4 http://www.chinaangel.org/system/article/SpecialReport.
5 Xiaoyan Li. *Why I invest in you* [M]. Beijing: China Commercial Publishing House, 2012.
6 Yingmei Shang etc., 2013.
7 *Z-park Science Park Builds the Most Attractive Center for Entrepreneur* (2013), Y.M. Xu, Angel Investment in Z-park of Beijing, http://www.pedaily.cn/Item. aspx?id=219665.
8 Gang Wang, 2013.
9 Jiangsu: *Suggestion on Encouraging and Guiding Angel Investors to Support Small and Medium-sized S&T Enterprise* (2012), Chengdu: *Science and technology development of small and medium-sized enterprises* (2012), Ningbo: *Angel Funding* (2012).

Turkey

Baybars Altuntas

THE ANGEL ENTREPRENEURIAL ECOSYSTEM

The 2014 Global Entrepreneurial Report (GER) by the Oracle Capital Group ranks Turkey as the second most entrepreneurial of 33 countries.[1] In common with most of the other developing economies in the report, Turkey scored low on fear of failure, and well on attitude to risk and early stage business activity. Moreover, Turkey was found to have the best attitude toward self-funding. Willingness to self-fund allows Turkish entrepreneurs to pitch to angel investors in a shorter period of time, due to already completed "demos." This is corroborated by the 2013 EBAN Angel Investment Market Growth Report, which ranked Turkey as the eighth biggest angel investment market in Europe.[2]

ANGEL INVESTMENT ECOSYSTEM IN TURKEY

Like many countries, the early stage market in Turkey is comprised of angel investors, angel networks, incubators, accelerators, banks, VC firms, co-investment funds, government grants, universities and

BAYBARS ALTUNTAS is a global entrepreneur, best-selling author, angel investor, columnist, star of the Turkish version of the television show Dragons' Den, President of the Business Angels Association of Turkey, President of Deulcom International, Vice President of the European Trade Association for Business Angels, Seed Funds, and other Early Stage Market Players (EBAN), and the World Entrepreneurship Forum's Ambassador to Turkey and the Balkan countries.

business plan competitions. Important players in the public policy arena include: the national angel association and the global voice of Turkey's early stage market, the Business Angels Association of Turkey (TBAA)[3]; the Under Secretariat of the Treasury; the SME Development Department of the Government (KOSGEB); and the Istanbul Stock Exchange (Borsa Istanbul).

GOVERNMENT POLICIES TO PROMOTE BUSINESS ANGELS

There have been four major developments in the Turkish angel ecosystem: a new Angel Investment Law; a fast-developing angel investment community; TBAA's global performance; and attempts by Borsa Istanbul to create more liquidity for start-ups.

SMEs in Turkey have limited access to finance because of their size, lack of collateral, and in some cases the low financial literacy of entrepreneurs, many of whom may need mentoring to develop their businesses. Financial institutions are reluctant to provide credit to start-ups and early stage companies due to the very high risk involved. According to a 2008 World Bank Group Survey, access to finance is the biggest problem of SMEs in Turkey. SMEs also struggle with lack of professional management and institutional capacity.

In 2013, the Under Secretariat of the Treasury implemented a new system to encourage angel investments in Turkey by targeting SMEs in early development stages with funding difficulties. The law aims to increase professionalism and ethics among angel investors, make angel investments more attractive through state support, and ultimately make angel capital an institutionalized and trustworthy source of finance. Under the law, the Turkish Treasury licenses business angels who want to benefit from tax incentives for their investments. (Accredited angel networks can provide the license applications.) Accordingly, 75 percent of the participation shares of qualifying Turkish resident joint-stock companies held by angels can be deducted from the angel's annual income tax base in the calendar year the shares are held. The maximum annual deductible amount is TL1 million The deduction ratio is 100 percent for those angel investors investing in companies whose projects are supported by the Ministry of Science, Industry and Technology; the Scientific and Technological Research Council of Turkey; and the Small and Medium Enterprises Development

Organization. To get a deduction from their taxable income, investors must hold the stocks for at least two years.[4] There are also a number of investment limitations on the part of investors, such as maximum investment amounts and number of investments, and on the SMEs (e.g. a turnover of less than TL5 million; less than 50 employees).

There are two criteria to get an angel license for this support scheme. An investor must either be of high net worth (have an annual gross income above TL200,000 or possess net assets above TL1 million) or "experienced" (have two years of experience as a manager/director in a financial institution or a company with a TL25 million turnover, have one year of membership in a local business angel network with shares in three SMEs, or have TL20,000-plus investments in three technology companies supported by an incubator).

Matching angels and start-ups has proven to be problematic. An efficient way to increase angel investments is therefore to build a network that gets angel investors and entrepreneurs together, increasing both funding capacity and investment capability. For this reason, the Turkish Treasury created an accreditation mechanism for angel networks that are willing to work on licensing and tax incentive applications, and provide data about their members' investments. The initiative defines an angel investor network as an association founded according to Turkish Civil Code, the Law of Obligations and the Turkish Commercial Code. The networks are required to have:

- a convenient physical place to meet with entrepreneurs,
- a minimum of one expert to process the applications of entrepreneurs,
- a minimum of five licensed business angels and five angel investments of those members in total, and,
- a functional web page and data base.

The Angel Investment Law has definitely helped foster the ecosystem. By October of 2014, there were 264 accredited angel investors and 10 angel investment groups. Turkey's global angel presence has also grown. Turkey's angel representative was elected to be an EBAN board member in the 2011 elections in Moscow and elected unanimously as the Vice President of EBAN in the 2013 elections in Dublin. Turkey is also has a board member on the WBAA—World Business Angels Association in the UK.

In 2014 Borsa Istanbul and other parties signed the European Early Stage Investments Financing Support Cooperation Protocol,[5] which aimed to increase mutual cooperation in creating employment and innovation. Private Market, designed to offer a new marketplace that brings together entrepreneurs and investors within Borsa İstanbul in order to solve their financing and liquidity problems, started accepting members in 2014. This Market brings start-up companies and rising companies together with qualified or business angel investors, and therefore offers them equity financing and liquidity facilities without going public and without being subject to the requirements of the Capital Markets Board. Shareholders can sell their existing shares on it to increase their liquidity. It also provides investors with the opportunity to find buyers and liquidate their investments. In Private Market, companies can completely control their shareholder structure and choose their new shareholders. They can manage and control the information flow and find counter-parties anonymously. They can also benefit from services including legal and financial consultancy, valuation, and brokerage provided by Private Market member partners at reasonable prices. Companies and investors can also be matched algorithmically, and negotiate in a secure environment through the "data and deal room application."

ANGEL INVESTMENT TRENDS

Many changes have occurred in the world economy since the 1980s. Technology is assuming an increasingly important role, service industries are growing, the world economy is more open to competition, and outsourcing is creating an opportunity for small firms. These changes have transformed the way in which business is conducted. Niche markets are being developed to cater to changes in customer preferences and/or technology. There has also been a shift from the concept of the "marketplace" (physical business activities) to the "market space" (business done electronically). This has helped small businesses gain competitive advantages over large competitors. Moreover, the independence and the relatively small size of entrepreneurial companies gives them the flexibility to change and innovate in response to customer demands. The entrepreneur is at the core of the process and as such, the social and cultural environment and attitudes of a country are important factors influencing its entrepreneurial activities. It is therefore important for policymakers to promote entrepreneurship and provide an encouraging environment that allows potential entrepreneurs to flourish. Access to finance for entrepreneurs and access to talent for angel investors are very important in achieving start-up success stories.

There is a wide agreement on the importance of entrepreneurship and early stage finance for economic development. Start-ups backed by qualified angel investors drive and shape innovation, and speed up structural changes in the economy. They also introduce competition that contributes to productivity and job creation. Encouraging entrepreneurial activities in the early stage market is vital for economic development in Turkey. Start-ups backed by angel investors will flourish in an environment where the individual is encouraged to take risk, where innovation is supported by public policy, and where a potential entrepreneur is backed by the technical and managerial skills of qualified angel investors, incubators, techno-parks and accelerators.

Acknowledgements

This report could not have been compiled without the support and help of the TBAA—Business Angels Association of Turkey, the Under Secretariat of the Treasurey of Turkey, the Development Bank of Turkey, and Borsa Istanbul.

Endnotes

[1] The report measures the opinions, attitudes, experiences and activity that contribute to entrepreneurism, http://orcap.co.uk/online/media/Entrepreneurial-report-final.pdf.
[2] http://www.eban.org/wp-content/uploads/2013/08/OECD-Financing-High-Growth-Firms.pdf.
[3] http://www.melekyatirimcilardernegi.org.
[4] Business angels cannot be controlling shareholders either directly or indirectly in the companies they invest in.
[5] http://www.ebaf2014.org/node/5.

Italy

Eng. Paolo Anselmo and Luigi Amati

ITALIAN ASSOCIATION OF BUSINESS ANGELS

The Italian Association of Business Angels (IBAN) was founded in 1999 through a project promoted by the European Commission, Business Angels Europe (BAE)[1] and the World Business Angels Association (WBAA). IBAN is the institution that best understands and represents the perspective of informal venture capital investors in Italy. It is focused on the development and growth of the angels, which it encourages through angel networks, investor clubs, individual angels and professionals who match investors with entrepreneurs.

In addition, IBAN has ties to the Italian Venture Capital Association (AIFI) as well as local and national associations of entrepreneurs. The association receives and examines about 300 company ideas per year and selects about 100 of those, which are then presented to registered angels. In brief, IBAN's expertise includes:

ENG. PAOLO ANSELMO is president of the Italian Federation of Business Angels (IBAN) and a senior advisor to local, national, and regional organizations on the preparation of research, policies and legislation affecting angel investors in Italy and throughout Europe. LUIGI AMATI is vice president of Business Angels Europe, the Confederation of European Angel Investing, a board member of IBAN and a member of the European Commission Advisory Group on "Access to Risk Finance."

- Increasing the sources of financing for unlisted SMEs and start-ups;
- Scouting and helping the financing of start-ups and SMEs;
- Recruiting angels and facilitating the creation of angel networks and clubs;
- Organizing investment forums between investors and companies that seek capital;
- Organizing training through the Business Angel Academy;
- Fostering the sharing of experience among angels networks and encouraging best practices.

IBAN has created a strong network of relationships covering the entire value chain of early stage firms. In doing so, IBAN has effectively supported start-ups in both growth and value creation, and developed and coordinated the activities of informal, risk-capital investors in Italy and Europe. IBAN has also encouraged the exchange of experiences between angel networks, promoted the recognition of angels and their clubs as subjects of economic policy, and, for the last 10 years, monitored investments made by angel investors. Today IBAN represents more than 500 informal investors throughout all regions of Italy.

In 15 years of business, IBAN has had a number of achievements:

- Assessing angel investing through its annual survey;
- Improving European best practices through collaboration between IBAN and BAE partners;
- Helping increase the number of deals closed, especially in the last five years;
- Publishing a "white paper" on innovation under the auspices of the European Charter of Lisbon and presenting proposals in the Ministerial and Community seat. This has helped angels gain acceptance and foster a more favorable tax regime (DL 112/08, Article 3), wherein the capital gains tax is waived if funds are reinvested in another start-up;
- Being approached by Banca d'Italia and the Ministry of Economic Development in 2012 to help develop measures to support the sector;
- Participating in more than 350 seminars and conferences througout Italy and abroad;

- Receiving positive recognition from the Italian government, the Consob, the Italian Stock Exchange, the Chamber's system, the Industrial Districts Club, various regional and provincial administrations, as well as the business community;
- Being the subject of many articles in the press;[2]
- Creating www.iban.it, which averages 10,000 visitors each month.

Angel Investments in Italy
Volume and Number of Projects

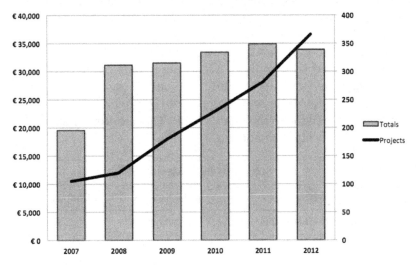

Only 18 percent of 1,963 closely examined projects were invested by the IBAN sample of angel investors (compared to 23 percent in 2011). This highlights the growing rigor of the valuation process, which has increasingly focused on the quality of the investee companies at the expense of quantity. A larger capital pool has allowed some angels to invest more in larger start-ups and a wider array of industries while also reducing their risks. Meanwhile, a growing number of small investments have been made by single investors. About 76 percent of angels invested amounts of less than 10 percent of their own "cash" assets and about 76 percent of their investments in firms were less than €60,000. Angel investments targeted mainly the energy and environment sectors, followed by ICT and medical technology, industries characterized by high potential growth and high innovation. The survey also found that angels widely dispersed across Italy.

STATE OF THE ART OF ANGEL INVESTING IN ITALY

IBAN conducted an online survey between January 14th and March 28th, 2013, to assess the national angel investing market. The 262 respondents were IBAN members, either directly or indirectly through a IBAN member club, or investors targeted by IBAN.[3] The survey found that total angel investment in 2012 amounted to about €33,810,000 among 94 start-ups. Several newly formed clubs took part in the survey. As a result, IBAN found significant changes in the results, e.g., the average amount of single declared investment went down (€92,400 vs €124,000 in 2011), while the average total amount of investment in a targeted company went up (€360,000 vs €231,000 in 2011). The angel market has a significant share of the Italian early stage market, which is an estimated €169 million. According to data collected by IBAN and AIFI, angel investments amount to about 72 percent of all registered investments, while representing only 20 percent of the value invested. These results indicate the vitality and VC presence of Italian angels in seed and early stage financing.

SURVEY OF IBAN MEMBERSHIP		
Metric	2012 Results	% Change from 2011
Sample (52% IBAN Members)	262 Answers	16%
Total Invested	€33,810,000	(3%)
Individual Investments	366	30%
Invested Companies	94	(37%)
Analyzed Projects	1,963	59%
Individual Invested Amount	€92,400	(25%)
Declared Exits	24	71%

The typical Italian angel investor (92 percent) is a male between the age of 50 to 55 with a higher education degree. More than 75 percent live in Northern Italy. Moreover he is a "serial" professional investor: about 20 percent of the IBAN sample had made more than six investments during the preceding years. About 80 percent of the angels declared personal assets greater than €500,000, and one fourth declared assets between €2 million and €5 million. More than two thirds of angels regularly invest between 5 percent and 10 percent of their "cash" assets, and 36 percent believed that their invested assets would grow in the near future. These trends point toward an optimistic growth forecast for Italian angel investing. Most of the investments to date, 81 percent, have been made in Northern Italy. In 2012, Italian angel investing in Europe was 31 percent, a small decrease on the previous year. Twenty-four exits were declared, 10 more than in 2011. It is clear that the current economic environment is influencing investors' behavior. Many exits were delayed, waiting for better economic conditions. The preferred exit strategy was a sale to other investors (47 percent). Other significant exit strategies were a sale to a company or a merger (31 percent), or sale to management (16 percent). Usually, at the time of initial invesment, most targeted companies have between zero and five employees. At exit, most firms have grown to a size of six to ten employees. Based on that estimate, the 62 exits in the past three years should have fostered the creation of about 650 jobs.

INTEGRATION OF CROWDFUNDING AND ANGEL INVESTING

According to the Commissione Nazionale per le Società e la Borsa (CONSOB, the regulatory agency for Italian financial markets), institutional investors (lead investors) are to be given an important role in equity crowdfunding. In order to close the fundraising of an innovative start-up, institutional investors have to buy a minimum of 5 percent of its equity. IBAN holds that angel investors are best positioned to take this role, as in the large majority of investment situations they are significantly more professional and sophisticated than traditional private investors. However, if angels were to be classified as an institutional investor, they would not be able to take advantage of the fiscal benefits assigned to private investors. IBAN has proposed that angels should be designated as "halfway subjects," positioned for policy purposes between the institutional and private investors. This would recognize their professionalism while at the same time allowing them to benefit from the available fiscal advantages.

PUBLIC POLICIES TO PROMOTE ANGEL INVESTMENT

The Italian government launched "Decreto Crescita" in October 2012, a package of tax breaks to support the creation and development of innovative companies. It provides tax incentives for investors who choose to invest economic resources in innovative start-ups. Since then, IBAN has maintained close contacts with the Italian Ministry of Economic Development, advising and contributing to the published final text on the implementing provisions for tax and fiscal incentives. The new regulation introduces fiscal incentives in the form of tax deduction. Individuals can deduct 19 percent, subject to a maximum of €500,000. A "legal person" can deduct 20 percent subject to a maximum of €1,800,000.

Endnotes

[1] BAE is the organization that represents angel networks and seed funds in Europe.

[2] See www.iban.it/press-area/about-us.

[3] About 50 percent of the sample were not IBAN members, but they still recognized it as their representative institution.

Australia

Jordan Green

Angel investing started in Australia in the mid-1990s. Bob Beaumont, an Australian engineer and businessman, returned from a prolonged period living in the US, where he had pursued an entrepreneurial career before becoming a venture capitalist and merchant banker. Along the way, he became familiar with the emerging practice of angel investing and was intimately involved in the early years of the movement in the US and Europe. When he returned to Australia, Bob established its first formal angel group. That first angel group started in Melbourne, Victoria, and continued for 15 years based on a five-year commitment cycle from its members.

Rick McElhinney is another Australian engineer who lived and worked for many years in Canada and the US There he become involved in angel investing and enjoyed successes such as the co-founding of Autodesk. In 2001 Rick established the Founders Forum in Queensland to generate qualified deal flow using experienced business people and angel investors to coach and mentor founders. In 2006 Rick established the Angels Institute as a national for-profit angel group. The Angels

---

JORDAN GREEN has helped found and grow technology-based ventures in Australia, Europe, and the US. As an early stage investor, he led a successful VC firm and drove the formation and growth of the angel investor community in Australia. He writes and speaks widely on angel investing and has advised governments on developing their entrepreneurial ecosystems.

Institute operated for several years, developing a strong reputation for the delivery of high quality training.

In 2005 Jordan Green, another internationally experienced Australian engineer and entrepreneur turned venture capitalist and angel investor, set out to build an angel investor community in Australia. He sought out other individuals who shared that vision, and in 2007 they established the Australian Association of Angel Investors Limited (AAAI), a not-for-profit national professional body. In 2006 and 2007 the founders of the AAAI started angel groups in their home cities:

- BioAngels (Adelaide, South Australia)—John Ballard
- Brisbane Angels (Brisbane, Queensland)—John Mactaggart
- Capital Angels (Canberra, Australian Capital Territory)—David Malloch
- Melbourne Angels (Melbourne, Victoria)—Jordan Green

The AAAI was founded as a professional association with individuals as members. This was a new development in the angel world as national angel associations in other countries were often established as trade or industry bodies with groups as members. The AAAI was also a significant departure from the experience of other countries in another way—it was entirely a grass roots endeavor. Created to foster and support a national community of angel investors, the AAAI has never received operational financial support from government or corporate sponsors. The organization grew its service and profile through the same entrepreneurial spirit that spurred its founders and members to become angels. In 2008 the Angels Institute merged its training operations into the Australian Association of Angel Investors (AAAI).

GROWTH AND DEVELOPMENT OF ANGEL INVESTING

With the proactive support and encouragement of the AAAI, angel groups have continued to form, and there are now 16 angel groups operating in ten Australian cities. The AAAI runs a national angel conference every year which includes angel training programs, government consultation and engagement sessions, panel-based conference sessions, and occasional key note speakers. The conference moves from city to city to provide variety and support local groups through profile-building, pre-conference engagement programs in the host city, and publicity to attract prospective members. The conference has been held in:

- 2008: Canberra (Australian Capital Territory)
- 2009: Brisbane (Queensland)
- 2010: Glenelg (South Australia)
- 2011: Newcastle (New South Wales)
- 2012: Melbourne (Victoria)
- 2013: Gold Coast (Queensland)

The conference has evolved to include entrepreneur showcases and entrepreneur education, as well as collaboration with local governments and universities to promote and showcase the regional early stage ecosystem. From the outset the AAAI has been actively engaged in the international angel community and has developed strong ties to its peers around the world. It was a founding member of the World Business Angels Association and has actively supported the formation of angel communities in several Asian countries. The formation of the AAAI also inspired New Zealand angels to create their own national association. Close working relationships with the national angel associations in Europe and North America have been supported by international exchange visits. Leaders of angel communities visit each others' countries to speak at national conferences, share experiences and discuss collaborative efforts to sustain and grow the global community.

ENTREPRENEURIAL ECOSYSTEM

Australia is the largest island in the world, the smallest continent and the only continent entirely occupied by a single nation. It is a country of 23.5 million people, 90 percent of whom live in the capital cities of its seven states and territories. As one of the most urbanized countries in the world, Australia is also one of the most sparsely populated, which creates significant challenges for domestic infrastructure and transportation. The 21st century brought with it a convergence of influences that ignited the entrepreneurial spirit:

- Historically, Australia has been both an effective early adopter of technology as well as a tier-one originator of new technologies. For example, WiFi, Bionic Ear, photocopying and refrigeration are all Australian inventions.

- The pivotal role Australian scientists and engineers played in the early spread of the internet opened up new opportunities to combat the tyranny of distance.
- A generation of engineers and businessmen nurtured in the successful Australia of the late 20th century, have enjoyed success living and working overseas in places such as Silicon Valley, London, New York and Hong Kong. They have returned home enthusiastic about the entrepreneurial opportunities in Australia.
- Australia enjoys continued growth through the immigration of highly skilled migrants driven to build a new future for themselves and their families through entrepreneurial endeavors. This has resulted in a truly multicultural society that values diversity.
- Australia benefits from privileged access to substantial opportunities in the emerging economies of Asia.
- The failure of the domestic venture capital experiment is being addressed by the rise of the angel investor as the primary source of risk capital for early-stage, high growth ventures.
- Entrepreneurial education is being promoted through world-leading institutions such as the Australian Graduate School of Entrepreneurship in Melbourne, and at the high school level with new programs encouraging young people to think of potential futures in entrepreneurship.

Working together these influences encouraged a new wave of entrepreneurs and early stage investment. However, for most ventures the domestic market is too small to deliver the scalability required for success. The corporate sector also lacks the skills and appetite to be persistent acquirers of technology-based businesses. As a result, entrepreneurs tend to focus on ventures that are "born global."[1]

ANGEL GROUP STRUCTURES AND ORGANIZATIONS

The Australian Associaton of Angel Investors Limited[2] (AAAI) does not engage in investment activities itself but creates resources to assist

AAAI Fellow Eligibility

Prerequisites	Annual Requalifications
Made at least 4 angel investments Exited at least 1 angel investment Completed approved angel investment training	Earn CPD points (25) Declaration of Involvement

Category	Fulfillment		
Total of 25 CPD Points Required	Activity	Points	Earning Cap
Structured Development	AAAI Conference	1	10
	Overseas Nat'l Angel Conference*	1	5
	Training Program/Workshop*	1	8
	Deliver Training Program/Workshop*	1	8
Unstructured Development (Experience and Skills)	Screening /Pitch Sessions	0.25+	4
	Angel Group Meeting/Leadership	0.50	6
	Angel-Entrepreneur Networking Event	0.50	3
	Angel Portfolio Governance/ Mentoring	0.25+	5
*AAAI approval required + Measured per company, not per hour			

members in investment activities. These start with the AAAI Code of Conduct,[3] which underpins the professional conduct of its members, providing protection and professionalism for both investors and entrepreneurs. Building on the code, the AAAI introduced "fellow" status in 2011 for members who have achieved and maintained a level of experience and expertise. Another investor or an entrepreneur dealing with an AAAI Fellow can be confident that they are dealing with a person of integrity and experience who has achieved recognition through peer-based review and continued professional development. The AAAI offers a range of international and home-grown professional education programs, investment document templates, and relationships with overseas angel investors for possible collaboration and co-investment. The AAAI undertakes a national survey of angel investing each year, the only such study in Australia and one of the first of its kind anywhere. It supports new angel groups by providing them both with information based on the experience of the community, as well as introductions to angel group leaders to encourage peer-to-peer collaboration. In 2011 the AAAI developed a syndication treaty which was launched in collaboration with the Angel Association of New Zealand[4] (AANZ) to create a basis for angel groups in Australia and New Zealand to syndicate investments. While the AAAI receives no financial support from government or business for its operations, the annual national angels conference receives modest sponsorship support.

THE ANGEL GROUP CONTEXT

While different groups have experimented with various forms, most Australian angel groups are member-led organizations with volunteer leadership and a not-for-profit incorporated structure.[5] One group has a manager-led structure and another invests on a one-in-all-in model using pre-committed pooled funds. Most groups receive no financial support for operations from the national, state, territory or local governments, but many do get modest financial support from local business sponsors, usually professional services firms. One notable exception is Scale Investors,[6] which was formed in Melbourne in 2013 with support from the AAAI. It is the first women-focused angel group in the country and is modeled closely on the US-based Golden Seeds[7] group, which was started by an Australian expatriate, Stephanie Newby. The female Minister for Innovation, Services and Small Business in the state government of Victoria awarded Scale Investors $600,000 over three years to fund their operations, including a full-time CEO. It is the only angel group in the country to receive such substantial financial support from any source and, as such, is the only one to employ a full-time executive. While such substantial government support is an important milestone, it is unclear whether it will constitute a precedent as the support was not awarded for angel investing, entrepreneurship, or economic development.

Both national and state or territorial governments offer a range of grants for innovation and commercialization.[8] The most important grant program relevant to angel investors is the federal government Accelerating Commercialization program.[10] Most grants require matched funding and so are somewhat like co-investment for angel investors. However, since the grants are uncertain and competitive, they are not the same as an actual government co-investment fund, which does not exist in Australia.

When considering both organizational structure and investment vehicles Australian angels must be aware of the requirements of the Australian

Financial Services regime administered by the Australian Securities and Investments Commission (ASIC).[11] The rules for a company raising funds may have an impact on who can invest and how that investment can be made.[12] Only one angel group has established itself as a licensed financial services provider and most Australian angel groups do not require members to make a formal declaration to attest to their status as sophisticated investors. Angel groups typically operate under the ASIC Class Order that provides a licensing exemption for organizations that introduce investors to investment opportunities without taking a pecuniary interest in the outcome of the introduction.[13] For this reason Australian angel groups do not receive transaction or success fees on investments made by members.

Of the 16 angel groups in Australia, two are dormant at the time of this publication, working on their portfolios but not making new investments. In five groups, a for-profit service provider gathers investment opportunities and makes them available to a mailing list ("network") of private investors. One group, Hunter Angels,[14] is a committed, pooled fund structure that results in a one-in-all-in investment model. The members are committed to transferring into the common pool a pre-agreed and equal amount of capital at predefined dates. A small portion of the funds are allocated to operating expenses but the significant majority are for investment. The group members are responsible for all phases of the investment, and investments are decided by a super-majority vote. Group members are allowed to co-invest with the central fund but the fund is the lead investor. In all other groups, members make an individual investment decision on every opportunity. They vary in how they conduct themselves, however. Brisbane Angels[15] and Melbourne Angels[16] have led the way in developing structures that allow syndicates of members to invest in each deal as a single shareholder. This has some real benefits for both the company and the investors. A structured investment vehicle makes it easier to focus and manage communications between the portfolio company and its investors. A single shareholder can be valuable to the portfolio company as, under Australian corporate law,[17] the company must become a public company once it has 50 shareholders which results in higher compliance costs and less agility in governance.

Originally angel groups adopted the Unit Trust model, which is a tax-transparent entity that allows angels total control of how they handle the tax implications of their investments and gives them uninhibited access to both gains and losses. A new single-purpose Unit Trust was created for each new portfolio company and a new single-purpose corporate trustee was established for operation of each trust. This proved to be a significant administrative burden as the number of investments grew, so Brisbane Angels led the adoption of a new model using a Bare Trust structure. This centralizes and simplifies the administration while still giving portfolio companies and angel members the benefits of a structured investment vehicle. Melbourne Angels is pursuing a different approach that does not rely on the trust structure, but still delivers the benefits of streamlined communications and expedited shareholder response to company requests for decisions.

Sydney Angels was the first group to establish a sidecar fund. Due to the Australian Financial Services licensing regime, it was necessary for Sydney Angels to contract with an external fund manager to establish and operate the fund. The fund manager selected the Early Stage Venture Capital Limited Partnership vehicle for the fund.[18] This vehicle required a fund of at least $10 million, which was successfully raised in 2011-12 from private investors outside the angel group. As part of the model, the fund management and transaction fees are split between the fund manager and the Sydney Angels, providing a modest revenue stream to assist the group in funding its operations. Interestingly, the sidecar fund has had the effect of isolating the Sydney Angels for two main reasons. There is no pressing incentive for the group to seek external funding for its investments, and the fund process imposes delays on deal flow processing that make it unappealing for entrepreneurs and other angel groups interested in syndicating deals. This is unfortunate because it deprives the Sydney Angels and their portfolio companies of the significant intellectual capital benefits that derive from syndication.

ORGANIZATIONS SUPPORTING ANGEL GROUP ACTIVITIES

There is very limited sponsorship of angel groups in Australia. Most groups get some in-kind support from a professional services firm or government agency by way of hosting meetings. A few groups get some token cash sponsorship from local professional services firms.

Two groups received substantial cash and in-kind support from the "Big Four" accounting firms, but each of those firms then decided that supporting one group satisfied their appetite. Given that these are billion-dollar companies it is a sad comment on their true support for the early stage ecosystem. On the other hand, none of the large corporations in Australia provides any support to angel groups. Local governments are more inclined to help but historically this has been piecemeal and usually attached to discrete events rather than sustained support for operations. There is no financial support for angel groups from any of the entrepreneur associations and organizations.

EQUITY CROWDFUNDING

The Australian Small Scale Offerings Board[19] (ASSOB) is a specialized platform founded in 2005 with a customized license for operation of a securities market. In modern parlance ASSOB can be seen as equity crowdfunding platform, and indeed the World Bank Group has identified it as the first equity crowdfunding service in the world. The Australian government has been consulting with industry to inform policy on the regulation of crowdfunding in general, and equity crowdfunding in particular. The AAAI has been a prominent contributor to the consultation as the leading advocate for the entire early-stage ecosystem. New legislation governing equity crowdfunding is expected in 2015.

Australia is home to the third largest pre-purchase crowdfunding site in the world, Pozible.[20] There are now a number of new ventures launching equity crowdfunding services within the current regulatory framework, and others that are poised to launch pending the anticipated regulatory change. An interesting aspect of the emerging platforms is that they are generally being delivered by either financial services experts (typically fund managers) or entrepreneurs. The former view platforms as another way to generate transactional fees, while the entrepreneurs usually believe they are changing the world. In any event, none of these teams has significant expertise or success in early stage investing. The general view is that equity crowdfunding will be an important part of the early stage ecosystem within the next five years. Most experienced early stage investors expect some major "debacles" along the way and are concerned that these might spawn ill-considered knee-jerk regulatory responses.

However, there is no pervasive view that unintended or criminal episodes will derail the eventual growth of equity crowdfunding.

GOVERNMENT POLICIES TO PROMOTE ANGEL INVESTING

In Australia, there are no government policies specifically designed to promote angel investing. Most levels of the Australian government recognize the existence of angels and, in some cases, pay lip service to their importance. In general, Australian politicians are ill-informed about the practice of business and the early stage ecosystem. Their most common response to discussions of angel support is that angels are "a bunch of rich guys," and they would be ill-advised to provide any public assistance. Senior policy bureaucrats are, for the most part, better informed and supportive of the value of promoting angels.[21] This is good to know in case a politician is elected who has a better understanding of the ecosystem and the courage to break new ground.

TAXATION

In Australia, the taxation that governs companies and personal investment is entirely centralized in the federal government, so there are no state-based opportunities for incentives to drive early-stage investment and innovation. On the national level, there is a generous tax incentive for R&D that assists founders and can be an effective multiplier on investor funds.[22] There are no specific tax incentives for angels though. Under the Employee Share Scheme any stock option or grant of stock as in-kind payment to an employee, director or investor is treated as cash income at a value set by the Australian Taxation Office, and is taxable in the hands of the recipient for the year in which it was received.[23] This has effectively killed the use of equity to attract, retain and reward staff in Australian companies, especially start-up companies. It has made start-ups in Australia more expensive because it necessitates cash salaries at competitive market rates. Consequently it makes early stage investment more expensive for angels.

Australians pay income tax using a marginal rate system under which income over certain thresholds is taxed at increasingly higher rates.[24] Australian investors pay Capital Gains Tax (CGT) on any return received from an asset held for more than 12 months. A return in less than 12 months is treated as income tax. An angel receiving a positive return on an investment held in his own name for more than 12 months will pay CGT on 50 percent of the gain at the top marginal rate. The majority of Australian angels invest from their retirement funds that are held in a Self-Managed Superannuation Fund.[25] This offers significant tax advantages including greatly reduced CGT liabilities. Australian angels who realize a capital loss on an investment made in their own name may be able to offset that loss against any contemporary or future capital gains they realize from other similar investments.

GOVERNMENT FUNDING

The federal and state governments offer a range of grant programs for companies, but there are no assistance or subsidy programs for angel investors. Moreover, there is no public funding targeted at angel-backed ventures and no government sidecar fund. There are a variety of grant programs at federal, state and local government levels that support early-stage ventures, most of which require matching funding. Historically, the Australian government and two state governments, Victoria and South Australia, have provided capital to private sector VC funds that were able to attract matching funds from private sector investors. Various federal government programs have been run over the years but none has proven successful if measured by return on capital, or by the quality of the VC firms sustained by those funds. Another form of matched funding has been through grant programs specifically targeting commercialization. The most recent version at the national level is Accelerating Commercialization, a market-driven program supporting the transition of innovative intellectual property from working prototype to first sales.[26] This program delivers both cash and expertise to grant recipients who must apply through a commercially competitive process. While not specifically targeted at angels, this program does offer them an attractive opportunity, as grant funds are not equity investment, i.e. non-diluting. The Victorian government Technology Voucher Program is a much smaller program with more limited funding, but serves a similar purpose.[27]

PUBLIC SUPPORT FOR CONFERENCES AND RESEARCH

In the early years of the Australian angel community, there was modest sponsorship support for the annual national conference from the federal government. That fell away quickly but was replaced for a few years by state government support. Recently, governments have ceased all support for the conference. This is despite each conference being a success and being recognized internationally as one of the premier events of its type. Again, this is mostly due to the influence of political leadership unfamiliar with and unwilling to support the early-stage ecosystem.

The Australian government funded a study of the angel market in 2006.[28] The government also commissioned and funded an OECD report on angel investing published in 2011. There is no current or planned government funded research into the angel space, nor any government support for the research conducted annually by the AAAI.

ANGEL INVESTMENT TRENDS

Angel investing is gathering momentum, and the general public is increasingly aware of its benefits. The number of organized angel groups will probably plateau, but the number of members should continue to grow steadily. Angel investing has already established itself as the primary source of early stage risk capital for high-growth ventures in Australia. In dollar terms it may be exceeded by equity crowdfunding platforms in five to ten years, but these platforms will not offer the intellectual capital contribution of angels. Moreover, angel groups may operate their own crowdfunding programs. Angel investors will continue to provide the key thought leadership for the evolution of the early stage ecosystem. They will be the glue that drives more effective collaboration across market sectors (industry, academia, institutional investors, and entrepreneurs). Angels will increasingly form co-investment or sidecar funds to give passive private investors access to the angel capital asset class.

Acknowledgments

This report could not have been compiled without the support and encouragement of the Australian Association of Angel Investors[29], or the help and information made available from the Melbourne Angels[30] and Brisbane Angels[31] groups.

Endnotes

[1] "born global," now in common usge, was first coined in 1993 by an Australian.

[2] http://aaai.net.au.

[3] http://aaai.net.au/code-of-conduct.

[4] http://www.Angelassociation.co.nz.

[5] In Australia, this means the organization may not distribute any surplus (profit) to its owners or members and, upon liquidation, any assets must be transferred to another not-for-profit in the same type of work.

[6] http://scaleinvestors.com.au.

[7] http://www.goldenseeds.com.

[8] http://www.business.gov.au/GrantFinder/GrantFinder.aspx.

[9] http://grants.myregion.gov.au.

[10] http://www.business.gov.au/advice-and-support/EIP/Accelerating-Commercialisation.

[11] http://www.asic.gov.au/asic/ASIC.NSF/byHeadline/Licensing.

[12] http://www.asic.gov.au/asic/ASIC.NSF/byHeadline/Fundraising.

[13] http://www.asic.gov.au/asic/pdflib.nsf/LookupByFileName/co02-273.pdf/$file/co02-273.pdf.

[14] http://HunterAngels.com.au.

[15] http://www.BrisbaneAngels.com.

[16] http://www.MelbourneAngels.net.

[17] http://www.comlaw.gov.au/Details/C2013C00003.

[18] http://www.ausindustry.gov.au/programs/venture-capital/esvclp/Pages/default.aspx.

[19] http://www.assob.com.au.

[20] http://www.pozible.com/.

[21] Note that the Australian government commissioned and funded the OECD study of Angel investing published in 2011 but, the Australian government has never formally acknowledged or acted on the report, see http://www.oecd.org/sti/ind/49320041.pdf.

[22] http://www.business.gov.au/grants-and-assistance/innovation-rd/RD-TaxIncentive.

[23] http://www.ato.gov.au/A-Z-index/AZItems.aspx?id=3668&category=Employee+share+schemes+(ESS).

[24] http://www.ato.gov.au/Rates/Individual-income-tax-rates.

[25] http://www.ato.gov.au/Super/Self-managed-super-funds.

[26] http://www.business.gov.au/advice-and-support/EIP/Accelerating-Commercialisation.

[27] http://www.business.vic.gov.au/industries/science-technology-and-innovation/programs/technology-voucher-program.

[28] http://www.innovation.gov.au/innovation/reportsandstudies/Documents/BusinessAngelReport.pdf.

[29] http://aaai.net.au.

[30] http://www.melbourneangels.com.

[31] http://www.brisbaneangels.com.au.

Belgium

Reginald Vossen and Claire Munck

Seven angel networks emerged in Belgium in the 1998–2001 period. Together they completely covered the Belgian area: four in Flanders, two in Wallonia and one in Brussels. In the beginning of 2004, the four Flemish networks merged into one private non-profit organization: BAN Vlaanderen.[1] In 2007, one of the Walloon networks merged with the one in Brussels to become a single private entity: Be Angels.[2] As of April 2015, there are now two remaining networks in Belgium, one in Flanders and one in Wallonia. Together these represent around 400 angels and receive over 750 projects annually. Approximately 200 of these projects are presented at 35 investment events, resulting in 40-50 annual deals and a total of €8 million. Both networks also organize entrepreneur and investor training activities, such as business angel days.

NATIONAL ASSOCIATION—BeBAN

The two Belgian networks join forces in BeBAN, the Belgian Association

---

REGINALD VOSSEN was the founding secretary of the Limburg Business Angels Network in 1999 and became its manager the following year. Since the merger of four Flemish BANs into BAN Vlaanderen vzw in 2004, he has been the general manager of this network of about 225 business angels. Over the past few years, BAN Vlaanderen has generated about 25 investment deals per year. CLAIRE MUNCK is Chief Executive Offivcer and Director of Be Angels, a 15-year-old business angel group based in Belgium for the French-speaking part of the country and one of Europe's largest and most active groups. Her key responsibilities include business development, recruitment of new investors, deal making, and the management of a women angel group she created last year as a subsidiary of Be Angels.

of Business Angels Networks. BᴇBAN's main goal is the promotion of angel finance and networks in Belgium. It has also drafted a code of conduct which has been signed by the two existing networks. BᴇBAN facilitates cooperation between the Belgian networks and the public and private organizations active in the field of risk capital. For instance in 2002 the Federal Participation Fund launched a new product to give favorable subordinated loan collateral to network member deals. This "business angel+" loan has been intensively used as a co-financing mechanism for Belgian angels.[3]

Since 2000 BᴇBAN has represented the networks in discussions with the Finance and Banking Commission over the scope of angel intervention, and angel compatibility with Belgian legislation on public offerings and prospectus requirements. Currently business proposals cannot be submitted to more than 100 people. At a regional level both networks actively lobby for a more favorable angel environment, including aspects such as fiscal incentives, co-investment mechanisms, training support, and support for women angels.

PUBLIC SUPPORT

Both Belgian networks have secured financial support from regional government for their day-to-day operations. This support varies from region to region due to the fact that economic policy is a regional responsibility in Belgium. The support of all regional authorities constitutes an official recognition of angels' contributions to the economy. For instance, a guarantee scheme for angel investments was created through Sowalfin, the public financing agency in Wallonia. Also important is the aforementioned federal business angel+ loan scheme.

The European Commission has supported several initiatives in the conceptual phase of angel networks. First, the Junior Chamber International coordinated ten awareness seminars in the late 1990s in Bruges, Kortrijk, Gent, Antwerp, Leuven, Hasselt, Brussels, Mons, Liège and Wavre. Second, two feasibility studies were co-funded in Belgium: one by GOM Vlaams-BraBANt and NCMV, and another by PYTHAGORAS n.v., a private company. Third, DG Enterprise supported a pilot project in Belgium benefitting Vlerick Leuven Gent Management School. Fourth, the European Regional Development Fund supported the Limburg BAN vzw network, which later merged into the Flemish network, BAN Vlaanderen. Fifth, three Belgian organizations (BAN Vlaanderen, SOCRAN and WfG Ostbelgien), together with a German (AGIT) and a Dutch (LIOF) partner started the Interreg-project EuBAN in January 2004. EUBAN was a tri-national network in the Euregion Meuse-Rhine, which aimed to generate more angel activity in the region and enhance cross-border investments. EUBAN was partially subsidized through Interreg III-funds. Sixth, Be Angels was part from 2013 to 2015 of a consortium led by Business Initiative (Luxembourg) to stimulate cross-border investment in the Greater Region (Luxembourg, Lorraine in France and parts of the Walloon Region in Belgium) called Seed4Start. Last, Be Angels (at the time through BAMS), participated as a partner in the Ready for Equity project. This helped create European-wide training programs for angels and entrepreneurs.

PROMOTION OF ANGEL INVESTING

The Dutch-speaking economic daily newspaper *De Tijd* regularly publishes articles on angel networks in Flanders. The French-speaking daily *L'Echo* does the same for the Walloon network. Economic magazines such as *Trends/Tendances* and *PME/KMO* regularly publish pieces on Belgian angel activity in both French and Dutch. The 2004 creation of BAN Vlaanderen raised a great deal of attention in the national media and enhanced knowledge about angel networks. Since then a large publicity campaign with commercials, advertisements and a region-wide road show has expanded the angel group concept throughout Flanders. BAN Vlaanderen also launched a funding platform—www. angel4me.be—to allow online matchmaking. Both networks organise many angel training activities such as angel bootcamps to introduce new investors to angel investing. Be Angels refurbished its website in 2013 to promote deals financed by its members and to raise public awareness about its role and activities. It started publishing press releases that are distributed to the daily press and specialized magazines. Be Angels also recently participated in an interview regarding angel financing for *Euronews*'s feature Business Planet.

GOVERNMENT POLICIES

In Belgium capital gains derived by individuals not engaged in business activities are generally not taxable; otherwise they are taxed at an income tax rate of 33 percent. Capital gains derived from shares are normally tax exempt. Dividends received by a Belgian resident from a company are subject to a taxation of 25 percent. Under certain conditions, the tax rate amounts to only 15 percent.

In July, 2015 a tax incentive to encourage investments in Belgian start-ups was launched. By this means, start-ups will have easier access to financing and dormant savings in savings accounts will be activated. This measure is similar to the Cooreman-De Clercq Act, but for start-up companies. The tax incentive comprises a tax relief in the personal income tax that an investor/natural person receives when he/she invests in a young entrepreneur or a start-up fund. More specifically this concerns: a tax relief of 45 percent in the personal income tax for new shares of a start-up (EU definition micro-enterprise); and a tax relief of 30 percent for new shares to be issued by a starting SME. To qualify for the tax relief, the shares need to be kept for four years. The maximum investment per investor per year is €100,000. The maximum per company invested is €250,000. For crowdfunders, the granting of capital up to maximum €7,500 and loans up to maximum €15,000 will be subject to tax support via a regulated crowdfunding platform thanks to tax relief in the personal income tax and an exemption from withholding tax on the interest of the loans.

In Flanders, a number of financial incentives are applicable to angels. The "win-win" loan is a tax credit of 2.5 percent per year that encourages the public to provide loans to friends starting businesses. The loan must run for eight years and is capped at €200,000. Flanders also allows firms to deduct interest on long term debt financing from their income tax. Moreover, a "notional deduction" allows companies to reduce their taxable base when making investments from their own resources. The deductible amount equals the fictitious interest cost on the adjusted equity capital. There is also an indirect incentive for angels who form a group fund. The PRICAF regime offers a tax transparent vehicle wherein shareholders pay practically no tax on capital gains. BAN Vlaanderen operates two private PRICAF funds: the ARK Angels Fund and the ARK Angels Activator Fund.

OTHER PUBLIC POLICIES

The national finance supervisory authority (Bank Commission) provided clear guidelines for the operation of angel networks. This has given angel networks a more professional and recognized image in the market, allowing groups to grow quickly in terms of member numbers and deal flow.

THE FLANDERS REGION: BAN VLAANDEREN

BAN Vlaanderen is the sole angel network operating in Vlaanderen (Flanders), the northern part of Belgium. As noted earlier, it was established in 2004 as a merger of four mostly regionally oriented networks. The Flemish government has been subsidizing the operations of these organizations since 1999. This support continued with the inception of BAN Vlaanderen and now equals approximately 40 percent of the operational budget of the network. Besides this structural support (which is renewed every 3-4 years), BAN Vlaanderen has been given ad hoc subsidies for projects on consolidated financing, support of growth companies ("gazelles"), M&A support and the implementation of an angel portal. BAN Vlaanderen has also partnered with the Regional Development Agency and the Flemish Ministry of Economy for several studies and pilot projects on alternative finance, crowd funding, and SME-internationalisation, among others. All subsidy agreements are subject to an extensive and constructive negotiation process between the network and the government officials ('Agentschap Ondernemen'). Recently, BAN Vlaanderen was selected to be one of the main strategic partners of the Agentschap Ondernemen in the economic development policy for Flanders. This is a major recognition of the important role angels play in entrepreneurship and risk financing.

Since its inception in 2004, BAN Vlaanderen has grown in both quantitative and qualitative terms. BAN Vlaanderen started with 75 affiliated angels and has grown to 225 members. In the past ten years these angels were brought into contact with 959 entrepreneurs, through carefully established and transparent processes. The 959 screened entrepreneurs were selected from 4,361 applications, indicating that capital-seeking entrepreneurs in Flanders are increasingly finding their way to BAN Vlaanderen. Of the 959 projects, 188 first rounds were funded by BAN Vlaanderen members. This 25 percent success rate is high in comparison to VCs. A large part of this is due to BAN Vlaanderen's "deal making services". Since 2008 BAN Vlaanderen has offered members and entrepreneurs a free, full-service package of guidance and juridical expertise in the negotiation process following the matchmaking phase. After projects are presented to angels, one of eight neutral dealmakers (all seasoned lead investors) is available to guide the due diligence and investment process. These "go-betweens" use their experience to enhance the chance of success and speed up the process. Currently one in three companies that enter this guided deal-making process receive funding, and the time to conclude a deal has been reduced by 50 percent. Moreover, 73 of these deals were able to make use of business angel+ loans, and 18 received supplementary funding through BAN Vlaanderen's PRICAF funds. By doing so a total flow of €44 million in risk capital was realized over the 10-year period. Taking into account an estimated €60 million leveraged from other sources, the total investment into the Flemish economy was about €100 million.

As noted, BAN Vlaanderen initiated two consecutive co-investment funds. The Ark Angels Fund (investment period 2007–2011) co-invested with angels in 16 companies. The capital for the fund was provided on a 50-50 basis by a group of 41 angels and the Flemish government through the Arkimedes I fund under the umbrella of the PMV (Flemish Participation Company). It is now in the phase of exiting from its investments, with two successful recent exits. With the Ark Angels Activator Fund (investment period 2012–2017) the Flemish government (again through PMV) participates alongside a group of 56 angels and the ING Bank. Each of the three groups of shareholders contributed a third of the total amount of €15 million. This fund is in investment mode and plans to invest in 15 to 20 angel backed companies with a leverage of up to four times the angel investment.

The Participation Fund is a federal financial institution that supports self-employed professionals who would like to start their own businesses. It provides financial, technical and administrative services to other institutions, alone or with the collaboration of other organizations. Its business angel+ loan is intended for entrepreneurs whose company is in the launch phase or at a stage of strategic development, and whose innovative risk profile means it is better fit for angel funding than traditional bank loans.[5] The business angel+ loan program benefits from a guarantee issued under the European Community's Competitiveness and Innovation Framework. The fund has signed an exclusive cooperation agreement with the angel networks. Its projects are preselected by the networks, which propose them to potentially interested angels. The fund gets involved when the "matching" nears completion.

WALLOON REGION: BE ANGELS

Be Angels is the sole structured business angel network operating in the Walloon Region. It also operates on the Region of Brussels along with BAN Vlaanderen. It celebrated in 2015 its 15th anniversary. Be Angels is the result in 2007 of the merger between BAMS, a private-led business angel group formed by businessmen around the area of Louvain-la-Neuve, and Business Angels Connect, a business angel group linked to EEBIC (incubator and fund manager) and the Solvay Business School. Be Angels benefits from the support of the Walloon Region and the Brussels Region to cover part of its operation costs. Today, Be Angels gathers some 170 members (13 percent of these members are women) and proposes a number of services to entrepreneurs and investors among which:

- Deal flow pre-selection
- Deal making
- Angel training
- Entrepreneur training
- Services to facilitate pooling by new and/or more passive investors
- Co-investment opportunities
- International contacts: member of the Business Angels Europe Club and organizer of the Seed4Start cross-border investment forums

Every year, Be Angels receives circa 300 business propositions. Through a careful selection process, 40 to 50 are presented to its investors during a monthly investment event. In 2014, 22 deals were closed for circa €2,5 million of angel monies, leveraging approximately 2 to 3 times that amount in public co-investment and bank loans for the companies.

CASE STUDY: CROWDFUNDING IN BELGIUM

As in all Western European countries, a number of new crowdfunding initiatives have been initiated in Belgium. BAN Vlaanderen and Be Angels welcome these initiatives as potential partners in promoting young entrepreneurship. Many crowdfunded projects probably will need an angel at a later stage who can take the company to a higher level. Although crowdfunding is often confused with angel investment, there are clear differences between the two forms of funding.

Crowdfunding has played a welcome role in drawing attention to daring entrepreneurs and has proven its value in the creative industries, where young talents get the opportunity to enter the market through fan sponsorship. For their support these sponsors receive either nothing or a small gift which is usually associated with the funded project. This form of crowdfunding (donation-based, reward-based and loan-based) is straightforward, and the parties involved know what to expect and act accordingly.

There is more risk related to the newer equity-based crowdfunding, where small equity portfolios of start-up companies are offered to micro-investors in a public manner. Good start-up funding goes beyond simply providing short term money. Equity crowdfunding may hinder the company's growth and "time to market." Besides money, entrepreneurs also need guidance so that attention and resources go to the right priorities. Starters should be given more "smart money," which combines financial input with a good portion of investor commitment and entrepreneurial experience. The legal context must also be clarified urgently. Supervisory authorities provide a number of rules regarding protection of depositors. In Belgium these rules hold that platform funds should only be directed to projects with a clearly defined maximum desired capital of €300,000, with a maximum investment of €1,000 per investor, which may not be split into sub-projects. Often the projects on a crowdfunding platform are not so precisely defined, and thus create a de facto infringement against the rules. Currently it is not clear who can be held liable in this case—the entrepreneur, the investor, or the platform?

Moreover, there is a real risk of unbalanced appreciation for the new shareholders. Normally entrepreneurs and investors negotiate to determine the business value and share price. With crowdfunding a unilateral proposed price ("take it or leave it") is proposed to the investors, and neither party gets to discuss their valuation issues. In order to avoid unpleasant surprises, a solid and balanced shareholders' agreement and articles of association are of crucial importance. For a company with growth ambitions, the early spread of capital over a large group of investors is not an ideal starting position for further funding rounds. Excessive distribution of shareholding capital makes strategic decisions and the entry of new strategic investors more difficult. The same is true for exits if not treated properly in the shareholders' agreement.

It is hoped that crowdfunding initiatives tackle these issues and that their legal position is clarified, so they can play a constructive role alongside angels. Specific attention should go to the selection of the proposed investee companies. A great deal of projects looking for money are turned down by professional investors after serious due diligence. These projects might now "try their luck" with the less informed and less professional crowd.

Again, crowdfunders are not angels, since angels do much more than just provide finance. Besides capital participation they also provide commitment and added value to the invested company by putting their knowledge, network and operating expertise at service. For this, they draw on their extensive business experience and therefore enjoy credibility with other funders. Crowdfunders lack these additional assets. An erosion of the concept of "business angel" would be unfortunate, precisely because of the positive role that many angels play in young companies.

Likewise, a crowdfunding platform is usually a very open structure where project sponsors and investors can easily join and place or select projects. This contrasts with angel networks where projects are presented and invested with discretion. For example, angel network files are not accessible on any website. This protects both ideas and promoters. Entrepreneurs are able to control those who enter into the shareholders' structure of the company, a very important issue often overlooked in crowdfunding! Entrepreneurs are also confident that the project is only presented to a group of selected accredited investors—"like-minded" peers. Entrepreneurs are also provided with a comprehensive package of training and coaching by the network team, so the project can be developed and presented under optimal conditions. In addition, the recognized structure of the network guarantees that there a sustainable model behind the investment, with clearly defined procedures and responsibilities.

Within the network of BAN Vlaanderen more than 200 investments in Flemish innovative companies were realized from an inflow of more than 2,800 projects. The average investment of €120,000 is just above the current legal €100,000 limit of the crowdfunding (similar size as Be Angels at an average deal size of €150,000). It is hoped that the transparency and the legal framework surrounding crowdfunding quickly rises to the level that allows cooperation with angel groups. It is uncertain whether crowdfunding platforms will prove strong enough to self-regulate. It is hoped that a clear win-win situation will be reached, where co-investment between the crowd (bringing market validation) and angels (bringing professionalization in due diligence and post-investment coaching) combines the best of both worlds, with full respect of the strengths of each party.

Be Angels published and promoted during the spring of 2015, along with two crowdfunding platforms (Crowdfin—donation and lending and Look&Fin—a lending platform) a White Paper concerning the stimulation of private savings in order to support the real economy. This White Paper described the current lack of access to finance by SMEs in Belgium, and the tools which are made available by business angel networks and different crowdfunding platforms, clarifying the targeted needs and amounts sought. Finally, the White Paper proposed a number of recommendations concerning the introduction of fiscal incentives for angels and smoother regulation allowing private individuals to invest via crowdfunding platforms.

Endnotes

[1] BAN Vlaanderen vzw; Mr Reginald Vossen, CEO; T: +32 11 870 910; info@BAN.be; http://www.ban.be.

[2] Be Angels SA ; Ms. Claire Munck, CEO; T: +32 10 48 50 22; info@beangels.be; http://www.beangels.eu.

[3] BeBAN can be contacted through its current president, Reginald Vossen (info@ban.be).

[4] The subsidy is composed of an annual fixed part of 90 percent of the total support and a variable, output related part of 10 percent of the total.

[5] Characteristics of the loan: subordinated; fixed interest rate; period of five, seven or ten years; one to three years of capital repayment grace; maximum of €125,000, by means of a contribution from the angel(s) and the creator/entrepreneur(s) higher than or equal to the participation fund's loan.

Spain

Juan Roure and Amparo De San Jose

Angel investment, in particular organized through networks, is a recent phenomenon in Spain. Despite a slow take-off in the early 2000s, more than 50 networks had been created by 2013 and the number is expected to grow. The last years of the economic crisis, as well as increasing media coverage of entrepreneurship, have brought attention to angel financing. Incubators, accelerators, and crowdfunding platforms are sprouting, offering angel investors opportunities and multiplying deal flow. In Spain, the best years of angel investment are yet to come.

The start of the organized angel movement in Spain dates back to around the turn of the century. Through a pioneer program in 1997, the European Commission helped create the European Angel Network Association (EBAN), which helped catalyze the market in its early years. The first European-wide event took place in 1999 with the participation

---

JUAN ROURE is President of the Spanish Association of Angel Networks, a Professor in the Entrepreneurship Department and has been a member of IESE's International Advisory Board for the last ten years. He also currently sits on the International Advisory Board of IAE (Argentina). He was a Visiting Professor at Stanford University, INSEAD, Harvard Business School and CEIBS (China). AMPARO DE SAN JOSE is the Director of IESE's Business Angel Network. The network has gathered a portfolio of 98 companies with more than 24 million invested. She also contributes to research at IESE Entrepreneurship Department. Previously she worked at the InterAmerican Development Bank and the Centre for European Policy Studies (Brussels).

of representatives from the Spanish public sector. They were the first to call attention to angel investing to the country. Particularly interested were members of ACCIÓ—the Agència Per A La Competitivitat De L'Empresa—which early in 2002 started to promote angel investment in Catalonia. In continental Europe the early adopters and promoters of angel networks were public agencies and institutions. In 1999, after the first European congress, the number of networks grew to 110 networks according to EBAN, roughly double the figure in 1998, which to that point had been dominated by networks in the UK.

Through an existing service to facilitate access to finance for small and medium-sized entreprises, ACCIÓ started to promote the first meetings between investors and entrepreneurs. However, the meetings did not generate as much investments as expected. ACCIÓ decided to launch the first training initiative for business angels and, in the following months, helped grow three of the early networks in the country.

Notwithstanding this lack of organized activity, angels were finding and closing successful deals. Some of the pioneer angels, are still widely recognized by the market as reference investors. Rodolfo Carpintier and Luis Martín Cabiedes, for example, have deals dating back to the late nineties such as Olé, MyAlert (which had an IPO in the Italian market in 2003), Kelkoo (sold to Yahoo for $600 million in 2004), and also more recent success stories BuyVip (sold to Amazon in 2009) and Tuenti, the most popular social network in Spain among youth.

The Spanish angel market has grown significantly in the past five years. The number of networks has continuously risen for the past five years to an estimated 50-60, 30 of which belong to the Spanish Association of Angel Networks (AEBAN). However, the exact scale of activity is unknown due to the lack of agreed statistics. Through direct observation, networks affiliated with AEBAN have invested modest figures: 86 investments corresponding to €17.7 million in 2012.

Using a different methodology, Global Entrepreneurship Monitor España (GEM), estimated in 2012 that 0.2 percent of the population was involved in angel investment, which would be the equivalent of more than 60,000 business angels. According to GEM figures, that would make Spain the fourth most active country in the world in terms of angel activity, just behind the US A more conservative estimate would put the number of professional and active angel investors—the "visible" market of angels—below 1,000. Estimating the "invisible" market is very difficult.

While the early days were dominated by open networks able to attract a larger number of potential investors, more recent years have witnessed the increase of small, club-type groups, which are centered around business or friendship bonds.

The preferences of Spanish angel investors differ somewhat from more mature angel markets such as the US While sectors such as the internet and communication-related companies still dominate, the healthcare sector (services, medical equipment or biotech), which is very popular in the US, is less popular. Indeed, the most active Spanish angel networks specialize in internet companies.

A FEW HINTS OF AN ENTREPRENEURIAL ECOSYSTEM

The economic crisis in Spain has put entrepreneurship at the forefront of public policy, media coverage and the political agenda. In the past three to five years, there has been an explosion in the number of business incubators, accelerators, awards and contests promoted by the public sector, corporations, academic institutions and sector agents. These numerous public and private initiatives have raised awareness of entrepreneurship, but flaws and difficulties still exist. Spain aims to be a country where entrepreneurship—starting a business to earn a living—steadily increases. Some progress is being made. The GEM survey and the Entrepreneurship Barometer confirm growing entrepreneurship activities. Nevertheless, the aspirations of entrepreneurs and policymakers alike still face challenges and restrictions in terms of the nation's culture and its regulatory and economic environment. While more people are involved in start-ups, roughly a third (35 percent) of Spainards say that, if they could choose between different kinds of jobs, they would prefer to be self-employed (EU, Entrepreneurship Barometer, 2012).

Regardless of what they prefer, fewer Spainards (21 percent) than Europeans (30 percent) consider self-employment to be feasible. The current economic climate seems to be the main reason. Fear of having to declare bankruptcy amid Spain's economic crisis is surpassed only by a fear of losing one's property or home (55 percent in Spain vs. 37 percent in the EU). Spain is the only European country where this is the main fear.

In the current crisis, financing is increasingly a problem for SMEs, both innovative and traditional types, so Spanish companies are highly dependent on bank lending and have one of the lowest levels of equity financing among EU nations. The use of equity financing is only lower in Slovakia, Hungary and the Czech Republic.

A FEW LEADING ANGEL NETWORKS

There is not a dominant form of angel networks in Spain, and there is no formal legal system to classify them into different types. Many club networks are loosely organized groups of friends who create a new investment vehicle for each investment. Some are initiatives or departments within larger institutions such as business schools, and there is an increasing number of groups that have management teams while allowing individual members flexibility to decide whether to invest in particular deals. A few of the most popular ones are Keiretsu Forum (with ties to US Keiretsu), ESADE BAN (run by alumni of ESADE Business School), the Crowd Angel (linked to an early stage consulting and investing group), and Faraday (a manager-led angel club). Some of the most notable ones are:

- Digital Assets Deployment (www.dad.es). DaD was created in 2006 by Rodolfo Carpintier, an entrepreneur and internet investor since 1994, and seven other angel investors. Today the network facilitates investment for 96 business angels, many of them with internet experience. Currently DaD has investments across three continents and a total of 40 investees, more than 20 of which are in Spain. DaD has been an early investor in several companies: Buyvip, which was sold to Amazon in 2010; Tuenty, sold to Telefonica the same year; and XPLANE, sold to US company Dachis in 2010.

- IESE Business Angel Network (www.iese.edu/businessangels).

This network, created by the Instituto de Estudios Superiores de la Empresa Business School, became in 2003 the first nationwide network. Although it is centered around the strong alumni network of a leading academic institution, it is open to entrepreneurs and investors not affiliated with the business school. It does not operate as a club or a fund; investment decisions are made by each individual. Its portfolio holds 65 investments of more than €16 million of angel money. The network is based predominantly in Spain but chapters are being launched in locations with a strong alumni bases and cooperation with associated business schools in Latin America is being developed. Among the most successful exits of the IESE BAN are: Privalia, the largest outlet online; Buyvip, which was sold to Amazon; and Quiterian, which was sold to Actuate Corporation.

- Seedrocket (www.seedrocket.com). SeedRocket is a rapidly growing hub and angel club. Since 2008 Seedrocket has trained more than 600 entrepreneurs and contributing to financing 32 start-ups, representing more than €12.5 million. It places special emphasis on working with former internet start-up founders, and has 45 investors. A few of its best performing deals are: Offerum, Marfeel, and Kantox, which have closed deals over a million euros. It specializes in seed stages, often with a participative loan. The network is financially self-sustaining, funded by a combination of fees from investors, subsidies and sponsors.

PUBLIC POLICIES OF ANGEL INVESTMENT ACTIVITY

Public support for angel investment in Spain is a patchy landscape characterized timid fiscal measures in different regions. Currently there are only two programs to foster the creation and strengthening of angel networks, both of which are funded by grants:

- DGPYME (www.ipyme.org). Since 2010 the Ministry of Economic Affairs has managed a support program for the creation and development of angel networks. The first call in 2010 attracted 47 applicants, 30 of whom received a maximum of €30,000 as a grant. Two years later, the number of applicants grew to 71, but only 16 received grants, as the total program budget was €350,000. For the most current year at the time of this publication, 2013, the Ministry divided applicants between new networks and existing networks, and reduced the scale of funding to €150,000 euros for the latter while increasing it to €450,000 euros for new networks to help foster creation of networks in regions that have had low angel activities.

- ACCIÓ (www.acc10.cat/ACCIO). The regional agency for economic development in Catalonia launched the first support program for angel networks in Spain. In fact, in 2002, ACCIÓ sponsored the first training program for angels organized by a business school in Europe. Catalonia, one of the regional economic powerhouses of Spain, has a population of 7.5 million today and some 10 angel networks. The ACCIÓ program was launched in 2003 to support new angel networks in the region. The incentives were initially tied to performing certain activities (matchmaking events, training for investors, or dissemination and communication efforts) and the networks' capabilities to close deals. Currently only the best performers in terms of deals closed receive public support. ACCIÓ primarily seeks to help networks become self-sustainable. The maximum ACCIÓ grant to a network currently amounts to €12,500 a year. ACCIÓ also tries to foster cooperation and exchange among networks to raise the profile of angel groups. Since 2003, networks covered by the program have facilitated a total of more than €50 million in investments in start-ups.

CO-INVESTMENT SCHEMES

Spain has a limited number of co-investment schemes:

- ENISA (www.enisa.es). ENISA, an agency under the Ministry of Industry, has a cooperation agreement with AEBAN. Under this agreement, companies raising financing from a business angel can complement their financing with participative loans up to the capital raised (which can be between €100,000 and €1.5 million). This scheme was recently extended to work with international investors under the Spain Start-Up co-investment fund. In particular, the AEBAN networks' agreement has catalyzed an additional €7 million into 27 deals. ENISA also lends to companies that secure financing from business angels outside networks, venture capital funds or capital raised from entrepreneurs. Overall, the total lending figure for ENISA since its creation in 1995 totals €500 million, complementing a total of €2.8 billion of external resources. ENISA participative loans do not require personal guarantees and offer advantageous interest rates based on the stage of the company.

• IFEM (Financial Instruments for Innovative Companies, SL) is led by a government agency that supports SMEs with a combination of Spanish and EU public funds. The co-investment program, established at the end of 2012, initially had €12 million available for co-lending. The program allows companies to match capital raised with a participative loan. IFEM performed well in its first year: angel capital on average was €250,000; co-lending funds applied for amounted to €150,000 per company, and IT and e-commerce represented three quarters of the deals. Relative to the US market, there have been proportionately fewer bio and healthcare deals (8 percent). Deals tend to be rejected most often because of insufficient cash flows or having insufficient capital to sustain the investee companies between investment rounds. IFEM works only with angels associated with 11 business angel networks, which helps to strengthen those networks in particular.

TAX INCENTIVES

Despite long-promised fiscal incentives that would recognize the role of angel investors alongside that of venture capitalists, progress was still halting at the time of this book. However, some changes are a step forward: the bankruptcy law for individual company owners, for example, which now recognizes "entrepreneurs" as a distinct category, represents a cultural change. Recent reforms include a personal income tax deduction of up to 20 percent subject to a maximum of €50,000 per investment. However, the measure excludes investments delivered under societal vehicles—the preferred form of professional angel investment—and the deduction is limited to investments performed as an individual subject. Capital gains obtained in a period from 3 to 12 years are tax-exempt if reinvested in a newly created company.

Regional governments, meanwhile, have been able to introduce their own incentives, such as a 20 percent deduction (30 percent in Catalonia and Navarra), but limited to investors and investees subject to tax in the same region. Nevertheless the sector still calls for more favorable measures in light of the support available to angel investors in other European countries.

Acknowledgements

The authors would like to acknowledge research contributions from Teresa Torres, IFEM, Oriol Sans and Sergi Mora from ACCIÓ, and José Herrera from BGM Associates.

Endnotes

[1] http://paulcollege.unh.edu/center-venture-research.

[2] *Flash Eurobarometer 354. Entrepreneurship in the EU and Beyond*: http://ec.europa.eu/enterprise/policies/sme/facts-figures-analysis/eurobarometer/index_en.htm.

[3] http://www.ipyme.org/es-ES/SubvencionesAyudas/RedesBusinessAngels/Paginas/ImpulsoRedesBusinessAngels.aspx.

[4] Ley 14/2013 September 27th, Apoyo a los emprendedores y su internacionalización.

United Arab Emirates

Heather Henyon

A BRIEF HISTORY OF ANGEL ACTIVITIES

Angel investment as a structured form of investing is in very early stages of growth in the Middle East and North Africa region. While family offices have traditionally invested in club structures, the type of investing is very different from angel investing (i.e. majority ownership is expected, only finance family members' companies, etc). There have been informal angel investors who invest as individuals and may work with others to increase access to deal flow but even groups like these are limited. In the UAE, an angel group called the Arab Business Angels Network (ABAN) was started in 2005 under Dubai International Capital (DIC) and Dubai Holding, an initiative sponsored by the government. There was interest in the concept and pitches held at the Dubai International Finance Center (DIFC) were well attended. However, very few investments were made. There are other similar government sponsored platforms in the Gulf. Silatech launched SILA

HEATHER HENYON is a socially motivated finance professional who has lived and worked in the UAE, Egypt, Lebanon and Palestine. She is the founder and managing partner of Balthazar Capital, a microfinance investment advisory firm for the Arab region. Prior to launching Balthazar Capital, Heather was the founding general manager of Grameen-Jameel, a regional social business jointly owned by Grameen Foundation and Abdul Latif Jameel Group. In 2013, Heather founded and chairs the Women's Angel Investment Network (WAIN), the first women's angel investment group in the Middle East.

Angel Investment Network in Qatar in 2012 to connect Qatari angel investors with entrepreneurs. While there are large amounts of wealth held by family offices and private investors especially in the Gulf countries, the challenge has been in attracting angel investors who have both capital and professional experience that they can leverage to add value to start-up companies. Entrepreneurs need early stage investors who are willing to open up their networks, help with business strategy and provide the mentoring support needed by entrepreneurs at the start-up stage.

An angel investor group called Envestors from the United Kingdom started to work in the UAE in 2008. They hold open pitches and invite individuals to attend and have an investor base of about 150 members in Dubai. There are other informal angel groups in the UAE such as VentureSouq, which has organized entrepreneur pitches since 2013 and has raised almost $2 million for 8 companies.

WAIN (Women's Angel Investment Network) is one of the new acts on the Middle East start-up scene. WAIN is composed of women investors from the region who want to invest both capital and their time in women-led companies. The angel group, the first of its kind in the Middle East, was started in response to a need voiced by Arab entrepreneurs for more active mentors and investors. WAIN invests in early stage companies in which a woman has a significant equity stake as a founder and holds a C-suite role. WAIN started in Dubai in 2013 with a group of women who were interested in piloting the model and determining whether the women-led companies in the region are investment-ready. They knew that there was a large number of women entrepreneurs in the region but they were not sure of the quality of the companies. The results were overwhelming: within two weeks of informally circulating an investment application, the Dubai group received 50 submissions. The pitches were equally impressive, especially the Jordanian entrepreneurs, reflecting the deep investment in the entrepreneurial ecosystem over the last two years in Jordan.

ENTREPRENEURIAL ECOSYSTEM IN THE UAE

The region has witnessed a huge jump in the resources available for entrepreneurs—incubators, accelerators, co-work spaces, boot camps and universities. Impact Hub, a gathering space for entrepreneurs with locations in over 40 cities, opened its doors in Dubai in 2013. Turn8, in5 and Dubai Silicon Oasis are active business accelerators and incubators in Dubai. Most recently, Flat6Labs from Egypt has opened a branch in Abu Dhabi in partnership with twofour54, a media trade zone. Co-work spaces like Pavilion and MAKE Business Hub have been in Dubai for the last few years. New co-work spaces such as the Dubai Mercantile Mining Commodities (DMMC) partnership with AstroLabs and Google

Angel Investor Groups in the Middle East and North Africa (2014)

Country	Angel Group	Year Formed
Bahrain	Tenmou	2011
Egypt	Cairo Angels	2011
Lebanon	Lebanese Business Angels (Bader)	2010
Saudi Arabia	SIRAB	2013
United Arab Emirates	Envestors	2008
United Arab Emirates	VentureSouq	2013
United Arab Emirates	Women's Angel Investor Network (WAIN)	2103
United Arab Emirates	WOMENA	2014

are due to open in 2015. Endeavor, the SME platform, recently opened an office in Dubai, its seventh location in the Middle East and North Africa region.

There is a flurry of entrepreneurial activity across the region. Dave McClure's 500 Start-Ups has announced a regional partnership with Tenmou in Bahrain. Oasis500 is an incubator that was started in Jordan in 2011 to create 500 new start-ups in the country. The GrEEK Campus, the first technology and innovation park in Cairo, is supporting ICT entrepreneurs. The MIT Enterprise Forum Arab Startup Competition is in its eighth year and is receiving close to 5,000 entries from 21 countries per application round.

Meanwhile, the funding ecosystem for entrepreneurs has significantly grown over the last few years. Crowdfunding is playing a key role for investors with Eureeca at the helm of equity investment. Other crowdfunding platforms in the region include Beehive, Liwwa, Emerging Circle, Zoomal and Aflamnah. Venture capital funds are increasing in the region (N2V, Dash Ventures, MEVP, Wamda Ventures, Jabbar Internet Group, Leap Ventures amongst others). Wamda Research Labs and the online news portal is helping to consolidate information and resources across the region.

KNOWLEDGE GAP

While there is growing support for entrepreneurs, there are not good learning resources and support for the other, and equally important, side of the equation—the investors. Government initiatives have attempted to create angel investment groups but without success in most cases. With the exception of WAIN, where members undergo learning modules on topics such as mentoring, due diligence, valuation and governance while simultaneously conducting the investment process (screening, evaluating, due diligence, negotiation and closing), most angel groups (formal and informal) are not offering an educational component to their members. One of the challenges faced by angel groups in the region has been convincing their members to go through angel education courses. Many investors view themselves as experienced investors without understanding the nuances of angel investing. In addition, without much experience to date, typical angel investment challenges such as exits have not been an issue for investors in the region. Tax liability in international jurisdictions is another area that is not well understood (e.g., Dubai consists largely of a free trade zone without income tax).

Global training groups such as Angel Labs and Startupbootcamp have made forays into the Middle East but their programs are cursory and are not providing the deep education needed by angel investors in the region. Without sponsorship, getting attendees for these kinds of programs has been difficult. The Kaufman Foundation and US Agency for International Development have provided some angel training in Egypt, Tunisia and Jordan, but the courses were not extensive nor financially sustainable.

With crowdfunding initiatives in the UAE increasing, there is concern that equity and debt investors are not informed of the high risk of angel investing. The platforms are concerned that one scandal that results in an early stage investor losing his/her money could result in restrictive regulation that may even prohibit angel investment.

GOVERNMENT REGULATION

Government regulation of angel investment is very light in the UAE. There are no investor accreditation requirements, which allows for many potential angel investors. However, without proper training and education, angel investors may not understand the high risk of angel investing and thus jeopardize their financial well-being. In 2014, DubaiSME, a division of Dubai's Department of Economic Development (DED), undertook a study of the SME landscape in the UAE including the funders. There is discussion around creating "soft" angel investor accreditation requirements but these are not yet clear.

Another issue for angel investors considering investing in local companies in the UAE concerns the local legal status. Onshore companies have local ownership requirements of 51 percent. Angel investors, especially if they are not citizens of the UAE, mitigate this risk by investing in offshore companies. However, this creates additional work and expense for the entrepreneurs. Accelerators and incubators are not setting up investor-friendly legal structures from the beginning, especially for investors who are not local.

One of the regulatory issues affecting entrepreneurs in the UAE and their willingness to start companies here is the lack of bankruptcy law. Without bankruptcy law, many entrepreneurs especially expatriates fear the risk of jail or deportation if they can't make their payments.

WOMEN: A NEW ASSET CLASS FOR ANGEL INVESTORS

As entrepreneurs take the Middle East by storm, new funding sources are starting to crop up across the region to meet the gap in capital. The latest is from women—following a trend where 30-40 percent of start-up entrepreneurs are women, the other side of the table is also starting to change.

While Silicon Valley and European VCs are predominantly men, it is no surprise to find a similar trend in a more socially conservative environment. However, what is surprising is the number of start-up companies that are women-led. There are lots of statistics in the US (3 percent of small businesses are women-owned, 12 percent of start-ups are founded by women, 13 percent of VC money goes to women-led companies); however, not a lot of data in the Middle East exists yet. There are the numbers from the accelerators and incubators in the region. In Jordan, for example, Oasis500 reports that while 10 percent of its applicants are women, 40 percent of its graduates are women. Forsa and Mowgli, two mentoring networks that are active in the Middle East, state that 38 percent of entrepreneurs in Jordan are women. No one is really sure why this is the case, but one possibility is that women face more difficulty entering the labor force and therefore find it easier to start their own companies. In the United Arab Emirates, women comprise 14 percent of the local labor force (defined as Emirati nationals) and make up 21 percent of the work force in Egypt.

EKeif, led by the dynamic winner of Cartier's prestigious 2013 Middle East regional award, is an online Arabic content company that provides "how-to" videos with a large user base in Saudi Arabia. Some of the companies can be considered social enterprises, where they are creating social impact in the education, arts or environmental sectors. Little Thinking Minds, a Jordanian company that produces Arabic educational media for young children, was started by two Arab female TV producers who were frustrated by the lack of original high quality Arabic educational content available for kids. Feesheh is the region's first musical instrument ecommerce site. Other companies, like Arabic online food company Zaytouneh and the Arabic content site for mothers, SuperMama, target the more traditionally "feminine" sectors. With the largest YouTube consumer base in Saudi Arabia, especially among women ages 25-35 years old, there is a thirst for Arabic online content that has been sorely missing from the internet until now.

THE FUTURE OF ANGEL INVESTMENT IN THE UAE

The UAE has become the regional hub for entrepreneurship. As such, there is an opportunity to also start a regional training center for angel investors as well as an umbrella regional network of angel groups in the region. This would greatly contribute to the coordination of angel efforts and also allow for some quality control around education and certification, which would provide a better outcome for entrepreneurs, their companies, investors and countries in the region.

Another area of opportunity for the government in the UAE is to follow the examples set in many countries such as the UK and New Zealand, where governments have invested in a sidecar fund managed by angel groups. In the UK, the UK Business Angels Network (UKBAN) manages £100 million in addition to its member investments and this fund not only co-invests alongside its angel members, allowing greater investment in the early stage sector, but also provides a management fee to UKBAN so that a full-time fund manager can run the fund. This is a very effective way to support private sector development while enabling angel groups to be financially sustainable.

United Kingdom

Jenny Tooth

A BRIEF HISTORY OF THE UK BUSINESS ANGELS ASSOCIATION

The UK Business Angels Association (UKBAA) is the trade body for angel investing in the UK. It was established in 2012, superseding the British Business Angels, which was set up in 2004. The main roles of UKBAA are to build the angel investing ecosystem, create better connections between the angel community and other sources of finance and support, act as a voice of the angel community to government and opinion leaders, and provide a hub for information, market intelligence and developments on the angel market. UKBAA focuses on England, Wales and Northern Ireland. It also collaborates with LINC Scotland which coordinates the angel syndicates and key activities in Scotland.

RECENT EVOLUTION OF THE UK ANGEL MARKET

The UK angel market has changed considerably in recent years and especially since the global financial crisis. Angel investing in the UK was traditionally organized through networks, often with quite extensive levels of angel members. However the angel market is now

---

JENNY TOOTH is the Chief Executive of the UK Business Angels Association, which represents more than 15,000 investors. In 2009, she co-founded Angel Capital Group and has been acting as MD for Angel Capital Innovations. She has more than 20 years of experience in SME finance, both in the UK and internationally.

much more diverse, with far fewer large networks and many more formal and informal syndicates, super angel funds, accelerators, online platforms and crowdfunding.

TECHNICAL AND REGULATORY FRAMEWORK

Angel investing in the UK has a relatively light-touch approach under the technical and regulatory framework of the Financial Markets Regulations. Under the Financial Services and Markets Act 2000, Financial Promotions Order 2005, angel investors are able to self-certify that they are either high net worth individuals (with annual income of £100,000 or more, or held, throughout the past financial year, net assets of £250,000) or sophisticated investors.[1]

SCALE OF THE ANGEL MARKET

How big is the angel market in the UK? Quite simply, we do not know! With such a diverse marketplace for angel investing, it is impossible to capture its size. While many attempts have been made to extrapolate figures, surveys to date have been relatively small-scale or unrepresentative of the market. One notable statistic has come from the use of the government Enterprise Investment Scheme (EIS), since all angels using this scheme must submit details of their investments. This latest figure is for EIS 2012 (which is always 12 months behind in terms of reporting) and shows that more than £1.1 billion was invested by investors in small businesses using this scheme in the financial year. This may not represent all straight angel-type deals, and it is important to note that not all angels use the EIS scheme, with potentially only around 70 percent of deals done through the EIS. This amount was the highest recorded since 2001, and significantly higher than the amounts recorded from 2008-11, so we can see that it reflects considerable current growth in angel investing. What is notable as a comparator is that venture capital investment in early-stage businesses in 2012 was only £323 million, going up to just more than £400 million in 2013, thus angel investing would seem to be about 2.5 times larger than the VC market for this stage of business.

In 2013, UKBAA conducted research on the angel market in collaboration with Deloitte that resulted in the publication of a report entitled "Taking the Pulse of the Angel Market."[2] The reported examined about 270 deals and interviewed more than 60 angel investors. Fifty-eight percent of the angels reported that they were investing more in 2013 than in previous years, with 20 percent saying they were maintaining the same level of investment, and 22 percent saying they were investing less.

Given the lack of robust research data on the angel market, UKBAA together with the Centre for Entrepreneurs sponsored more extensive research. The research report, entitled "Nation of Angels—The Unsung Heroes of Britain's Economy"[3] was carried out by the Enterprise Research Centre, which is a major new research hub on entrepreneurship and finance, and led by Warwick, Aston and Imperial University Business Schools. The research yielded key insights. One of the most significant findings was that angel investors have been getting younger, with nearly 45 percent of the angels in the survey under the age of 45, with 16.5 percent under 35 and a small number under 25. Angel investing in the UK remains a predominantly male field, who were 86 percent of the 395 respondents. However encouragingly, 14 percent of angels were women, which is roughly double the figure of previous estimates (5 percent to 8 percent). Clearly, there is along way to go to attract more women into angel investing. Of note, there are more women-focused investor groupings, including Angel Academe, Incito Ventures, and a UK branch of Astia. Whilst the majority (77 percent) of angels identified in the survey are British by ethnicity, almost a quarter (23 percent) are not. Asian angels account for a large portion (46 percent) of non-British angels.

Angels' experience, measured by the number of years investing as a business angel, ranges from 1 to 42 while a high proportion started angel investing only after 2000. Angels vary in their approaches, with some engaged full-time and others part-time. Some describe themselves as active investors, and others are passive. While angel investing has frequently been perceived as very locally focused, 58 percent of angels in the survey said they now invest outside their home region in the UK and 22 percent are investing outside the UK entirely.

SECTORS ATTRACTING ANGEL INVESTMENT

Angels are investing in a vast range of sectors, ranging from high-tech to traditional sectors, from manufacturing to service sectors.

Funding choices often reflect the sector interests and professional experience of the angel. Our research shows that high-tech accounts for a large proportion of angel deals, with a strong focus on healthcare and medtech, digital media, as well as B2B and B2C services such as e-commerce and m-commerce. Angels are also taking an interest in software, especially notably in software as a service and big data. In London and other key cities, fintech is also emerging as a strong focus, reflecting the fact that an increasing number of angels came from the financial services sector following the crisis.

INFLUENCERS AND DRIVERS FOR ANGEL INVESTMENT

As noted, UK angels have been uniquely supported by a major tax relief scheme, the Enterprise Investment Scheme.[4] This scheme has been in operation for almost 30 years, showing the extent and depth of government support for business angels across both the Labour and Conservative parties. The EIS scheme offers a tax break (currently 30 percent , increased from 20 percent in 2012) for an investor who makes an investment in an unquoted qualifying business with a significant trading base in the UK. Not only does the scheme offer tax relief on the deal, but also offers a deferral of capital gains tax made on subsequent gains and a deferral of tax on gains that are subsequently reinvested and also in relation to inheritance tax. An investor can invest up to £1 million a year using this scheme but cannot be connected before making the investment and must be a UK taxpayer, whilst some trades are excluded.

In 2012, the government decided to give a further boost to investing in small businesses and not only raised the EIS tax relief but made a bold decision to support start-ups and seed stage businesses by initiating a new Seed Enterprise Investment Scheme (SEIS), offering a new 50 percent tax break for investments in seed-stage companies The scheme enables investors to invest up to £100 thousand per year in seed businesses offering also the same capital gains deferrals. Among other incentives, if an investor makes any gain through the sale of a business or property sale that is subsequently used to buy equity in a seed-stage business, they qualify for a 50 percent exemption from capital gains for life. However, an investor cannot own more than 30 percent of the company's issued share capital, which offers important protection for the company. The company cannot take on more than £150,000 in total of SEIS, and must have been trading for less than two years with less than 25 employees and no more than £200,000 gross assets. Under both EIS and SEIS, if a company fails, the remaining loss after up-front tax breaks can be set off against other income up to the highest rate of tax relief paid by the investor. This can mean that around 70 percent of the overall investment is covered by the government through these tax breaks!

This tax break scheme has been widely used by many UK investors and offers substantial mitigation to risk. The Seed SEIS scheme has effectively kick-started angel investing in much earlier stage businesses. UKBAA research in 2013 showed that for many investors the existence of these tax breaks was a key factor in determining whether they would take risks: 74 percent of angels believed the tax breaks were significant or highly significant to their decisions. Our 2014 research reinforced this picture, with nearly 8 out of 10 having used the scheme. Several statistics from Her Majesty's Revenue and Customs ministry are worth noting:

EIS latest figures (2011-12):
- £1.1 billion invested by angels through EIS-an 87 percent increase from 2010-11
- 2,596 companies raised funds under EIS (an increase of 27 percent from previous year), of which 1,498 companies were raising funds for the first time
- 52 percent of investments were over £100 thousand

SEIS Stats (2013)
- 1,100 companies raised funds under SEIS
- Over £82 million invested
- Average investment £72,000 (max £100 thousand per investor)

SYNDICATION AND CO-INVESTMENT FUNDS

Syndication of angel deals has been a growing trend for angel investors. UK investors are forming both structured and unstructured syndicates. This has enabled them to pool risks, share due diligence and pool their finance, leading to larger deals and more opportunities to invest in further rounds. Consequently angel syndicated deals are frequently being done at around £1 million-plus in the first round. Co-investment funds have helped encourage syndication. A successful angel co-investment fund operated through the Scottish Investment Fund, for example, has resulted in a substantial number of angel groups emerging in the Scottish region. The year 2012 saw a further catalyzer for syndication for the rest of the UK angel market in the form of a new Angel Co-Investment Fund supported by public funding. The Angel Co-Fund, originally set up at £50 million and later increased to £100 million, is aimed at leveraging syndicated angel investment. The fund, managed by British Business Bank (previously Capital for Enterprise Ltd) can offer between £100 thousand and £1 million of co-investment alongside angel syndicated deals. The fund, which is not a VC fund, but operates as a "super angel" alongside angel money. It cannot take more than 49 percent of the investment but can offer follow-on investment. This fund, similar to the Scottish co-investment fund, has had a substantial role in encouraging more angel syndication and a structured approach to deals. Recent UKBAA research has shown that 82 percent of angels have invested as much or more in syndication than in previous years. The latest figures show that 7 out of 10 deals in the UK are done in syndication.

Overall indicators so far from the new Angel Co-Fund have shown that there as been at least a 3:1 ratio of angel money leveraged, which is encouraging larger deal size among syndicates and often bringing in a range of co-investors. A key factor has been the lead angel, who is seen as vital to building support for syndication. Having proven successful, the Angel Co-Fund model is now being emulated around the UK by regions seeking to set up similar approaches. The London Region is supporting a new £75 million Angel Co-Fund for entrepreneurs, and the Greater Manchester region is also introducing a new angel co-investment model to leverage syndication. Of note, a number of angel groups are successfully using EIS/SEIS funds to co-invest alongside their angel deals. This often enables angels to put some of their annual investment funds directly into a managed fund that offers them the same 30-50 percent tax breaks. This is also suitable for more passive angels and assists in leveraging syndication and helping to close deals. In some cases angels remain involved in the decisionmaking on EIS Fund deals, or they may take a more passive role.

THE CHANGING LANDSCAPE

The UK scene for angel investing has become much more diverse and wide-ranging. The longstanding notion of a "ladder of finance" has been largely discarded, and angels are recognized as playing a role across multiple forms of investment across the value chain. Angels are investing from very early seed stages right through to initial public offerings, and through multiple models alongside many types of different co-investors, from crowdfunding to private equity. Early stage VCs increasingly want to connect with angels, both for deal sourcing and offering follow-on finance (Series A). Challenges still remain for angels in relation to dilution, especially for deals using the EIS scheme which requires them to take ordinary non-preferential shares, except for a liquidation preference allowed under EIS. Nevertheless, there is evidence of angels and VCs collaborating, especially VCs that operate publicly funded funds. Nesta's research in 2012 revealed that 41 percent of VC deals include angels. Some VCs now also maintain high-powered angel pools, which sit alongside their own deals as co-investors.

Perhaps more surprisingly, private equity firms have been known to directly engage angels and angel syndicates not only for deal flow or cross-referral, but also for seeking angel-backed businesses as good prospects for private equity (Series B) funding, with a view to getting in early. There is also evidence of private equity firms appointing experienced high-profile high-net worth angels with strong sector experience as chairmen or non-execs to guide the private equity portfolio businesses through growth and expansion and prepare for exit. Several private equity fund managers are also angel investing in their own time.

One of the more interesting recent developments is that of the corporate angel. Corporates have been setting up their own venture capital funds for several years, but there are some enlightened corporates now recognizing the opportunity to co-invest alongside angels. They can offer additional access to markets, customers and technical infrastructure to help strengthen deals, and help develop a path to exit.

As in the US, successful UK entrepreneurs often re-invest in other small entrepreneurs, what has been called the Silicon Valley effect. While this approach is still not as widespread in the UK as it is in the US, some great entrepreneurs have done this, often using fund vehicles with the backing of the EIS scheme to offer additional tax breaks, and bringing direct hands on support and market connections. Some are developing accelerator schemes alongside their investing. Examples of such entrepreneurial investors include: Brent Hoberman (ex-Last Minute.com), who has set up Profounders Capital; Stephan Glaenzer (ex-Last FM) and Eileen Burbidge (ex-Beebo) who have set up Passion Capital; Ex Skype Brothers have set up Atomico; Richard Reed and co-founders (ex-Innocent Drinks) have set up Jam Jar investments.

ACCELERATORS

An increasing number of angels are getting engaged in accelerators. These offer an opportunity to identify bespoke deal flow and get in early, as well as enabling angels to take stakes in deals in return for assisting through mentoring, support and market access. In some cases, entrepreneurial angels are directly backing and setting up accelerators, or helping to mobilize other investors, including corporates. These accelerators are burgeoning in both London and around other larger cities, often around tech clusters or science parks, with a growing number having a direct sector or market focus. This approach has directly affected angels' approaches to deal flow, offering angels the opportunity to directly curate pipelines of start-up and early stage deals.

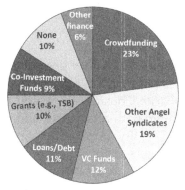

WHO UK ANGELS INVEST ALONGSIDE

CROWDFUNDING

As in the US, crowdfunding has grown exponentially in the last three years. Equity crowdfunding platforms in the UK have been required from the outset to be regulated under the Financial Conduct Authority (FCA) and required to set up a similar regulatory and compliance framework as venture capital funds. During 2013, the UK government also carried out a consultation on the regulatory and technical environment for all crowdfunding platforms, including lending and donation. This led to a relatively light-touch framework, with an emphasis on ensuring that individuals engaged in crowdfunding were sophisticated and understood the risks they were taking. In recognition of the interest in crowdfunding, the role such platforms play, and the number of angels involved, UKBAA has enabled regulated equity crowdfunded platforms to become members of the trade body.

A significant number of experienced angels have also directly invested in the crowdfunding platforms as growth businesses, and there is clearly a significant number of angels investing in and alongside deals on such platforms. The "Nation of Angels" research even shows that crowdfunding plays a relatively bigger role than other types of financing. Our research has also shown that angels investing alongside crowdfunding are likely to be somewhat younger than angels in general, with half being under the age of 45. Equity crowdfunding deals are growing in size, with many deals being funded at levels comparable to angel deals, with some deals attracting over £1 million first round and attracting leading investors alongside the crowd. For example, the deal for Lovespace, a storage company, which won the UKBAA Equity Crowdfunded-Angel Deal of the Year 2014. Lovespace was set up by Brett Akker, who is the founder of the successful Zipcar and also an angel investor. Lovespace raised £1.6 million from a combination of business angels, VC funding and the crowd.

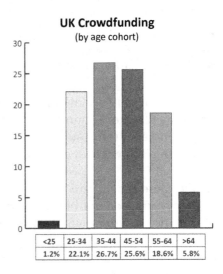

UK Crowdfunding
(by age cohort)

<25	25-34	35-44	45-54	55-64	>64
1.2%	22.1%	26.7%	25.6%	18.6%	5.8%

ONLINE PLATFORMS

Angel investors are increasingly using the internet and online platforms to access deal flow that might supplement their offline investing. However, a relatively small number of angels are using platforms for online deal transactions. Some angel groups and networks are also building their own online communities for deal sharing and structuring. UKBAA, for example, has also set up its own "Members-Only Angel Deal Sharing Platform" in partnership with an FCA-regulated online platform, JustInvesting, to enable the closing of deals by members that have already been partially funded to attract investment from other investors, syndicates or funds. There is also a growing interest among angels in being part of a broader online community to share deals. A significant number of UK angels now participate in Angel List. Targeted online communities have been formed, such as Seedcamp (which has an international focus) and CapitalList (focused on the London region). Online investment communities may yet reap more cross-border deals.

SUMMARY

What are the challenges for the growth of angel investing in the UK? Angels are, in the main, optimistic about their portfolios at the time of this writing, with more than 50 percent reporting good to high growth and expecting positive exits. However, angels in the UK continue to face challenges in scaling up funding companies and achieving exits. The angel market continues to lack options for liquidity, with many angels and syndicates supporting businesses through multiple rounds of funding, but without a clear opportunity for realization of returns.

At the same time, there is a clear recognition of the need to support the realization of the high-growth potential for their portfolio and ensure the growth of world-class businesses and avoid selling out too early. This provides an ongoing dilemma for the angel market. The opportunities for angels to work alongside other key players in the ecosystem, including private equity, the alternative investment market, and the wider business and market expansion schemes. A key further area of concern for the angel community is the need to increase access to talent and skills for their portfolio, i.e., to ensure the right team is in place to support high growth.

There have been one or two notable exits for angels in recent years, e.g., DeepMinds, a big data company acquired by Google, and Brandwatch, the social media monitoring company, which offered a 1x return partial liquidity event for the angel investors through its latest Series B round. And there have been a number of notable angel-backed e-commerce deals successfully listing on the alternative investment market. Nevertheless, there remains a low level of exits through trade sales, with corporates in the UK still not making sufficient acquisitions at this level. The new £2.5 billion Business Growth Equity Fund, which was set up with backing from the top five UK banks in 2012, is offering angels partial liquidity for deals that meet their threshold of around £2 million-3 million turnover. The government has supported some useful concessions to simplify access to the alternative investment market, again offering a potential partial or full exit for angels. In sum, the UK angel market is strong and has substantial government backing, but there remains much to be done to support portfolio companies in achieving their high-growth potential and enabling increased access to exits and liquidity for angels.

Endnotes

[1] See http://www.legislation.gov.uk/uksi/2005/1529/schedule/5/made.
[2] "Taking the Pulse of the Angel Market," UK Business Angels Association and Deloitte, 2013. http://www2.deloitte.com/content/dam/Deloitte/uk/Documents/about-deloitte/deloitte-uk-taking-the-pulse-of-the-angel-market.pdf.
[3] "Nation of Angels—The Unsung Heroes of Britain's Economy," UK Business Angels Association and The Centre for Entrepreneurs (2015). http://www.ukbusinessangelsassociation.org.uk/sites/default/files/media/files/cfe_ukbaa_nation_of_angels_report.pdf.
[4] http://www.hmrc.gov.uk/eis/part1/1-1.htm.

India

Ashish Dave and Mohit Agarwal

As pioneers of groundbreaking technology that now covers a myriad of industries, the financial equivalent of the "angels of Broadway" have come a long way. This chapter examines the evolution of this avant garde investment movement through the experience of India. Academic literature has volumes on venture capital and its efficacy, but there is little on angel investing,[1] which accounts for more than half of the equity financing for new projects. VC started before the development of the stock market when wealthy families supported emerging businesses. In India it took off in 1987 when the government-funded Indian Industrial Development Bank (IDBI) set up a VC scheme.[2] Over the years, venture capital has maintained an elitist and quantitative approach to investment.

Angel investment both in India and abroad started to grow because of angels' relatively lighter controlling hand and a focus on trust rather

ASHISH DAVE joined Kalaari as an Investment Associate in 2014 and focuses on investment opportunities in mobile, internet, e-commerce, and education companies. Some of the portfolio firms he works with include Zivame, Grabhouse, Vyome, AppsDaily, Via, and Crowdfire. Prior to joining Kalaari, he co-led efforts at Mumbai Angels, where he analyzed seed stage ventures in similar sectors. MOHIT AGARWAL majors in electronics and electrical communication engineering at the Indian Institute of Technology. At IIT Kharagpur, his study focuses on computer vision and image processing. He is interested in the fast-growing angel and VC industry in South Asia and Southeast Asia.

than stringent rules.[3] One study has illustrated the positive influence of angels on investee firms in areas such as business contacts, knowledge gaps and follow-on finance.[4] The competition for angels' financial leverage has also improved the efficiency of firms. Even though angel investors are sometimes criticized for entering "too small and too early,"[5] their relative scarcity increases the quality of start-ups. Angel investors and venture capitalists work in a synergy: angels come in at the later technical development stage or early market entry stage, and venture capitalists engage next.

Mumbai Angels, founded in 2006, was the first angel organization to be created in the Indian peninsula. Sasha Mirchandani, co-founder of Mumbai Angels, ushered in what was to become an eventual mushrooming of private angel investing firms around the country. A national angel group, India Angels, was set up in the same year with branches around the country. These networks enabled Indian white-collar professionals to invest surplus income, if not wealth, into ideas that could potentially change the consumer market or at least give a 30-40 percent return per annum. This was supported by an accelerator program, the mentorship of The Indus Entrepreneurs network of Silicon Valley, and other partnerships such as MentorSquare, a network of experts and mentors. The Indian Angel Network (IAN), now touted as the nation's largest angel investing group, has further helped foster the ecosystem for entrepreneurs.

The industrial topography in the subcontinent is also being developed through many technology centers and science parks. Genome Valley in Hyderabad and Science Park in Pune are two of the prominent ones. IKP Knowledge Park in the South of India has five dedicated innovation corridors, and is revolutionary in India as it is the only dedicated space for multinationals to operate within the region. IKP also works as an incubator for new business in the field of pharmaceuticals and biotechnology.

Another noteworthy field is impact investing. The Acumen Fund that addresses poverty and Investor's Circle, which originates from the US and has its own angel investing group, are two examples. These all point to a move away from the traditionally more risk-averse and numbers-focused Indian culture.[6]

When India opened to the world in 1991, it offered a new market with a massive number of consumers and a dedicated working class. As a hub for cheap labor, it received low-priced outsourcing. However, as London Business School professor Nirmalya Kumar highlighted in his recent book, India's invisible innovation was responsible for its success. This innovativeness was also highlighted by the 2013-2014 Halo report of the Silicon Valley Bank, which noted that 95 percent of angel investing in India happens in brand new companies.

Why? With rising income inequality and high sustained rates of unemployment, self-employment is seen as a tactical solution. As a result, the 2014 government budget has emphasized the importance of start-ups and started a 10,000 crore VC fund.[7] A recent report by Wharton business school noted foreigners' apprehensions about investment due to the difficulty of obtaining exits.[8] This might be eased by new entrepreneur-friendly bankruptcy laws, tax incentives for small businesses and special loans in certain areas. The government has also started the "Skill India" progam, which fosters skill-building. India has a substantial rural population, while 50 percent of angel investments are concentrated in the cities of Bangalore and Mumbai. So the government has started a 100 crore fund for the "Start-Up Village Entrepreneurship Program" that aims to broaden entrepreneurship. Government investments have also revamped special economic zones, expanded digitalization of the economy, and allocated 2,500,000 crores into economic development over the next five years.

International private equity investing is growing, with organizations such as the Canadian Pension Plan Investment Board partnering with Indian Piramal industries on projects. Indian private equity firms are also managing international capital. Renuka Ramnath, founder of the $400 million Indian private equity fund Multiples, touts the resilience of the Indian market especially during the 2010 financial slump. Sensing the growth potential of India, international private equity funds such as Walden and Baring have also set up offices in the country.

ENTREPRENEURSHIP IN INDIA

As entrepreneurship continues to grow, a thriving ecosystem has developed to provide services, support, mentoring and funding. India has a somewhat rigid family system, which has made entrepreneurship a young man's game. Most entrepreneurs in the country tend to be college students, fresh college graduates or graduates with one to three years of professional work experience. India's entrepreneurs are therefore young and hungry but come with little money in the bank. This has necessitated the development of a mature funding and support environment—from standalone angel investors to angel groups and incubators to late-stage venture capital funds.

Recognizing that the average Indian entrepreneur tends to be younger than his US counterpart and thus needs more assistance, support organizations have sprouted up around the best engineering and business schools. The Indian Institute of Technology is a chain of the best engineering schools in the country, while the Indian Institutes of Management produce the business leaders. Both these university chains have recognized the stream of entrepreneurs emerging from their institutes, and set up incubators, funding schemes, deferred placement facilities, "entrepreneurship cells" and nationwide business plan competitions[9]. Recent years have also seen a rise in Science and Technology Entrepreneur Parks[10] (STEPS) across the nation. Technology Business Incubators (TBIS) and STEPs function as specialized incubators and accelerators, with the objective of creating technically skilled entrepreneurs. STEPs tend to be located in universities, as most technical ventures in India haves roots in engineering colleges. Success stories include the STEPs in BITS Pilani, IIT Roorkee and IIT Kharagpur.[11]

Beyond universities, major cities in India have numerous incubators and accelerators. Eighty percent of entrepreneurial activity is based in three cities—Mumbai, New Delhi and Bangalore. Most incubators, angels and VC firms set up offices in these locations, sometimes in all three, and the cities boast of having the most advanced entrepreneurship support ecosystems in the nation. Incubators and accelerators operate through multiple models, but all have a single-minded focus on helping young ventures overcome the hurdles of running a "tight shop."[12] These incubators are indicative of the increasing popularity of entrepreneurship among India's youth. The difference between the accelerators and incubators in India has been aptly summarized by authors at Inc42: "Accelerators accelerate the speed of your business, in most cases an existing business or an idea.

Major Start-up
Incubators and Accelerators

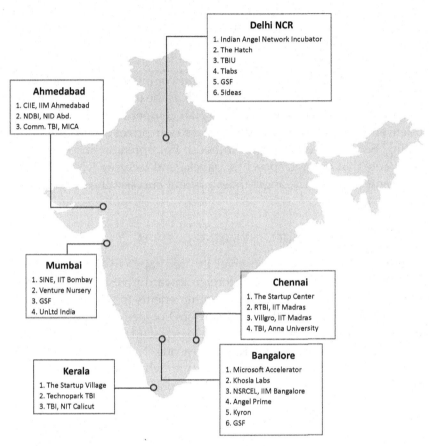

Delhi NCR
1. Indian Angel Network Incubator
2. The Hatch
3. TBIU
4. Tlabs
5. GSF
6. 5ideas

Ahmedabad
1. CIIE, IIM Ahmedabad
2. NDBI, NID Abd.
3. Comm. TBI, MICA

Mumbai
1. SINE, IIT Bombay
2. Venture Nursery
3. GSF
4. UnLtd India

Chennai
1. The Startup Center
2. RTBI, IIT Madras
3. Villgro, IIT Madras
4. TBI, Anna University

Kerala
1. The Startup Village
2. Technopark TBI
3. TBI, NIT Calicut

Bangalore
1. Microsoft Accelerator
2. Khosla Labs
3. NSRCEL, IIM Bangalore
4. Angel Prime
5. Kyron
6. GSF

The programs are short and intense. They help you hone your idea and build it out. Whereas incubators incubate your early pre-product idea, help you make a prototype, and further make a product out of it. The engagement is longer than an accelerator."[13] Success stories in the incubator and accelerator space[14] include the IAN incubator, TLabs, GSF, The Hatch, Khosla Labs, Microsoft Accelerator, SINE (IIT Bombay), Venture Nursery, Startup Center, Morpheus and CIIE (IIM Ahmedabad).

Although the Indian entrepreneurship landscape has a series of local competitions, internet globalization has meant that Indian entrepreneurs increasingly look to international business plan competitions for wider recognition and access to world class venture capitalists. Recent examples include an Indian team participating in the Rice Business Plan competition, and many Indian entrepreneurs traveling to Ireland to present at "The Summit," an event bringing together VCs, entrepreneurs and Fortune 500 CEOs from around the world.

Universities also benefit from innovation competitions and business plan events. Technology universities such as the IITs and the BITs boast of technology festivals and business plan competitions where young student entrepreneurs present their ideas to win prizes and occasionally funding. Some universities with in-house Entrepreneurship Cells also host events that include speeches, panels, and lectures. These E-Cells often invite Tier A VCs, angel investors and successful entrepreneurs to talk to students.

ANGEL INVESTING IN INDIA

The Indian economy only loosened its "red tape" in the early 1990s when a policy overhaul allowed foreign inward investment. The shift also paved the way for Indian-bred entrepreneurs to set up businesses that have become behemoths. As businesses boomed so did the number of businessmen with disposable income to invest. Many looked to invest in young start-ups for three primary reasons. First, they understood these businesses. For instance, businessmen who had built successful technology companies looked to invest in small technology companies. Second, they wanted high returns. Most investors were not content with the eight percent offered by fixed deposits or the movement of the Sensex, the benchmark index of the Bombay Stock Exchange. By investing in early stage high-risk high-return companies, they could use their knowledge to hedge risks. Third, most successful businessmen cannot make large private investments in large companies, real estate or private equity because too much capital is required. Instead, investing in an early stage start-up costs about 5-10 lakhs, which is disposable income for a successful businessman.

Historically most initial investments in India have been "informal" angel investments, made through connections of friends and families. Angels would often invest a token amount that would complement the money that entrepreneurs had already obtained from friends and family.

A succinct representation of angel investors is provided by the NEN:[15] "A lot of angel investors are retired executive or business owners who have spare money to invest and who would like to make use of their years of experience as a mentor to others or keep abreast of developments in a particular area which interests them. An angel investor who is knowledgeable about your company is a godsend and can prove very useful in giving valuable advice about how to run things. They might also know some useful contacts. The better your company does, the better your angel investor does, so he will have the company's best interests at heart."

In spite of seed capital providers and VCs in the country, a huge financing gap between seed and VC investments remained. These investments ranged from 50 lakhs to 5 crores, and were too large a sum for an individual angel investor. This precipitated the birth of angel groups.[16] Early stage investments accounted for 68 percent of all VC investment activity, and 44 percent in value terms for the twelve months ended December 2013.[17] As of the writing of this book, the most notable and active angel investment groups in India are the Mumbai Angels, Bangalore Angels, the Indian Angel Network, Hyderabad Angels, Kolkata Angels, Powai Lake Ventures, and Harvard Angels. Of these Mumbai Angels and the Indian Angel Network are the most well known in the nation (Bangalore Angels is a sister concern of Mumbai Angels). Recently, *The Economic Times* covered Mumbai Angels and the Indian Angel Network, providing a profile for both these groups:

Mumbai Angels:[18]

- Founded by Sasha Mirchandani and Prashant Choksey in 2006, it is India's most high profile, city-based angel network.
- It has invested in roughly 50 start-ups, including e-commerce, education, finance, gaming, mobile, healthcare and technology.
- Notable exits have been from the mobile ad network InMobi, online fashion retailer Myntra, and the e-commerce venture Exclusively.in.
- Its biggest names are Qualcomm Ventures' Karthee Madasamy, Patni Computer Systems' Amit Patni, and Fame Cinema's Shravan Shroff. There are more than 200 members.
- It is typically interested in seed-stage and early-stage ventures,

investing between 50 lakh and 2 crore per transaction. It also co-invests with other investor groups.

- It provides a platform for start-ups to get funding from corporates, entrepreneurs and venture capital and does not invest as an entity.

Indian Angel Network:[19]

- Set up in 2006, IAN is the country's first (and Asia's largest) angel network.
- It has recently launched operations in the UK, and has made investments in Sri Lanka, Europe, Singapore, Canada and Hong Kong.
- It is sector-agnostic, typically investing less than $1 million in early-stage ventures, with an investment life-cycle of between three and five years. It has invested in 60 start-ups.
- Prominent members include HCL co-founder Ajai Chowdhry, Genpact's Pramod Bhasin, Google India MD Rajan Anandan, and Rehan yar Khan.
- The IAN Incubator supports technology-focused early stage ventures.
- Portfolio companies include social gaming venture HashCube, critical data protection venture Druva, and distance-learning company Aurus Networks.

Regional Angels:[20]

- Outside of the two big angel networks, Hyderabad Angels is possibly the best known city-based angel network.
- It invests between 25 lakh and 2 crore with an investment cycle of between three and five years.
- It has invested in education technology company Edutor, energy solutions venture GIBSS, and social hiring application WhistleTalk, among others.
- Kolkata Angels and Bangalore Angels are rather new and not as well known, partly because of lack of entrepreneurial activity in their cities.

Beyond institutional angel groups, there has also been a substantial rise in the number of angel investors in India. An analysis of AngelList data[21] revealed 670 registered angels based in India who were looking to invest in Indian ventures, and 3,020 angel investors in India and around the world who were interested in Indian start-ups.[22]

PROGNOSIS FOR THE FUTURE

The future promises even more capital injections for budding entrepreneurs in India. As the capital gap between seed and venture capital money is bridged by angel groups and consortiums in the country, entrepreneurs will have access to capital and guidance at every stage of their journey. The means and mode of funding are also being innovated. As VCs and angels fight over the good deals, entrepreneurs have begun exploring crowdfunding as a way to raise capital, sometimes choosing crowdfunding over seed investments from friends, family and angel investments. Global crowdfunding sites like Kickstarter expose start-ups to early adopters who are willing to pay inflated prices for a first shot at products or services. They allow successful firms (mainly those focused on global solutions) to market their products while raising non-equity capital. India also has a few local crowdfunding platforms that cater to the India-focused ventures. They offer goods for pre-purchase and include sites like Ignite Intent, Start51, and TheHotStart.

Endnotes

[1] *Angel Finance: The Other Venture Capital* by Andrew Wong (2002), http://papers.ssrn.com/sol3/papers.cfm?abstract_id=9412288.
[2] http://www.smoothridetoventurecapital.com/.
[3] Fairchild, R. 2007, "Angels vs. Venture Capitalists—The Effect of Value-Adding Abilities, Fairness, Trust, and the Legal System," http://www.angelcapitalassociation.org.
[4] Macht, S. and Robinson, J. 2009, "Do Business Angels Benefit Their Investee Companies?" *International Journal of Entrepreneurial Behaviour & Research*, Vol. 15 (2).
[5] http://smallbiztrends.com2014/09/venture-capital-trends-four-years-later.html.
[6] Banerjee, S. 2008, "Dimensions of Indian Culture, Core Cultural Values and Marketing Implications: An Analysis," *Cross Cultural Management: An International Journal*, Vol. 15 (4).
[7] http://ibnlive.in.com/news/full-text-finance-minister-arun-jaitleys-maiden-budget-speech/485007-3.html.
[8] http://knowledge.wharton.upenn.edu/article/indias-new-wave-private-equity-investments/.

[9] In India, the jobhunting process is more inward than outward. Most hiring happens on campuses of universities, during the final year of a student, during a time called the "placement season." By allowing a student to defer his "placement season," the university encourages entrepreneurship, while offering the possibility a chance of a host of jobs on the other end. Entrepreneurship Cells, or E-Cells are student run organizations that lead a host of entrepreneurship support activities on campus. These organizations also organize a "fest," equivalent to a large fair, focused on start-ups.

[10] Refer to http://www.ijbmi.org/papers/Vol(2)2/Version-1/F223948.pdf for more details on the impact of STEPs on the nation. The paper also elaborately studies the successes, shortcomings and a critical analysis of the various TBIs and the STEPs of India.

[11] A full list of all the STEPs in India maybe found here: http://www.nstedb.com/institutional/step-centre.htm.

[12] A detailed coverage of all incubators and accelerators in India maybe found here: http://inc42.com/resources/50-amazing-startup-incubators-and-accelerators-in-india/.

[13] Ibid.

[14] Ibid.

[15] http://nenonline.org/content/angel-investors-india.

[16] The history and the story behind the birth of Mumbai Angels, India's most active angel investment group is, however, different.

[17] http://articles.economictimes.indiatimes.com/2014-04-26/news/49422658_1_indian-angel-network-hyderabad-angels-mumbai-angels.

[18] Ibid.

[19] Ibid.

[20] Ibid.

[21] https://angel.co/.

[22] https://angel.co/india/investors.

The Netherlands

René A.G. Reijtenbagh

THE SCOPE OF ANGEL ACTIVITIES

Angel investing is making a significant economic contribution in the Netherlands. Although precise details of the Dutch angel market are unavailable, data from the Netherlands Federation of Angels Networks (BAN Nederland) can give an indication of the scale of the market. Thirteen networks, comprised of 3,200 angels, are members of BAN Nederland. In 2012, these angels invested in 118 deals (with an average deal size of €290,000) for a total amount of €34 million. These figures represent only part of the market as not all groups are members of the federation, and many angels operate independently or in small unaffiliated groups. It is estimated that only 8 percent of EU angel deals take place via networks.[1] Extrapolating from this, the Dutch angel market could represent an investment volume of €272 million. If one instead assumes that the federation represents 16 percent of the Dutch angel market, the investment volume amounts to €212.5 million. Either way, it is clear that angels represent a substantial contribution to the provision of private capital, especially if one takes into account that the year 2012 was a year of recession in the Netherlands. The table below lists the groups that are members of BAN Nederland.[2]

RENÉ A.G. REIJTENBAGH is the Senior Business Angels Network Manager at the Development Agency East Netherlands (Oost NV), where he founded "Masters of the Future," a business angel network for the region.

Three major Dutch banks have also now established their own informal investment service for their wealthy clients: ING Bank, ABN Amro, and Rabobank (under the name Money Meets Ideas). A number of local development agencies have also established angel networks including the Northern Development Agency (NOM) and the Brabant Development Agency (BOM). These establishments have followed the successful approach taken by the Development Agency East Netherlands (Oost N.V.) with its angel network Meesters van de Toekomst (Masters of the Future). These agencies focus on linking angel networks with university applied science programs, using revolving co-invest participation funds. Angels are viewed as possible sources for the 50 percent co-investment requirement.

MARKET DEVELOPMENTS

Each year the Dutch Ministry of Economic Affairs conducts a survey of angel investors in order to monitor the informal investment market.[3] This survey is non-representative but does offer some indication of market developments and angel perceptions. Fifty three percent of survey participants invested in young businesses showing exponential growth, and a further 26 percent invested in existing companies. Twelve percent have invested in management buy-outs and buy-ins, and a small percentage have invested in reorganizations. The ICT sector proved most popular among respondents, with software being identified by 49 percent of investors as an attractive sector. The internet enjoyed 44 percent interest and IT services, 36 percent. Almost 40 percent of respondents indicated investment interests in healthcare and medtech, 11 percent in the environment and cleantech, and 16 percent in the creative industries. These results point to a marked preference for high-tech sectors. With respect to co-investment, the most eye-catching result is the important role played by venture capital funds (38 percent) followed by the banks (33 percent). Regional funds occupy third place at 19 percent, and corporate investors fourth, with 17 percent. Family and friends of the entrepreneur provided co-financing in 15 percent of cases. In 55 percent of the investment opportunities, the surveyed angels invested alone.

One noticeable outcome of the survey was that deal activity in 2012 remained reasonably on par with previous years, despite the period of recession and growth stagnation. Thirty percent of respondents expected to conclude the same number of deals in the survey year, as compared to 40 percent in the previous year's survey. Thirty-five percent of investors expected to conclude fewer deals in 2012, whereas the previous year's percentage was 25 percent. In other words, future expectations for investment showed a slight downward trend. The main reason cited for this was disappointing returns from existing participations (53 percent), followed by the poor economic climate (33 percent), and lack of quality propositions (32 percent).

TRENDS IN THE DUTCH ANGELS MARKET

While solid research data is limited in availability, a number of trends can be identified in the angel market.[4] Angels have always played an important role in the financing of young, promising start-ups. However, angels are particularly at risk of becoming the victim of the current financial crisis. Banks are increasingly unwilling to provide growth financing to existing companies, so established entrepreneurs are turning en masse to angels. As a consequence, angels are moving up-market and increasingly financing propositions that in the past were the realm of banks and participation companies. After all, why invest in a high-risk start-up with no track record, if an angel can with equal ease acquire a position in a proven business? This shift is making it very difficult for start-up companies to acquire angel financing. A clear exception can be made for so-called "intrinsically interesting" start-ups, i.e., those with intrinsically interesting intellecutal property that is considered valuable. These (mostly) spin-offs from universities and major businesses continue to successfully attract angels. Entry-level amounts for participation are directly related to milestones in execution, however. This results in numerous investment rounds and relatively low investment amounts.

Companies with little experience often have to finance their start-up phase with the founder's personal savings or financial assistance from family and friends. The gap between this and formal bank capital has grown in the Netherlands, revealing a clear role for the government in reducing the risk for investors by means of co-financing funds. In the Netherlands a few crowdfunding platforms are also entering the capital market for start-up companies.

OVERVIEW OF ANGEL NETWORKS IN THE NETHERLANDS				
Network	Year Founded	Members	Participation Values	Stage
TIIN Capital	1998	600	330k–2m	growth
Investeerdersclub	2009	45	50k–500k	seed, start, growth
Informal Capital Network	2003	400	up to 1m	growth
BID Network	2005	115	10k–1m	all
FLIIN	2007	60	50k–500k	start, growth
Meesters van de Toekomst	1996	230	50k–1m	start, growth
Mind Hunter	2006	n.a.	>100K	all
Women Professionals Group	2010	n.a.	25k–300k	start, growth
Money Meets Ideas	2002	n.a.	100k–1.5m	all
Nextstage	2004	100	50k–1m	seed, start, growth
Investormatch	2010	>500	50k–2m	all
ABN Amro Informal Investment	1999	350	100k–3m	all
Pepperbase	n.a.	n.a.	n.a.	n.a.
Matchinvest	2008	300	50k–500k	all except seed
Successity	2011	20	50k-500k	early

The previously referred to trend among angels, namely the shift towards large deals with a lower risk profile, ties in with two other observable trends: syndication and internationalisation. It is increasingly common for angels to operate in syndicates, conducting due diligence together and investing jointly in a single business. This allows angels to spread their individual risk and invest larger amounts, sometimes in excess of €1 million. The angel market is also developing more of an international character. The new generation of angels are relatively young and far more accustomed to thinking and traveling internationally. The same applies to entrepreneurs in search of venture capital for growth. For example, it is extremely useful to bring a German investor on board if the growth strategy is focused on accelerated introductions to the

German market. This counsel holds for the life sciences and high-tech sectors, in particular. Another observable trend is that exit strategies in certain niche markets are increasingly internationally-oriented. In considering whether or not to invest, the exit strategy is growing in importance. The more probable the exit strategy, the greater the likelihood of finding an angel. In the Dutch angel market only those propositions with a low risk profile and high market potential are likely to find an angel. Prior to the crisis, there was more willingness to undertake more high-risk investments, because investors were aware that those same investments could easily generate a high return.

The personal spark between investors and entrepreneurs remains crucial. There is clear evidence that angel networks are offering selected propositions on open and closed platforms via the internet, and that such offers are always accompanied by an in-depth personal introduction in either a formal or informal setting. Social investment, namely investing in activities with a clear social or environmental impact, is becoming an increasingly important element in the decisionmaking process of some angel investors. This has nothing to do with charitable considerations. There is evidence that companies that take social and environmental elements into account enjoy more commercial success. And at the end of the day, the investor is interested in commercial success above all.

GOVERNMENT POLICIES TO PROMOTE ANGEL INVESTMENT

Since the late 1990s, the Dutch government has been focusing attention on angels. Initially the emphasis was on financial support for informational meetings for entrepreneurs and novice angels. In 2006, the Business Angel Program (BAP) was launched to support existing and new angel networks that supply information to angels and entrepreneurs wishing to raise capital. In other words, BAP was aimed at start-up businesses in search of venture capital, and angels on the lookout for good propositions. The eventual goal of BAP was to link businesses and angels, increasing the level of investment in technological start-ups. BAP features four action programmes: awareness; readiness; cooperation between angel networks; and research and monitoring. To date BAP has helped organize about 500 information meetings for more than 2,000 angels and 7,000 entrepreneurs, 63 percent of whom acquired new contacts as a result. At the same time the Dutch government launched the SEED facility for investors. The SEED capital scheme makes it possible for investors to assist technological and creative start-ups in turning their knowledge into usable products and services. The SEED scheme allows closed-end participation funds to qualify for a loan the maximum size of which matches the private contribution amount from the fund, up to a maximum of €4 million. These loans are subject to a flexible repayment regime. This scheme makes investing in technological and creative start-ups not only socially responsible, but also financially attractive. As soon as income is generated, the fund repays SEED 20 percent, until their own investment has been paid back. If the fund continues to enjoy income flows after the Ministry of Economic Affairs has recouped its initial 50 percent investment, any additional income is shared in an 80:20 ratio between the fund and the Ministry. The total budget for SEED applications in 2013 was €20 million.

In 2013, an investment fund of €150 million was established for innovative companies. This fund will invest approximately 20 percent of its total in other funds, as long as they obtain the remaining 80 percent of their capital from private financiers. As a result, the €150 million can catalyze €5750 million in venture capital for innovative companies. The fund is financed by €100 million by the Ministry of Economic Affairs and €50 million by the European Investment Fund (EIF). The same year, the Dutch government announced two further new instruments: early phase financing, and investments by angels in young and small businesses.[5] Early phase financing is intended for innovative start-up companies or existing innovative SMEs with ambitious plans for growth. This financing will enable these businesses to produce an initial prototype and develop their business models with a view to independently attracting follow-up investment. For these two instruments, the government has reserved a total of €75 million. By offering co-financing for investments by angels in young, innovative and small businesses, finance is made available to a group of companies currently experiencing difficulties as a consequence of the tightening up of financial regulations under Basel III and the economic crisis. These two instruments tie in neatly with one another, thereby offering support for the difficult-to-finance initial growth phase of innovative start-up companies and ambitious existing SMEs.

Endnotes

1. As indicated by Marianne Hudson during the 2012 conference of the Dutch Federation in Utrecht, www.dagvandeinformal.nl.
2. Evaluation of EU Member States' Angels Markets and Policies, 2012, Centre for Strategy & Evaluation Services, UK. The last two networks are added by the author and are therefore recent.
3. Informal investment in Nederland 2- Meeting, Tornade Insider, May, 2013.
4. It should nonetheless be noted that these trends are based purely on personal observations and experience of the author.
5. See letter Ministry of Economic Affairs, to the parliament DGBI/13156534.

Singapore

Poh-Kam Wong

BRIEF HISTORY OF ANGEL ACTIVITIES

As in other newly industrialized Asian economies, angel investing in early stage start-up companies is relatively new to Singapore. High tech start-ups are themselves relatively new to Singapore, having only really taken off in the late 1990s as the Singapore economy began its shift towards a knowledge-based, innovation-driven economy.[1] While angel investments are known to have existed in the 1980s and early 1990s, they were mainly in the traditional trading and manufacturing sectors, according to a study of 29 angel investors.[2]

While there are no reliable statistics on the number of angels and their contribution to venture investing in Singapore, some indicative figures can be culled from the annual Global Entrepreneurship Monitor study on Singapore that the author conducted for the period 2000-06.[3] As can be seen in Table 1, the prevalence of informal investment[4] in Singapore

POH-KAM WONG is a Professor at the National University of Singapore (NUS) Business School and founding director of NUS Entrepreneurship Centre, where he oversees the expansion of entrepreneurship teaching as well as schemes such as the NUS Incubator and NUS Venture Support. He initiated the annual Start-Up@Singapore national business plan competition in 1999. He was a co-founder of three companies in Malaysia before joining NUS and has been active in angel investing in Singapore, Silicon Valley and China. He has been the chairman of Business Angel Network (Southeast Asia) since 2001.

RATES OF ENTREPRENEURIAL ACTIVITY IN SINGAPORE		
YEAR	INFORMAL INVESTMENT RATE (% OF ADULT POPULATION)	TOTAL ENTREPRENEURIAL RATE (% OF ADULT POPULATION)
2000	1.3	4.2
2001	2.0	6.6
2002	3.6	5.9
2003	1.6	5.0
2004	2.7	5.7
2005	3.5	7.2
2006	3.0	4.9
SOURCE: WONG ET AL, GEM SINGAPORE REPORTS, 2000-06		

appears to have increased over the 2000-06 period, with the informal investment rate rising from 1.3 percent of the adult population to a high of 3.5 percent in 2005, before falling slightly to 3.0 percent the following year. Nevertheless, this was still below that of advanced economies such as the United States and Asian newly industrialized countries in Asia such as Taiwan, China and Korea (Wong and Ho, 2007). As shown in the table above, the informal investment rate is somewhat correlated with the rate of entrepreneurial activity in Singapore, as measured by the total entrepreneurial activity (TEA) rate.[5]

Several studies of advanced economies[6] have estimated that the total amount of informal investment is several times the size of the formal venture capital industry.[7] Based on Global Entrepreneurship Monitor (GEM) estimates, Singapore is no exception. The relative size of the informal investment market is estimated to be several times larger than the market for formal VC investments. Although informal investment as a proportion of GDP has fallen from 2 percent of GDP in 2000 to just over 1 percent in 2006, it nevertheless far outweighs the amount of VC investment, which has generally been less than 0.2 percent of GDP from 1999 to 2005. The GEM data suggest that the majority of informal investments in Singapore are based on social ties. About 42 percent of informal investors in Singapore were related to the investees, with another 52 percent being social acquaintances (work colleagues, friends or neighbors), leaving only 6 percent socially unrelated (strangers or others). If one regards this last category to be true angel investors, then their incidence is probably in the range of 1 in 1,000.[8]

DEVELOPMENT OF THE ANGEL INVESTMENT COMMUNITY

There is no reliable data on the growth of angel investors in Singapore, but anecdotal evidence suggests that the first wave of angel investment in technology companies emerged in the mid-1990s, after a number of technology and manufacturing companies successfully achieved initial public offerings. Some of these successful entrepreneurs subsequently became angel investors, funding the next wave of technology-based start-ups that emerged in Singapore as part of the global dot.com boom.

For example, the three co-founders of Creative Technology, arguably the first successful Singaporean high tech firm and pioneer of the PC soundcard that became the global market leader, all engaged in angel investment activities after the company's IPO in 1994. One of them, Chay Kwong Soon, established a formal investment fund (Enspire Capital) to do so. Other examples of successful technology entrepreneurs who turned angel investors in the late 1990s include Gay Chee Cheong and Tommy Goh. After they led their contract manufacturing firm, JIT Electronics, through a successful IPO and subsequent acquisition by Flextronics in the late 1990s, they co-founded a venture investment fund (2G Capital) to invest in technology start-ups and growth companies.

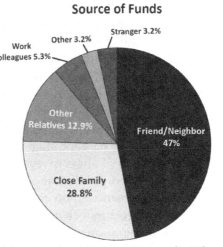

Source of Funds

Stranger 3.2%
Other 3.2%
Work Colleagues 5.3%
Other Relatives 12.9%
Friend/Neighbor 47%
Close Family 28.8%

Informal Investments By Source, Singapore (N=497)
Source: Wong et. al. GEM—Singapore Reports 2000-6

A number of prominent angel investors in this first wave included senior executives of global multinational corporation subsidiaries in Singapore and government-linked corporations (GLCS). For example, Mr. Koh Boon Hwee, an ex-Hewlett Package senior executive and later chairman of a number of GLCs such as Singapore Telecom and Singapore Airlines, has been known to play the role of "arch-angel," syndicating co-investments with fellow senior executives.

Another example is Ng Hock Ching, a senior vice-president of the GLC Natsteel Electronics, who became an angel investor in several technology-based companies after the 1998 Natsteel Electronics IPO. After the dot.com crash in early 2000, the number of high profile angel investment deals appears to have dwindled. In their place, a number of new angel investors have emerged who have focused on smaller deals in early stage high tech start-ups, including spin-offs from local universities and public research institutes. There has also been a noticeable trend towards the formation of angel groups and networks.

FORMATION OF BANSEA

The Angel Network of Southeast Asia (BANSEA) was established in Singapore in 2001 by a group of Singapore-based angel investors with loose ties to investor groups in Thailand, Malaysia, Vietnam and Indonesia. Inspired by the professionalism of angel groups like the Band of Angels in Silicon Valley and the Tech Coast Angels in Southern California, BANSEA's vision is to foster the development of a vibrant, professional angel investment community in Singapore by providing a platform for knowledge-sharing and deal syndication among investors as well as a platform for matching start-up deals with investors. Recognizing the nascent stage of angel investing in Singapore, the founding group of angel investors decided to organize BANSEA in the form of a limited public company, with membership open to all bona fide angel investors upon recommendation by an existing member. A board of directors is elected annually from among the members to govern the operation of the nonprofit company.

The core activity of BANSEA is a regular networking lunch, where three to four pre-selected start-ups pitch to members of BANSEA and other invited investment professional guests. BANSEA focuses on early stage companies seeking investment ranging from $100,000 to $1 million. Interested entrepreneurs can apply to pitch to the network by either submitting executive summaries of their business plans to the BANSEA website, or through the introduction of an existing member. Applicants who are not selected to make a business plan pitch may still opt to have their plans circulated to members online. In the early years BANSEA took a more inclusive approach, offering membership to angel investors with investment track records, rookies interested in learning about deals, and investment professionals such as investment brokers, consultants and deal lawyers. This led to membership figures of more than a hundred. In more recent years, BANSEA has shifted towards greater professionalism and instituted a two-tier membership (chartered members and ordinary members), with more stringent membership qualification criteria and an increase in membership fees. As such, membership now stands at about 50 serious investors.

In recognition of its growing professionalism and catalytic role in the venture ecosystem of Singapore, the government agency in charge of the promotion of start-ups (SPRING Singapore) has helped BANSEA with funding support since 2007. Under a scheme called the Incubator Development Program (IDP), SPRING provided funding for up to 70 percent of the qualifying cost of BANSEA operations. This public funding enabled the organization to employ a full-time executive director who could organize income-generating activities and provide services to members. As part of the professional upgrading, BANSEA introduced a Start-up Mentorship Program, whereby a pool of BANSEA chartered members offer to provide a face-to-face mentoring service to startup entrepreneurs in return for an honorarium. In addition, BANSEA organizes training workshops for entrepreneurs and angel investment forums for members. BANSEA also participates in various activities fostering the development of the entrepreneurial ecosystem in Singapore, with members serving as judges in various business plan competitions and providing input to government policymaking. Moreover, BANSEA successfully organized the inaugural Asian Angel Forum (ABAF) in Singapore in March 2010, which attracted more than 200 participants.

As part of the move towards professionalization, BANSEA began compiling data about the investment activities of its members in 2007. While admittedly incomplete, the data collected by BANSEA shows a total of 79 investment deals between 2007 and 2012 (of which 44 were local deals), with a total investment of S$18 million (of which S$15 million was invested locally).[9] The majority of the funded deals appear to be in internet technology, interactive digital media, information technology and biomedical devices.

Besides BANSEA, several loose angel networks have also emerged in Singapore in recent years. This includes an angel investment club established by the Hewlett Packard Alumni Society, and another angel network for alumni of the Nanyang Technological University (NTU). These networks have less regular activities than BANSEA, however, and no statistics are available on the volume of deal flow generated through them. More significant are emerging angel groups facilitated by various government support schemes, including the angel groups funded by the Business Angel Scheme (BAS) and Technology Incubation Scheme (TIS).

GOVERNMENT SUPPORT FOR ANGEL INVESTING

The Singapore government recognized that domestic venture financing (especially early-stage) was relatively weak compared to more advanced high tech economies such as Silicon Valley and Israel. After consultation with BANSEA leadership, government officials have introduced a number of support programs in recent years to address these weaknesses. With regards to angel investment, these programs can be classified into two groups: those that directly promote angel investment, and those that more indirectly encourage angel investment through the provision of early-stage venture capital.

The most established of these programs is a co-investment scheme to leverage private angel investors. The Start-up Enterprise Development Scheme (SEEDS) was introduced in 2000 by the Economic Development Board (EDB), but the administration of the program was subsequently transferred to SPRING. SPRING co-invests with third-party investors who are not related to the start-ups, with a minimum investment of S$75,000 required of the private investor. SPRING initially provided a 1:1 co-investment between S$75K to S$300K. However, the co-investment was increased over 2009-10 to 1.5:1 and S$750K (cumulative) in response to the financial crisis.

In the initial years the scheme provided an upside incentive to the third party investors when there was a positive exit. After recovering its initial investment plus accrued interest, the scheme offered one-third of any remaining surplus gains to be given to the third-party investors. In more recent years, this upside incentive has been withdrawn. More recently SPRING's co-investment ratio has reverted to 1:1, although the investment ceiling has been raised to S$1 million. Funding for the first round however, is usually limited to S$300K. As of 2012, SPRING had co-invested S$73m into 200 start-ups.[10]

A related government scheme seeks to promote the formation of angel groups. The Business Angel Scheme (BAS), also administered by SPRING, was introduced in 2005 and co-funds investment by pre-approved angel groups. Under BAS, SPRING would co-invest S$10 million with at least three experienced angel investors who collectively commit to invest at least S$10 million over five years. The scheme provides for a 1:1 co-investment of S$1 million per deal, with an option for investors to buy out SPRING's investment within five years at 1.25 times the original investment value. As with SEEDS, the co-investment terms were improved over 2009-10, to 1.5:1 up to a maximum of S$1.5 million per deal. Three angel groups have been co-funded under the BAS program so far: Sirius Capital; BAF Spectrum; and AccelX. BAS and SEEDS complement each other, so that start-ups that have already received funding under SEEDS can still apply under BAF for follow-on investment up to a maximum of S$1.5 million. As of the end of 2012, close to 30 ventures had been funded by the three angel groups supported by the BAS.

Angel investment depends on the availability of follow-on VC investment funds to take the start-ups to the next growth stage. Although Singapore has enticed a significant amount of VC funds to base their operations in Singapore, these funds are predominantly later-stage funds investing outside of Singapore. Thus a large proportion of the US$1 billion TIF fund-of-funds established in 1999 has gone to US VC funds, with extremely limited investment activities in Singapore. Moreover, most members of the Singapore Venture Capital Association (SVCA) do not invest in early stage start-ups.

In order to fill this gap, the Singapore National Research Foundation (NRF) has in recent years established two VC support schemes.[11] The first of these is the Early-Stage Venture Funding Scheme (ESVF) which was launched in 2008 and seeks to catalyze the formation of early-stage VC funds. Under the scheme, selected VC firms receive co-funding from NRF to invest in locally-based early-stage technology start-ups. Selected VC firms must raise at least S$10 million from third-party investors, and NRF matches S$1 for every S$1 invested. To date six funds have been selected for such co-funding: BioVeda Capital II; Nanostart Asia; Raffles Venture Partners; Tamarix Capital; Upstream-Expara; and Walden International (NRF 2008). However, most of these funds have tended to invest in deals that are above S$2million in size, thus leaving a gap for angel investment.

TYPES OF START-UP FUNDING IN SINGAPORE					
	PRE-SEED	**SEED**	**POST-SEED**	**GROWTH**	**PRE-IPO**
AVAILABLE SCHEMES	iJam: $40m TIS: $60m POC &TRD: $75m TECS & ACE: $95m SEEDS: $100m	SEEDS/BAS: $220m	ESVF II: $50m ESVF I: $120m Private Sector VCs: $320m	PUBLIC SECTOR: >$2B BANKS AND PRIVATE EQUITY FIRMS: >$250M PRIVATE SECTOR VCS: >$270M	
	Private Angels $20 million				
SIZE OF DEAL	$50K-$250K	$500K-$3M	SERIES A $3M-$5M	MORE SERIES OF FUNDING (SERIES B, C, D, ETC. >$10M)	

Source: Adapted from Cheok (2014)[14]

The second NRF scheme, the Technology Incubation Scheme (TIS) was launched in 2009 and is modeled on Israel's Technological Incubator Program. TIS aims to encourage local and foreign technology incubators to invest in early-stage high-tech start-ups in Singapore, nurturing them and preparing them to raise funds from VCs. Under TIS, NRF co-invests in Singapore-based high-tech start-ups accommodated in the selected technology incubators. As of 2013, 14 incubators have been funded under TIS: Red Dot Ventures; Small World Group; Plug and Play; Get2Volume; Jungle Ventures; Stream Global; WaveMaker Labs; Clearbridge Accelerator; Biofactory; TNF Ventures; Silicon Straits; Techcube 8; Golden Gate Ventures; and Incuvest. Notably, six of these were led by foreign investors enticed by the generous co-funding provided by the government. By early 2011, 21 ventures had been funded under TIS and in 2012, 40 start-ups received such funding.[12]

The National University of Singapore (NUS) also contributes to the availability of early-stage venture financing. The NUS Entrepreneurship Centre (NEC) secured commitment from NUS senior management to provide a S$5 million seed fund to invest in promising NUS-related spin-offs from its incubator (the NUS Enterprise Incubator or NEI). These funds are matched by a number of government schemes, including the SEEDS fund and SPRING's Young Entrepreneurs Scheme for Start-ups (YES! Start-ups) scheme (previously known as ETDF). NEC also helps start-ups apply for various government support schemes such as the EDB Cleantech incubator grant scheme, the SPRING Technology Enterprise Commercialization Scheme's Proof of Concept (POC) and Proof of Value (POV) grants, the Media Development Authority's micro-funding scheme, the NRF POC grants, and the NRF ESVF and TIS funds. NEC also maintains close contacts with BANSEA to introduce promising start-ups to BANSEA, SEEDS and BAS investors. Indeed, a disproportionate number of the investment deals by the ESVF and TIS so far have been in NUS-related spin-offs. Similarly, a number of notable deals by SEEDS and BAS investors that have attracted significant follow-on VC investment or corporate acquisitions were also NUS-related spin-offs.[13]

CONCLUSION

In line with Singapore's increasing shift towards a knowledge-based, innovation-driven economy, the angel investment community in Singapore has grown in professionalism and sophistication in recent years. The development of the angel investment community has been driven by both government support policies as well as the emergence of a nascent class of tech-savvy investors comprising of successful entrepreneurs, experienced senior executives from high tech multinational corporations and local firms, and entrepreneurially minded academia with connections to Silicon Valley. The cosmopolitan nature of the Singaporean economy and the government's open pursuit of foreign talent have also facilitated an inflow of foreign angel investors who add to the diversity and vibrancy of the angel community in Singapore. Going forward, a key challenge—and opportunity—for Singapore's angel investment community is to develop stronger global links with angel investors and VCs in leading high tech hubs in the world. Because of the small domestic market, successful start-ups in Singapore need to go global quite early, so the angels backing them also need to develop the skills to help them globalize.

Endnotes

[1] Wong, P.K. and A. Singh. (2008). "From Technology Adopter to Innovator: The Dynamics of Change in the National System of Innovation in Singapore," chap. 3 in C. Edquist and L. Hommen (eds.), *Small Economy Innovation Systems: Comparing Globalization, Change and Policy in Asia and Europe,* Elgar, 2008, p. 71–112.

[2] Hindle, K. and Lee, L. (2002). "An exploratory investigation of informal venture capitalists in Singapore," *Venture Capital* 4(2): 169–177.

[3] Wong, P.K. and Ho, Y.P. (2007). "Characteristics and determinants of informal investment in Singapore", *Venture Capital*, 9(1): 43–70.

[4] Informal investors are defined as those who have in the past three years invested in an entrepreneurial business venture started by someone else, excluding the purchase of publicly traded shares or mutual funds.

[5] The Total entrepreneurial rate (TEA) rate measures the proportion of a nation's adult population that is engaging in entrepreneurial activities in one of two ways: in the process of starting up a business or running a newly formed business less than 3.5 years old with significant ownership (Wong and Ho, 2007).

[6] Wetzel, W.E. (1983). "Angels and Informal Risk Capital," *Sloan Management Review,* 24, pp. 23-34.

[7] Bygrave, W.D. et.al. (2002). "A Study of investing in 29 nations composing the Global Entrepreneurship Monitor," paper presented at the Babson-Kauffman Entrepreneurship Research Conference, Boulder, Colorado, 6-8 June, 2002.

[8] Wong, P.K. et.al. (2000-2006). Global Entrepreneurship Monitor (GEM) - Singapore Report, various years (2000-2006).

[9] http://www.BANSEA.org/.

[10] SPRING Singapore (2013). *Enabling Transformation: SPRING Annual Report* 2012/13, http://www.spring.gov.sg/AboutUs/AR/Documents/FV_AR12_13/SPRING_Singapore_Annual_Report_2012_13.pdf, accessed 13 January 2014.

[11] http://www.nrf.gov.sg.

[12] Chng, G. (2013). "More seed money for budding start-ups," *Straits Times*, 21 February; Kok, L. (2011). "More funds on tap for start-ups," *Straits Times*, 27 March.

[13] More details about NUS' role in facilitating angel investment in Singapore can be found in Wong, Ho and Singh (2011).

[14] Cheok, J. (2014). "More money in pipeline for startups," *Business Times*, 11 March.

Canada

Ross Finlay and Blake Witkin

Angel investing was reported as early as 1994 in Canada, in an article of *The Financial Post*. At that time, information about early stage investing was largely anecdotal and tended to focus on the practice as if it were the domain of the privileged few. There appeared to be no links, either in existence or in development, between Canadian angels, venture capital firms, merchant banks, and other private investors. The Canadian mutual fund industry was in its infancy, and Canadians themselves had yet to wholeheartedly embrace direct investing as a means of creating and preserving wealth.

Since the 1990s, Canadians' knowledge and understanding of investing has advanced exponentially. It is now much clearer that angels and other investors have a great deal in common, with respect to objectives and appetites for risk and reward. The Canadian public has been quick to accept many different forms of investment and has become a captive audience for an industry of financial experts, consultants and advisors. Angel investors, however, have not enjoyed a similar level of information sharing and counsel. Angels by nature take significant

---

ROSS FINLAY is the co-founder and Director of the First Angel Network Association, Alanatic Canada's association for private investors. He has made more than 30 angel investments since 2000. BLAKE WITKIN is the Chair of the Board of Directors of The Network of Angel Organizations—Ontario. He is the chairman, president and an investor in Unified Computer Intelligence Corporation.

investment risk, but until recently have had to rely on personal advisors and their own tried-and-true practices for success.

In early 2000, a small group of angel investors banded together to form the National Angel Organization (NAO) to support angel investing in Canada. The NAO's mission was to help angel investors become more successful and thereby boost the economy. They began by building a diverse, broadly representative group of some 100 founders who spanned regions, industries, clusters, generations and cultures. Since 2002, NAO has held annual summits to bring together angels from across Canada so they can share best practices and learn about the angel investing environment. NAO members have been invited to speak at events from coast to coast, including national conferences encouraging business development in technology, life sciences and clean energy. In British Columbia, NAO helped kick off the country's first women's angel network. NAO regularly responds to Department of Finance requests for input regarding the federal budget. Furthermore, NAO has conducted roundtable discussions with more than one 100 angels in Halifax, Quebec, Montreal, Ottawa, Kingston, Toronto, Golden Horseshoe, London, Edmonton, Calgary and Vancouver.

In 2007 NAO was renamed the National Angel Capital Organization (NACO). At a meeting in 2010, with the Business Development Bank of Canada (BDC), NACO identified the need to provide potential venture capital co-investors with some comfort regarding the "professionalism" of Canadian angel groups. This would pave the way for more, and more efficient, co-investment with BDC and others. NACO established an education and best practices committee to develop programs and standards for angel groups. Standards were approved at the 2012 NACO annual general meeting. Since then, education programs have been developed and are being delivered by both NACO and the Angel Resource Institute (ARI) across Canada.

In 2013 the Canadian government launched the "Start-Up Visa" program. This program fast-tracks the permanent resident visa status of international entrepreneurs receiving funding to start their business in Canada from reputable, "designated" angel groups. The Angel Group Standards developed by NACO were used to "designate" groups able to participate in the Start-Up Visa program.

In Ontario, the provincial government provided funding to start the Network of Angel Organizations, Ontario (NAO-O), to support the development of new angel groups. This funding was later complemented with investments made by the Federal Economic Development Agency for Southern Ontario (FedDev). Approximately 25 groups have been formed to date, of which 21 remain in operation. By the end of 2013, these groups had funded 136 companies with roughly $93 million.

Atlantic Canada saw its first organized angel network created in 2005. The region is quite large geographically, encompassing the provinces of Nova Scotia, New Brunswick, Prince Edward Island and Newfoundland and Labrador. However, the population is relatively small, at some 3 million people. The First Angel Network grew from 16 members at start-up to almost 100 five years later. The organization has consistently made four investments per year and, as of this writing, has 25 portfolio companies and $10 million in investments. This investment has leveraged at least $70 million in follow-on investment. In 2007, the Newfoundland and Labrador Angel Network was formed to invest only in that province.

The angel ecosystem is supported by the federal government and several provincial governments across the country. At the federal level, support comes from Industry Canada, the Business Development Bank of Canada, the Federal Economic Development Agency for Southern Ontario (FedDev Ontario), the Federal Economic Development Initiative for Northern Ontario (FedNor Ontario), the Scientific Research and Experimental Development Tax Credit Program (SRED), and the Industrial Research Assistance Program (IRAP).

At the provincial level, angels are supported by tax credit programs offered in New Brunswick, Manitoba, and British Columbia. The government of Ontario supports Ontario angel groups by providing funding to cover administrative costs through the Angel Network Program. The Quebec government supports a single angel group, Anges Quebec, to manage three chapters across the province. The Quebec Government has also supported the establishment of an $80 million co-investment fund which Anges Quebec is entrusted to administer.

The NACO 2013 Report on Angel Investing Activity in Canada identified key trends in angel investment across Canada. NACO gathered survey and interview responses from angel group managers to determine Canadian angel investments and exits for that year. These responses were then compared with similar studies conducted in the 2010-2012 period to determine trends and create a longitudinal database of angel investment that tracks the status of each deal and company. These annual surveys have helped to determine how effectively angel groups are meeting the need for seed and early stage risk capital. The report also helps highlight the best practices and activities of Canadian angels, emphasizing their key role in the entrepreneurial ecosystem. In 2012 NACO began to examine the performance of another important aspect of this ecosystem, accelerators. Over the past four years the research report has covered 475 angel investments, totaling $180 million, and has made a significant contribution to Canadian entrepreneurship. The NACO report focuses on the activity of the most "visible" portion of the angel market, angel groups. It does not examine investments by angels who prefer to remain anonymous. In January 2014, an online survey was distributed to 33 angel groups—all 19 that had responded to the 2012 survey, and a further 14 angel groups identified by NACO. Of the 33 groups that were approached, 29 (or 88 percent) participated. Over 2,100 investors who were represented in the data, 55 percent resided in Central Canada, 40 percent were in Western Canada, and 5 percent were in Eastern Canada.

ANGEL GROUPS IN CANADA

With a median age of five years, angel groups are now an established institution in Canada. Slightly more than two-thirds of the groups (68 percent) are structured as not-for-profit organizations, 14 percent are for-profit, and 18 percent are not incorporated. Group size varies substantially with an average of 73.7 and a median of 40 members. About a quarter of the groups focus on only one or two sectors, while the rest consider investment opportunities in what the survey revealed to be the top three industry sectors in 2013: information and communications technology, life sciences and clean technology. In the majority of groups, individual members make their own investment decisions. Seventy-five percent of angel groups were established after 2007 and the size of the groups continues to increase:

- 45 percent of the groups now have fewer than 50 members (compared to 70 percent in 2011).
- 30 percent of groups had between one and ten members making investments in 2012 (compared to 60 percent in 2011).
- 20 percent of groups had between 51 and 100 active members (compared to 4 percent in 2011).
- 70 percent of groups indicated that they received more than 50 business plans in 2012.

THE ENTREPRENEURIAL ECOSYSTEM

A large number of organizations support the growth of entrepreneurs in Canada, and the number grows every year. For example, in 2005 there were 10 such organizations in Atlantic Canada. Today there are 26. These organizations provide entrepreneurs with the skills to run a business thus improving deal quality for angel networks. In particular, companies are better prepared to sell equity.

The number of incubators has risen across the country. A large number of them are supported by the Canadian government and organizations such as the Business Development Bank of Canada (BDC) and the National Research Council (NRC). Their policies differ, but they generally produce well-groomed entrepreneurs who have often received seed funding from supporting organizations and/ or innovation competitions. In addition to incubators, entrepreneurs in Canada are also supported by accelerators, science parks and technology centers.

The Canadian government (through Industry Canada and the NRC) is supporting the growth of angel groups in many parts of the country. Some groups receive money for direct operating expenses. To earn this support many groups consult for these government agencies and provide services such as education and information provision. In addition, some provincial governments have established sidecar funds to support angel investment in their province.

CASE STUDY: ONTARIO ANGEL GROUPS

Prior to 2006, most start-ups found it difficult to access angel capital in Ontario. There was also very little awareness of angels. Although this situation began to change after the 2006 NACO Summit, Ontario angel activity remained very informal and was not well tracked or understood. In 2007 the creation of NAO-Ontario broadened the scope of angel activities, providing resources and education for the first three Ontario angel groups. Angels began to develop a public presence in Ontario. This accelerated in 2011 with the start of FedDev's Investing in Business Innovation Program (IBI). Currently, NAO-Ontario is affiliated with 26 angel groups, including 12 supported nonprofits and 14 clubs. Network members have directly invested $134 million ($106.7 million from the nonprofits and $22.8 million from the clubs). Altogether 871 angels have been involved in 380 investment rounds.

Two important programs have helped develop angel activities in Ontario: the Angel Network Program, which is a provincial program funded by Ontario's Ministry of Research and Innovation, and Investing in Business Innovation, a national program funded by the Federal Development Agency for Southern Ontario, FedDev. The first program funds NAO-Ontario, which gives competitive grants to nonprofit local angel groups for operational expenses, training, educational resources, events and due diligence administration support. The second program funds both NAO-Ontario and local angel groups directly. The money is used for outreach, communication, group operational expenses and other events. FedDev was established in 2009 and its Investing in Business Innovation program started in 2011. It provides low-interest loans to investee companies, matching half the amount invested by angel groups and registered VCs. The requirements for the program are: businesses need to be incorporated in Canada and headquartered in southern Ontario; projects are normally expected to be complete within two years; investors need to fund at least two-thirds of the venture; investors must be accredited members of NAO-Ontario organized groups or investment clubs; and there must be at least three investors.

From 2007 to 2014, a total of $466 million was invested in 236 Ontario companies: $134 million directly from angel members and $332 million from private sector co-investors. This investment is estimated to have created or preserved more than 3,200 jobs. The leverage ratio for this public support of angel investing is therefore 57:1.

Portugal

João Trigo Da Roza and Francisco Banha

A BRIEF HISTORY OF ANGEL ACTIVITIES

Angel activity formally started in Portugal in 1999 with the creation of Gesventure and the Business Angels Club (BAC), both led by Francisco Banha. In 2006 Associação Portuguesa de Business Angels (APBA) was created with the objective of boosting angel activity and visibility in the market and aggregating several angel groups, including more than a dozen very active angel syndicates with national coverage and the Centro Business Angels (CEC).

In 2007 the National Federation of Business Angels Associations (FNABA) was created, combining the BAC with four angel groups—Invicta Angels (Associação de Business Angels do Porto), Clube de Cascais (Business Angels de Cascais), Associação de Business Angels do Algarve and Associação de Business Angels da Covilhã, which comprised of 16 regional associations and 35 very active angel syndicates with national coverage.

APBA and the Business Angels Club are currently the largest Portuguese angel groups. In November 2007 Law DL 375 created a

JOÃO TRIGO DA ROZA is the current president of Associação Portuguesa de Business Angels. FRANCISCO BANHA is the current President of the Business Angels Club and served as president of National Federation of Business Angels Associations from 2007 to February 2015.

new legal entity that covered angels and venture capital investors (Investidor em Capital de Risco). In 2009 the public institution PME Investimentos launched the Compete co-investment fund with a base of €42 million (€28 million from European Union funds, €12,5 million from Portuguese angels and €1,5 million from Caixa Capital). This has helped angel activity grow significantly.

In Portugal, an angel is defined as a private investor whose investment strategy is oriented toward innovative projects. It is an investment with "smart money," which means that the capital is accompanied by both entrepreneurial expertise and financial advice. Angels typically invest between €25,000 and €500,000 and want to exercise their mentoring ability, expertise and network of contacts. They usually prefer to invest in a specific region of the country. Most use Portugal as a test market, but aim to help the start-up become a global company.

The development of angel activity increased sharply after 2010 when the Compete co-investment fund was launched. As required by the regulations governing Compete, many angel vehicles were created with a minimum of three angels as shareholders. For each project, the goal is to invest €750,000, with angel vehicles contributing 35 percent and PME Investimentos, 65 percent. Sometimes angels co-invest with VC funds, like Caixa Capital (FCR Empreender+), Caixa Tech (Transfer Accelerator Ventures), ES Ventures, EDP Inovação and Portugal Ventures (a public VC). The Compete fund substantially increased the number and size of angel projects. From 2010 until mid-2015, there were 192 co-investments made in 126 start-ups, totaling €25 million. This figure only refers to Compete, so the entire national angel market is obviously greater. February 2014 saw the launch of a second, €15 million angel financing line: €10 million from European Union funds and €5 million from Portuguese angels. By December 2014 the entire amount had been allocated among 42 start-ups, which demonstrated the demand for this kind of investment.

ENTREPRENEURIAL ECOSYSTEM

Portugese entrepreneurs are most active in sectors such as information technology, the web, mobile-tech, clean-tech and cloud applications. However innovative investment spans a broad range of sectors including agriculture, trade, tourism, finance, education, health and telecommunications. This innovation is supported by a network of public and private incubators that have existed in Portugal for more than a decade. Since 2010 this activity has been supplemented by accelerators, which are playing a key role in the entrepreneurial ecosystem by supporting the rapid investment and commercialization of ideas and business models. Accelerators may be public or private and include Fábrica de Startups, Beta-I, Startup Lisboa, Sanjotec, Instituto Pedro Nunes, DNA Cascais and Startup Braga.

In many cases they are associated with universities and sponsored by large companies and banks such as Caixa Geral de Depósitos. They are very active and effectively cater to the varied needs of entrepreneurs at various stages of development. The government has also launched several programs to support entrepreneurs such as the "Passport to Entrepreneurship." Numerous organizations sponsor contests and scholarships (with and without prizes), including:

- Large companies such as Premio EDP Inovação (APBA is a member of the jury)
- Large financial groups such as Caixa Geral de Depositos (Contest Caixa Empreender Award)
- Acredita Portugal, one of the largest contests in the world for ideas and start-ups with more than 14,000 participants each year (APBA is a partner)
- Universities, especially business and economics schools (all have entrepreneurship offices and ideas contests) with the participation of APBA and FNABA
- The public sector (Passport to Entrepreneurship, Portugal Ventures)
- Accelerators/incubators (demo days, Venture Day, Energy Portugal, and Seedcamp)
- Global Entrepreneurship Week, a project of the Ewing Marion Kauffman Foundation (co-sponsored by APBA and Associação para o Desenvolvimento Económico e Social (SEDES) in Portugal)
- Business Angels Week, a project of FNABA co-sponsored with IAPMEI and PME Investimentos;
- National Congress of Business Angels Community (organized by FNABA)

There are also several science parks and technology centers in Portugal. The parks mainly focus on R&D and coordinate to some degree through an association called TechParks.

ANGEL GROUP STRUCTURES AND ORGANIZATIONS

The largest networks in Portugal are APBA and BAC. These networks have many individual business angels as associates, but also several investment vehicles. The mission of both APBA and BAC is to foster the development of angels in order to develop the spirit of entrepreneurship and contribute to the growth of a sustainable and innovative economy. APBA and BAC have national coverage and almost 150 members.

APBA has a delegation in the north and associated networks, clubs and syndicates such as Business Angels do Concelho Empresarial do Centro, Busy Angels, Shilling Partners, Brains2Market, Brain Capital, Brain Invest, Eggnest, only to mention a few.

FNABA (www.fnaba.org) has 16 regional business angel associations with about 600 affiliated angels. Its mission is to represent the interests of networks in Portugal such as BAC, Invicta Angels (O'Porto), Investors of Cascais, Algarve Business Angels, Vima Angels (Guimarães), Santarém Business Angels, Alenbiz (Évora and Beja), Covilhã Business Angels, Open Business Angels, Famagrow (Famalicão), ABAC (Aveiro) and Business Angels Club de Lisboa.

In the last few years, APBA and FNABA have participated in different international organizations and events such as the EBAN board and the Angel Capital Association Congress. Since 2006 APBA, BAC and FNABA have participated several times on the board of EBAN and FNABA assumed the presidency of the board of EBAN from 2012 to 2014. During 2013 APBA also joined Business Angels Europe and both APBA and FNABA have a partnership with Portuguese-speaking angel organizations Anjos do Brazil, Gavea Angels and Cape Verde Business Angels. Moreover since 2008, APBA has organized Global Entrepreneurship Week Portugal with SEDES. FNABA, meanwhile, has hosted a yearly National Week of Business Angels since 2007, during which regional groups promote private investment in new business projects. They have also hosted a National Congress of Business Angels since 2011, which aims to leverage "smart" angel money to finance start-ups. Last, FNABA is a founding member of the World Business Angels Association (WBAA), created in 2009 and is part of its board.

APBA and FNABA participated in development of the angel legal framework, both in the approval of the tax benefits for angels and in the creation of the Compete co-investment program. In Portugal there are also some domestic crowdfunding platforms and a few international ones targeting Portuguese shareholders (e.g., ppl.com.pt; and seedrs. com). There is no legal framework for these platforms, however.

POLICIES PROMOTING ANGEL INVESTING

The 1989 Portugal Law (215/89) on fiscal benefits, Article 32 governs the taxation of venture capital companies and angels. Angels can deduct the lesser of 15 percent of their personal income tax or 20 percent of the value of the investment (either individually or as part of an investment vehicle). The total limit of the deductions is established each year in the government's annual budget. In the 2013 budget, the authorized amount was an insignificant €10,000. However, as of yet the government has not implemented these authorizations. Town halls can establish lower rates for taxes in local areas. Until now, none of the town halls have established specific reductions for angel investments.

There are other co-investment options beyond the Compete program. Portugal Ventures is a public venture capital firm that invests in seed, early and growth stages by taking a minority equity stake in a company. It co-invests with angels. Apart from these minority equity investments, Portugal Ventures has also funded accelerators and developed the Ignition Capital Network, through which angels can screen, monitor, invest and follow investments with Portugal Ventures. There are also several incentives to support entrepreneurial activity, usually managed by the Agency for Competitiveness and Innovation (IAPMEI), which also funds conferences.

POLICY SUGGESTIONS

The tax incentive is currently too low to be effective, so raising this would stimulate funding and growth. Moreover, in the future European framework of 2014-20, co-investment schemes should be reinforced.

The Compete program is a good example of an initiative with a very positive impact on angel activity.

THE PROGNOSIS FOR ANGEL INVESTING IN PORTUGAL

Angel activity in Portugal is growing at a sustainable pace. The evolution of the market has been very strong during the last three years with the creation of many angel investment vehicles that are professionalizing the activity. There are many new players in the ecosystem that are energizing the system and capturing synergies, enabling better projects and generating more investment. This trend could be accelerated by public policies that are more supportive of investors. The public finance situation in Portugal poses constraints. However, this can also be viewed as an opportunity because there is now a strong entrepreneurial dynamic in the country, and assets are at a good price for investors.

Acknowledgments

This report was produced by João Trigo da Roza, President of APBA, and Francisco Banha, the FNABA President from 2007 to 2015, with contributions from Fatima Cristovão and Diogo Cardoso, APBA Board Members.

New Zealand

Franceska Banga and David Lewis

BRIEF HISTORY OF ANGEL ACTIVITIES

In the early 2000s, angel investment was largely unknown in New Zealand. There were few "angel investors" as such, and no funds or formal networks. A few wealthy individuals and successful entrepreneurs from the 1990s technology boom invested in an ad hoc way, but this investment was sporadic, unstructured and largely below the radar. New Zealand's export profile resembled that of a developing country, not that of a developed one. During periods of high commodity prices and good weather, the primary sector was very profitable and the overall economy did well. But a volatile exchange rate and the cyclical nature of commodity prices led to stop-go economic performance. Successive governments sought to implement policies to foster a more innovative and diverse economy.

In 2001 the New Zealand government and leaders in the business and academic community held a major conference, entitled "Catching the

FRANCESKA BANGA has been a leading figure in the venture capital and angel investment market in New Zealand, having served as chief executive of the New Zealand Venture Investment Fund since its inception in 2001. DAVID LEWIS has worked with a number of private equity, venture capital and angel groups, including the New Zealand Venture Investment Fund. Previously he worked as a senior advisor for the New Zealand Prime Minister,and as a consultant to the New Zealand Treasury.

NEW ZEALAND YOUNG COMPANY FINANCE INDEX		
YEAR	AMOUNT INVESTED (NZ$)	NO. OF DEALS
2006	$21,366,964	30
2007	$29,518,348	55
2008	$32,569,403	41
2009	$43,238,580	75
2010	$53,109,861	112
2011	$34,798,049	103
2012	$29,896,789	102
2013	$53,230,971	116
	$297,728,965	**634**

Knowledge Wave," to develop policies to reduce economic dependence on agriculture, fisheries and forestry. A number of initiatives emerged. Incubators were established in major cities with links to university commercialization agencies. Universities and research agencies were asked to emphasize research that could be commercialized. An organization linking prominent expatriate New Zealanders (KEA-Kiwi Expats Abroad) was created to help build international networks. And the New Zealand Venture Investment Fund (NZVIF)[1] was established in 2002 to catalyze the creation of a venture capital industry.

The government allocated NZ$100 million to seed NZVIF's venture capital program, with the requirement that NZVIF invest into qualified venture capital funds alongside private investors. The fund has grown to NZ$260 million under management and made investments through nine venture funds. Capital returns can be reinvested in new VC funds. The VC market has changed and grown substantially, benefiting from limited partnership legislation enacted in 2007 and an active venture capital association. In 2005, the government asked NZVIF to complement its VC program by establishing an angel investment fund, the Seed Co-Investment Fund (SCIF), for angel funds and groups. Around the same time, a handful of angel groups started to invest, led by Sparkbox Ventures and Ice Angels in Auckland, and Powerhouse in Christchurch.

The SCIF, combined with a core of experienced angel investors willing to lead the sector, has fostered what is now a vibrant New Zealand angel community. Auckland, the largest city, has seven active groups, while others are located throughout the larger cities, often close to universities and major scientific research centers. In addition to investing, NZVIF helps develop the market by building capacity, supporting best practice investments, and collecting data on the formal angel market through the Young Company Finance Index. Angels invested NZ$53.2 million into young companies in 2013, a record high and an 80 percent increase on the NZ$29.9 million invested in 2012. Cumulatively, NZ$297.7 million was invested into young companies by angels between 2006 and 2013.

ENTREPRENEURIAL ECOSYSTEM

New Zealand has about 500 organizations directly involved in commercializing innovation. Fifty of these are major institutions: large universities, government research institutes, polytechnics and private sector companies. There are also many smaller science, engineering and technology companies; laboratories; university campuses; workshops, studios and factories. Business incubators are found in all the main centers, mainly founder-focused initiatives that foster the survival and growth of early stage, high-growth businesses. In 2014, the government launched a new type of technology-focused incubator aimed at encouraging more innovative, complex technology-based start-ups based on an Israeli model. The new incubators are privately owned businesses focused on the commercialization of complex intellectual property primarily sourced from publicly funded research organizations, such as universities and Crown research institutes.

New Zealand is regarded as a highly entrepreneurial country. It is currently ranked 11th in the Venture Capital and Private Equity Attractiveness Index,[2] an annual global survey undertaken by the IESE Business School in Barcelona. The survey assesses countries multiple factors—economic activity, capital markets, taxation, investor protection, corporate governance, and entrepreneurial culture, among others. New Zealand scores particularly highly in investor protections, and the human and social environments.

ANGEL NETWORKS

The Angel Association of New Zealand[3] was established in 2008 to allow business angel networks and early stage funds to begin working toward an agreed national vision. The Association comprises 14 formal angel groups, funds and networks:

- Auckland: Sparkbox Ventures, Ice Angels, Cure Kids, K1W1, Pacific Channel, Flying Kiwi Angels, Arc Angels[4]
- Tauranga: Enterprise Angels
- Palmerston North: Manawatu investment Group
- Wellington: Movac, Angel HQ
- Nelson: Venture Accelerator
- Christchurch: Powerhouse Ventures
- Dunedin: Otago Angels

The association runs programs on angel investing practices and an annual summit. Leading angel investors from the United States frequently attend, and they lead workshops on strengthening capability in New Zealand.

PROGNOSIS FOR THE FUTURE

Equity crowdfunding began to emerge in New Zealand in 2013. The government passed legislation, the Financial Markets Conduct Act 2013, which paved the way for the creation of platforms. Platforms must apply for a license from New Zealand's financial markets regulator, the Financial Markets Authority (FMA). Businesses are able to use an approved crowdfunding platform to raise up to NZ$2 million a year by issuing shares or borrowing from the public without issuing a formal prospectus or facing the usual regulatory scrutiny. The FMA granted the first two equity crowdfunding platform licenses in July 2014. This part of the market will develop over the coming years.

The links between public and private equity markets have improved significantly since 2012. The global financial crisis of 2008-2012 led to a dearth of activity in terms of initial public offerings on the New Zealand Stock Exchange (NZX). Since 2013, there has been a spate of new offerings, including a number of small technology companies. This activity is expected to continue, albeit at a lower, more sustainable level.

Having a growth or exit pathway is crucial, so the heightened IPO and sale activity involving growth companies has been a welcome feature, and should improve the flow of capital into young companies entering the pipeline. As investors sell-down or exit investments, they tend to re-invest in the next generation of start-up and growth companies. Creating greater churn is a key feature of a vibrant and sustainable early stage investment sector.

To encourage more small companies to list, the NZX proposed a new "NXT" market with fewer disclosure obligations in June 2015. The NXT platform is targeted at small to mid-sized businesses with market capitalizations ranging from $10 million to $100 million, whose growth potential may be constrained by a lack of expansion capital. Companies listing on the NXT through an initial public offering need to raise a minimum of NZ$5 million and have at least 50 shareholders (instead of 500). The NXT market allows for reduced complexity with a set of simplified listing rules and a less onerous approach to disclosure.

GOVERNMENT POLICIES TO PROMOTE ANGEL INVESTING

The corporate tax rate in New Zealand is 28 percent. All companies, whether resident or non-resident, are taxed the same. New Zealand does not have a capital gains tax as such. However, gains from the sale of real property (land and buildings) and personal property (including shares), in cases where the property is acquired for resale or as part of a dealing operation, are subject to income tax at normal rates. There are no special tax rules or incentives for angel investment.

Callaghan Innovation is a stand-alone government entity established in 2013. It administers more than NZ$140m a year in business research and development (R&D) funding through three programs, designed to help accelerate innovation by firms in New Zealand:

- R&D Growth Grants: designed to increase R&D investment in businesses with a strong track record for R&D spending;
- R&D Project Grants: designed to support greater investment by businesses in R&D, especially businesses with less established programs.
- R&D Student Grants: designed to support New Zealand

undergraduate and postgraduate students who want to develop technical skills in a commercial research environment and bring that capability into businesses.

A significant percentage of angel-invested companies have accessed (or plan to access) R&D funding from Callaghan Innovation.

	NZVIF SEED CO-INVESTMENT FUND			
	ANGEL PARTNERS	INVESTEE COMPANIES	NZ$M INVESTED	AMOUNT INVESTED (CUMULATIVE)
2006	2	1	$0.2M	$0.20M
2007	4	4	$0.70M	$0.90M
2008	8	18	$2.54M	$3.44M
2009	9	27	$3.27M	$6.71M
2010	11	41	$3.26M	$9.97M
2011	12	61	$4.99M	$14.95M
2012	14	77	$4.36M	$19.33M
2013	14	96	$5.20M	$24.53M

New Zealand Trade & Enterprise (NZTE) is the government's international business development agency. It offers a range of programs and services to companies growing globally, often including seed and early stage companies that use angel capital. Relevant programs include Beachheads (connecting participating companies to a network of private sector advisors in New Zealand and around the world) and Better by Capital (services delivered in partnership with private sector specialists to help New Zealand businesses access the right capital, at the right time, to fund their international growth).

The key government policy to promote angel investing is the NZ$40 million Seed Co-Investment Fund run by the New Zealand Venture Investment Fund. NZVIF established a SCIF in 2005 to support the development of angel investment. It is managed by NZVIF and is an equity investment fund aimed at small to medium-sized businesses at the seed and start--up stage of development which have a strong potential for high growth. The key objectives of SCIF are to enhance the development of angel funds and angel networks, stimulate investment into innovative start-up companies, and to increase capacity in the market for matching experienced angel investors with new, innovative start-up companies. It operates as a co-investment fund alongside selected angel networks (its SCIF partners) by providing matched seed funding for investment into start-up companies.

SCIF has a number of key features. Seed-stage and start-up investments are eligible for the fund, as long as the majority of their assets and employees are in New Zealand at the time of initial investment. However, this restriction does not apply to subsequent investments into a company by the fund. The fund excludes investment in financial intermediaries, property development, retailing, mining and hospitality industry businesses. NZVIF will invest up to NZ$4 million per co-investment partner with the potential for a further NZ$4 million subject to a partnership review. Investments through

SCIF by the Numbers (July 2014)	
Number of portfolio companies	115
NZVIF amount invested	NZ$29.9m
SCIF partner amount invested	NZ$61.5m
Other private investment	NZ$77.6m
Ratio of NZVIF to SCIF partner investment	1:2
Ratio of NZVIF to all private partner investment	1:4.6
Cumulative portfolio company revenue	NZ$100m
Average size of NZVIF first commitment	NZ$170.5K
Percentage of companies exporting	>80%

the fund are limited to a maximum investment of NZ$250,000 in any one company or group of companies, with the possibility of follow-on capital investments up to a maximum in any company of NZ$750,000, at the discretion of NZVIF. A 50/50 matching private investment is required for the fund to invest, and the fund acts as a direct investor on the same terms as the co-investment partner. As of 2014, some NZ$30 million had been invested by the fund.

Since SCIF's establishment, angel investing has become a small but important part of New Zealand's capital markets. To date, the fund has partnered with 15 networks, while a number of other active groups and individuals operate outside the SCIF framework.

SCIF has enjoyed warm support from angel groups and investors. It is seen as a consistent, dependable long term co-investment partner. This has given its angel partners the confidence to make long term plans to stay in the game, keep investing and develop their capability. It has enabled NZVIF to work with its angel partners, assisting in investor oversight, providing follow-on capital and protecting investors' positions to prevent or minimize dilution in later investment rounds. SCIF has also helped shape industry best practice, especially with respect to investment documentation (term sheets, shareholders agreements, reporting documents, etc.). This has facilitated an acceleration in angel group deal syndication in New Zealand.

ANGEL INVESTMENT TRENDS

Over the next five to ten years, a number of key drivers are expected to affect the New Zealand's angel market. Organized angel networks are expected to at least match the current funding level, around NZ$50 million per annum. This will be augmented by an increase in the number of organized angel investment funds (including sidecar funds and micro-venture capital funds). Angel investment by successful entrepreneurs should increase as they recycle capital from successful exits into start-ups. Meanwhile, New Zealand's equity crowdfunding market will continue to develop.

Endnotes

[1] http://ww.nzvif.co.nz.

[2] http://blog.iese.edu/vcpeindex/newzealand/.

[3] www.angelassociation.co.nz/.

[4] Arc Angels was established in October 2013 in Auckland. Its rules do not require all members to be women. Rather, its investments are into companies founded and run by women entrepreneurs.

Russia

Ivan Protopopov and Konstantin Fokin

In the last few years the Russian venture capital market has reached a number of important milestones. In 2013 Russia was the fastest growing venture capital (VC) market in Europe and fourth in size.[1] The number of high-risk, high-reward investment opportunities continues to grow, despite generally unfavorable economic conditions in the country. The VC community has a long way to go before these achievements are sustainable, however. Russia is in the investment phase of the cycle, with the large funds that were established in the 2006-2008 period just reaching maturity and starting to look for exits.

The times ahead will define the development of Russian venture ecosystem. With many large-scale venture fund managers looking to reboot their fundraising in the upcoming three years, deal flow issues are at the forefront of public discussions. The tentative consensus is that the current lack of adequate pre-seed and seed-round financing is fast becoming a major strategic issue. Although various state-sponsored grant schemes have been set up to catalyze investment, only

---

IVAN PROTOPOPOV served for more than four years as Partner at the seed-stage investing and accelerating firm Atom Partners, prior to joining North Energy Ventures. He has invested in energy, instrumentation and IT companies, including Dashboard and Aerogreen. He is also a board member of Fidesys and MedPro. KONSTANTIN FOKIN is President of the National Business Angels Association of Russia.

recently has the focus shifted to the early stage market and associated investors. Business angels—an elusive, attention-averse and otherwise peculiar breed—are fast becoming the industry's "chosen people" to take Russian venture capital to the next level.

THE WAY OF THE ANGEL

The Russian venture industry is very young. According to recent research, the typical investor has been active in the venture market for less than five years. There is a good reason for this. The 1990s saw a fundamental change in the way Russian society was organized. A new creative entrepreneurial class emerged that possessed youth, ambition and a previously unimagined freedom of decisionmaking. The shift toward a market economy after the collapse of the Soviet Union presented a myriad of under-served markets, from retail stores to the stock exchange, from jeans manufacturing to fast-food outlets. The young leaders created by this entrepreneurial boom laid the foundation of the angel movement that is only now starting to mature.

Economic wars raged for the control of the Soviet legacy of heavy industry (particularly in mining and aluminum). Powerful groups of mega-entrepreneurs vied for assets, and multi-billionaires were created. This left unattended the small niche markets, allowing them to blossom into sophisticated industries that now sustain the otherwise feeble post-2008 economy. For instance, the Russian IT, retail and financial industries were built from scratch by creative and visionary people. They are now recognized as world-class in a country where overall labor productivity is almost embarrassingly low compared to the other G8 economies. These industries in particular have been able to produce the modern angels that the venture ecosystem so desperately needs. This process needs more time to reach maturity, but in the meantime it has produced some interesting results.

The Russian business angel is younger and more active than his American or European counterpart. Research suggests the average Russian angel is in his mid-40s, as opposed to the mid-50s average for developed countries. He also has another source of income that needs constant attention, i.e. he is either an active entrepreneur with his own thriving business or a top manager of a large corporation. This has a substantial effect on his view of how to deal with investment opportunities and portfolio companies. This fundamental feature of Russian angels also affects the way they deal with the venture ecosystem. Having been actively involved in business activities in a setting where the rules of the game change on a yearly basis, they are wary of commitments to venture infrastructure, collaboration with government institutions and trusting the legal system. Of course there are exceptions. Russian IT is a lightly regulated industry, so it should not come as a surprise that it is particularly popular with Russian angels. This popularity is reinforced by the fact that many angels have an IT industry background.

Over the past five years a new group of angels has also emerged. This group seems keen on building a modern investment community and is prepared to promote the agenda of the angel investor with all the determination and grit that is required. They are open and public about their activities and ideas, assuming the role of industry representatives in dealing with other active institutions of the venture ecosystem, most notably the government.

THE LAWS AND THE FLAWS

As with any government, the Russian government's role can be divided into two broad categories: passive encouragement (determining the rules of the game) and active help (spending public funds on activities designed to yield breakthrough results). As far as passive encouragement goes, there are contradictory forces. Tax laws are very accommodating for a private individual investor. The personal income tax is set at a flat rate of 13 percent, while dividends are taxed at 9 percent. Recently the national business angel association also initiated a movement to pass a bill that would enable business angels to offset their personal income tax payments with their high-risk private investments. Although the proposed deduction is relatively modest (up to $100,000 per year), it would help the angel movement.

On the other hand, angel surveys strongly suggest there is a reluctance to invest privately for a non-controlling share of a company—which is the standard practice of angel investment everywhere else—because of the unpredictability of the legislative process. Under current legislation the power of the founders/executives to steer a company into a wrong direction can easily be upheld by local courts. This distrust of the legal system, often borne of an angel's personal experience as an entrepreneur, holds back the development of the angel investment movement. Although this perception remains entrenched, there have been significant changes in the way the venture industry is allowed to operate. Notably, the 2008-2009 changes in national corporate codes allowed for the emergence of shareholder agreements in a relatively modern form. This was designed to help investors structure venture deals in local jurisdictions. Moreover, in 2011 a breakthrough bill allowed for the incorporation of typical investment partnerships, a potentially great vehicle for early-stage investments. There is still a certain reluctance to accept these changes, but the government appears determined to bring the legislation up to speed with recent worldwide developments. Russia's legal system is based on so-called continental law, however, which allows limited room to accommodate venture investors' needs. (Anglo-Saxon law allows greater flexibility.) The goal, of course, is to help everyone in the investment community "get on the same page" and feel comfortable operating within their existing jurisdiction. The government also has a powerful tool to promote its jurisdiction through a number of special purpose venture vehicles.

THE VENTURE TRINITY

The presidency of Dmitri Medvedev (2008-2012) brought with it a consistent commitment to innovation and modernization as a whole, and to the development of the venture ecosystem in particular. Recent years have seen an unprecedented increase in attention and financing of the ecosystem, with clear and tangible results. Early on, these initiatives faced challenges because Russia's process was not geared toward state support of venture investment. The government tried different approaches to solve this and eventually ended up operating mostly through three large independent vehicles that wield between them a combined $5 billion: Rusnano, the Russian Venture Company, and the Skolkovo Foundation. The first two are structured as large corporations, while Skolkovo is regulated by legislation passed in 2010. There are other government initiatives in place, especially on the regional level, but this "venture trinity" is so large and powerful that it has become (in some cases unwillingly) the principal point of both state-supported venture activity and the entire ecosystem. Nowhere has the shift toward a recognition of angel investment been more apparent than in the work of the trinity with angels and their activities.

Rusnano was established in 2007 as a state enterprise dedicated to foster the growth of the Russian nanotechnology industry. The project was initially geared to support large-scale businesses such as the construction of large technology plants. However, being the first venture-oriented vehicle with a lot of political power (it is headed by political heavyweight Anatoly Chubais, who previously completed the reform of the Russian power supply industry), it ended up engaging in many complementary activities that are now handled by the Infrastructure and Educational Programs Fund. Ironically, despite its immense power, budget and ambition, Rusnano was the first to recognize the importance of angel investment, and it was instrumental in helping to set up the National Business Angel Association of Russia (NBAA) in 2009. It has been an active supporter ever since.

NBAA acts as an industry moderator and a focal point for the promotion of best practices, standards and the angel investment cause in general. It represents regional angel communities and associations, which are eligible to become members. NBAA in turn, acts as a channel between these associations and the venture community as a whole, which in large part represented by the government institutions. It also plays a crucial role in educating investors and potential investors about the ever-changing venture capital industry, organizing seasonal educational programs (called NBAA Universities) to promote the angel cause, and helping new community members get their bearings. A large part of this activity has historically been financed by Rusnano.

Russian Venture Company (RVC) was established in 2006 as a fund of venture funds, and to date it has invested in 13 funds (including two international ones) that collectively manage almost $1 billion. The vast majority of funds also have private investors. Most of the closings date back to 2007-2009, meaning that these funds are reaching a critical period in their maturity cycle, with important consequences for the industry as a whole. Similar to Rusnano, perhaps unsurprisingly, RVC started out with large-scale co-investments as its main strategic objective and ended up playing a more intensive role in the development of the Russian venture market. In RVC's case, its strategic overhaul coincided with the arrival of a new CEO, Igor Agamirzyan, in 2009. The new strategy included a focus on infrastructure and the establishment of a number of new RVC funds, most notably the RVC Seed Investment Fund (SIF). SIF is tasked with fostering early stage investment via a co-financing mechanism, with SIF supplying up to 75 percent of the investment requirement and the remainder supplied by accredited funds and investment companies. This mechanism has proven successful and more than 50 companies have received financing. SIF has recently launched a special business angel co-investment initiative and is able to supply up to $100,000 in an angel investment round. This opportunity is available to any business angel with previous investment experience in at least two portfolio companies. Research shows that some of angels are reluctant to take advantage of this opportunity, citing too much paperwork and obstacles in strategic decisionmaking as key reasons. Despite this, the leadership of SIF has expressed a determination to follow through with its plans to considerably boost angel investment.

The role of RVC in an angel's life is readily apparent through its extensive activities. The company co-organizes, promotes, and sponsors almost all start-up events in Moscow and other centers for venture communities (e.g., Novosibirsk and Kazan). There is no shortage of options for investors looking to find interesting projects, and teams looking for seed financing, and the number of events has been steadily increasing. This is especially true in the case of Moscow, where the local administration has also started promoting venture capitalism and new technologies through the establishment of the Moscow Innovative Development Centre.

The Skolkovo Foundation is the youngest of the venture trinity. The initial goal of the foundation was to establish a full-scale innovative community on the outskirts of Moscow, one that would have a population of more than 20,000 and state-of-the-art infrastructure exemplified by a giant glass dome in its center, all financed with $10 billion in funds. Although the project has recently been scaled down somewhat, the aim of building a self-sustaining venture community remains. At the heart of Skolkovo are its residents (about 1,000 are established at the time of this publication), who are engaged in groundbreaking research aimed at disrupting markets.

The participants, who are expected to move their offices to Skolkovo once the city's development is completed, enjoy an unprecedented tax regime—they are virtually exempt from all taxes—and have access to non-dilutive grant financing with up to four rounds of grants and $17 million available. The grants require co-investment, however, and while historically Skolkovo has tried to establish good working relationships with large venture funds, the reality is that the vast majority of the residents require smaller pre-seed and seed rounds that VCs typically do not provide. This was recognized by the fund managers and a new initiative called the Skolkovo Business Angel Club was established. This initiative encourages angels to invest in Skolkovo residents and has been steadily gaining traction, as the foundation has the resources to provide due diligence and lower risks for angels who choose to participate. The foundation also tries to foster connections between its residents, early stage investors and funds that are prepared to come in at later rounds. The goal is to proactively create potential exit opportunities, which are otherwise too few and far between. Skolkovo also constantly tries to reach out and establish working relationships with the high-tech community abroad: venture and angel funds, corporations that are strategic investors, and educational institutions, most notably the Massachusetts Institute of Technology. Angel investors that invest in Skolkovo residents can leverage these connections for their own benefit.

With all the trinity institutions, the key to establishing a good and longstanding relationship with angels is to overcome the mistrust that currently exists between the state and private high-net-worth individuals. Judging from the developments in the last three years, the process is going in the right direction. The hope is that no one will try to rush it unnecessarily with the aim of getting tangible results quickly.

THE 2014-2015 YEARS

The good start of the year 2014 did not last long for the angel market and Russian economy in general. The situation around Crimea and East Ukraine, as well as the resulting sanctions caused serious deterioration of investor confidence, both local and international. No precise figures will ever be available but NBAA estimates that over the course of 2014-2015 more than 50 percent of most active investors left the country.

Those who remained markedly limited their investments, choosing to focus on follow-on rounds for their existing portfolio companies. The preferred destinations for angel investors now are the Baltics, Israel, the US, Singapore, and Hong-Kong, and some of the leading Russian angel investors have quickly become a very integral, natural parts of those entreprenership ecosystems.

THE FUTURE OF ANGEL INVESTMENT IN RUSSIA

As long as there are bits and pieces of a market economy in Russia there will be business angels, more or less of them, who are more or less active, and who more or less positive about angel investing and the prospects of their own region and Russia in general. A few pretty good years of dynamic market growth before 2014 have clearly shown that Russia has a very sizable group (at least tens of thousands) of reasonably wealthy people with good business experience who are capable and potentially willing to engage in smart, positive angel activity. Further, this group has proven its responsiveness to positive market and political signals. From 2010 to 2013, for example, economic growth was so fast that Russia became the third-largest market in Europe.

What is coming? Nobody knows. NBAA believes that two dramatically different scenarios are equally probable in the next 10-15 years. First, one could imagine a skyrocketing of the Russian angel market into the ranks of the world's elite. This is a realistic and very appealing possibility should the country seriously change its political and economic climate. New angels will quickly engage and "old angels" will inevitably move back home. The second scenario, obviously a less positive one, would entail ever more degradation of the market and social freedoms in the country, resulting in a virtual collapse of the angel market as such.

Endnotes

[1] http://www.bloomberg.com/.

Colombia

Juan Pablo Rodriguez Neira

EARLY ANGEL ACTIVITIES

Although Colombia is not yet a paradise for funding start-ups, there has recently been a great improvement in access to capital for high-potential entrepreneurs. Financing options for different stages of business development have increased significantly and now include angel networks, venture capital funds, private and government seed capital, business accelerators and crowdfunding platforms. The entrepreneurial community has also developed significantly in recent years, so the demand for capital is still higher than the supply. Angel activities are not new in Colombia, but efforts to measure the progress of this sort of capital started only after the formation of the first two angel networks: the National Business Angel Network (RNAI) led by Bavaria's Foundation in Bogota, and Capitalia's Business Angel Network in Medellin. These were created in 2010 with support from the Inter-American Development Bank and the Multilateral Investment Fund.

JUAN PABLO RODRIGUEZ NEIRA is the Director of Colombia's National Business Angel Network (RNAI) and has developed different financing models for early stage entrepreneurs. As a mentor he has helped more than 300 entrepreneurs through the business plan contest "Destapa Futuro." He holds an Industrial Engineering degree from Los Andes University and Strategic Management specialization from La Sabana University.

After the creation of these networks, angel investing became more popular among new investors. Successful young entrepreneurs became angels and started to lead investment in promising start-ups. RNAI and the consulting firm Inspired profiled these investors and found that:

- 87 percent were men
- 70 percent had at least a master's degree
- 79 percent had experience as entrepreneurs
- The average age was 40
- They were able to invest $150,000 on average

In 2013 RNAI started to grow across the country and is now the most active angel network in the region, with more than 120 registered angels. During the last year it closed 10 deals amounting to $1.8 million.

THE ENTREPRENEURIAL ECOSYSTEM

The Global Entrepreneurship Monitor ranks Colombia as one of the most entrepreneurial countries in the world. According to Startup Angels, several factors support the nation's entrepreneurial ecosystem development. The government provides substantial resources for entrepreneurs through initiatives such as iNNpulsa, an agency that fosters economic growth. This is fueling the local start-up scene. Colombia is in sixth place, tied with the US, in the World Bank's investor protection ranking, and it has made great strides in reforming its regulatory environment, improving faster than any other Latin American state. There are comparatively low restrictions for foreign investment in new ventures and acquisitions, and a variety of government programs encourage foreign investment. Also, Colombia has a well-educated workforce that includes a strong base of software developers.

There are several incubators and accelerators across the country. Good examples of accelerators include Wayra (Telefonica Group), Hub Bog, Connect Bogota, Social Atom, and Dinamizar Pereira. Examples of prominent incubators include InQLab, Manizales+, InnoMaker, Inneo and Ruta N (a technology park). According to Colciencias (the national Department of Science, Technology and Innovation), technology centers in Colombia are focused on specific sectors of national interest ranging from industry infrastructure to agribusiness.

INNOVATION COMPETITIONS

Destapa Futuro is a national contest that has been held for the past eight years. Entrepreneurs throughout the country are encouraged to present business plans. Those accepted receive training and support in developing and testing their business plans. Once they have made significant progress, the best entrepreneurs are selected to be mentored by top executives of Bavaria and its partner organizations, and to compete for rounds of seed capital. During the past eight years 65,000 business plans have been evaluated, 4,700 entrepreneurs have received training, and 380 companies have received seed capital.

ANGEL GROUP STRUCTURES AND ORGANIZATIONS

Professional angel networks started to emerge a few years ago. Most of them are local groups in the main cities. For example, the National Business Angel Network and Hub Bog are based in Bogota; Capitalia and Rai-Cap, which are based in Medellin; and the Club de Inversionistas del Caribe in Barranquilla. There is one national angel group, the National Business Angel Network (RNAI), led by the Bavaria Foundation in alliance with two universities (Universidad del Norte and Javeriana Cali), one foundation (Bolivar-Davivienda), three Chambers of Commerce (Pereira, Cali and Bucaramanga), and a technology cluster (Creatic). The RNAI has operations in eight cities: Bogota, Medellin, Barranquilla, Cali, Pereira, Manizales, Bucaramanga and Popayan. The RNAI belongs to the regional network "Angeles del Pacífico" operating in Chile, Mexico, Uruguay, Peru and Colombia. This network has 320 registered business angels and has invested in 95 deals amounting to $30 million.

Angel investing activities in Colombia are actively supported by the Inter-American Development Bank, the Multilateral Investment Fund, the Xcala Program (Montevideo University Business School and Multilateral Investment Fund), and iNNpulsa-Bancoldex (a government agency and development bank in Colombia).

POLICIES TO PROMOTE ANGEL INVESTING

There have not been many subsidies for angel investment in Colombia, although recently iNNpulsa has instituted a matching grant program. Under this program, qualified angel investors present their investment proposals to iNNpulsa. If their proposal fulfills the program's requirements, iNNpulsa matches the amount invested by the angel, although the investor gets the full 20 percent of participation in the company. The objective of the program is to reduce the risk for investors and incentivize the culture of angel investment in Colombia. This can create moral hazard, however, as investors invest in riskier projects. Although in the short run this kind of program might result in higher investment totals and help more people enter into angel investment, the long run effects might be counterproductive. If riskier projects end up failing, the perception of angel investment might be tainted and investors might become more risk-averse.

PUBLIC FUNDING

RNAI conducted research on investment mechanisms that would foster business angel investment in Colombia. They identified two main lessons. Survey participants wanted mechanisms that would allow investors to co-invest and reduce their coordination costs. Specifically, they felt that angel investment funds would decrease the matching costs of finding the right angel investors for each project and would help investors diversify their risk. Success cases can be found in other countries such as Chile and Mexico, the latter being the most successful. In Mexico, angel funds have been able to combine portfolio diversification with smart capital by establishing a lead angel for each investment project. This leader was in charge of providing the "smart capital" required to reduce the risk of the project and increase the business profitability.

The second notable finding of the research was that one-third of those who wanted to invest in risk-capital markets were highly risk-averse. This has led them to evaluate many business opportunities but not invest in any of them. These risk-averse investors were willing to be part of an investment deal by negotiating a higher payoff in case of failure vs. a lower payoff in case of success. On average, these investors were willing to sacrifice 11 percent of their profitability in exchange for 17 percent of collateral in case of failure. This opens the door to new investment mechanisms such as warranty funds. These contingent funds could take a percentage of the deal if the business succeeds, against paying collateral in case of failure. This mechanism could attract more investors to early stage projects and decrease the risk associated with these kinds of projects. Nevertheless, they would require a good institutional design in order to avoid moral hazard problems and align incentives of investors and entrepreneurs. Although both mechanisms can be funded by private capital, legal uncertainty and transaction costs might be too high. Government support in developing risk capital markets could make these proposed mechanisms feasible and give legal certainty to the angel investors.

PLATFORMS FOR INVESTING

Angel investors in developing countries face significant difficulty in finding a developed capital market where they can execute their exit strategies. Currently the returns on investment rely on profits made by the company or, in just a few occasions, an acquisition by a large firm. To foster business angel investment in Colombia, public policies should not be solely focused on creating incentives or investment mechanisms. More work needs to be done in developing financial and stock markets, establishing clear investment laws, and easing the creation of venture capital and investment funds.

Acknowledgements

The author wishes to acknowledge several people who contributed to this chapter.

SERGIO ZUÑIGA BOHÓRQUEZ is the RNAI manager. He has been an entrepreneur, investor and government advisor for early stages financing programs. He holds a molecular biology degree from Lund University in Sweden, an entrepreneurship master's degree from the same university, and an international VC certification.

LOURDES ROMERO GÓMEZ is the regional coordinator and founding member of the RNAI. Her career has a clear focus on entrepreneurial early stage financing. She holds an Industrial Engineering degree from Javeriana University and a Finance Master from Los Andes University. Her prior experience within Bolivar Group involved operative risk, treasury and strategic finance planning at Leasing Bolivar.

ANA MARÍA FIERRO is the RNAI communications professional. Ana has experience in marketing and communications for big and small enterprises with high potential. She is a member of the RNAI located at the south west region. Among different duties she is responsible for changing the mindset of Colombian angels, promoting alternative asset classes as good investment portfolio opportunities.

MONICA LOZADA is the managing professional at RNAI. Monica gives operational support in daily tasks such as logistics, contracts, budget control and reports. She also supports the director of Bavaria Foundation.

SANTIAGO REYES is a great collaborator of the RNAI. Santiago is currently studying for his master's degree at The University of Chicago Harris School of Public Policy. He has developed impact measurements of business angel investments in Colombia.

Austria

Bernard Litzka

AUSTRIA WIRTSCHAFTSSERVICE GESELLSCHAFT

The Austria Wirtschaftsservice Gesellschaft (AWS)[1] is the Austrian federal development bank for the promotion and financing of companies. The bank provides approximately €1 billion per annum in financial aid, mainly as grants, loans and guarantees. The AWS has three statutory objectives: strengthening Austrian industry; securing and creating new jobs; and strengthening the international competitiveness of Austrian companies. The AWS focuses on enterprises from the pre-seed stage to the small and medium-sized stage.

THE AUSTRIAN BUSINESS ANGEL NETWORK (ABAN)

In 1997 the AWS founded i2 Business Angels[2], a matching service for equity-seeking enterprises and potential investors. It helps state-of-the-art start-ups raise equity while at the same time promoting early

---

BERNARD LITZKA is the director of the Austrian Business Angels Network & Federation (ABAF). He has developed several patented innovations during his stay in the US and later back in Austria. He has commercialized his patents successfully to national and international strategic investors. Since 2004 he has applied his practical knowledge and experience to improve ABAF and the Business Angels Matching Service i2—www.business-angels.at—on behalf of Austria Wirtschaftsservice GmbH, the national development agency owned by the Austrian ministry of economy.

stage funding and innovative business models. In turn, it enables investors to participate in new ventures. At the international level, i2 is a founding member of the European Business Angels Network, and since 2013, it has been full member of Business Angels Europe.

i2 SERVICES AND INVESTMENT FOCUS

AWS offers numerous types of assistance through the i2 program. It facilitates potential arrangements between i2 members and early-stage start-up companies, and provides mentoring and knowledge transfer to angel networks. i2 also supports the entrepreneurial community in Austria through networking events and workshops. Moreover, it conducts research and acts as a contact point for international business angels groups. i2 focuses mainly on innovative enterprises seeking capital between €100,000 and €1 million, in the DACH and CEE regions. Desirable companies have high growth potential, a scalable business model, and a distinct competitive advantage. Targeted industry sectors include unique consumer products and services, as well as all technological sectors such as medical services, mechanical engineering, chemistry, life sciences, IT, and digital media.

ABAN PORTFOLIO
(SEPT. 2013)

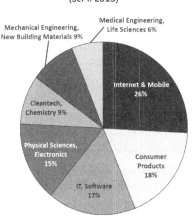

Mechanical Engineering, New Building Materials 9%

Medical Engineering, Life Sciences 6%

Internet & Mobile 26%

Cleantech, Chemistry 9%

Physical Sciences, Electronics 15%

Consumer Products 18%

IT, Software 17%

SCREENING PROCEDURE

i2 receives approximately 500 requests annually, from which it selects about 60. Proposals are required to meet strict criteria and are screened by an experienced i2 team to ensure quality standards. The i2 team verifies the details and assumptions stated in proposals. Thereafter i2 prepares an investment proposal and offers it to the business angel network. After all parties have agreed to conditions and a deal has been closed, the funding process begins. Funders then have access to the network of valuable public funding and co-financing instruments of AWS.

I2 TRACK RECORD

Apart from its 230 i2 angel members, ABAN is the connector for 65 strategic partners, including incubators, venture capital organizations, banks, consultants and lawyer offices. Since its founding in 1997, member angels have invested in over 105 start-up companies with an overall transaction volume of approximately €17 million. Currently 30 percent of the enterprises listed on ABAN find a suitable angel. In 2013, 18 out of 60 start-up companies struck a deal with an angel. For the first six months of 2014, 14 entrepreneurs were able to do so. These angels invested amounts ranging from €40,000 to €800,000, with an average of €156,000.

ALTERNATIVE FINANCING AND EQUITY

The matching service provided by ABAN is embedded in a wide range of AWS services and activities. The AWS Gründerfonds[3] is an independent venture capital fund for innovative and fast-growing enterprises with investment sizes ranging from €100,000 to €3 million. The AWS Business Angels Fonds is a financial instrument for private investors with a proven track record. The fund offers equity-in-trust to invest in start-up enterprises, doubling the initial private investment. With the AWS Double Equity Credit program, the AWS acts as a guarantor for commercial banks and takes over 80 percent of the guarantee. Since the beginning of July 2014, i2 also provides and maintains the AWS Equity Finder,[4] a free of charge, open access platform to connect seed, early stage, and SME companies with potential investors.

Endnotes

[1] http://www.awsg.at/deq.
[2] http://www.business-angels.at.
[3] http://www.gruenderfonds.at.
[4] http://www.equityfinder.at.

Finland

Jan D. Oker-Blom

Angel investing is probably almost as old as trade. In Finland people started supporting each other's businesses as soon as they had formed their first communities and built their first ships. The term "business angel" is young, however, and was adopted in the early 21st century in line with the US model. A substantial advantage of Finland's angel ecosystem is its open taxation regulations, which make it easy to find potential angels and grow networks. Tax information is publicly available. At the end of the tax year, people know who has sold a company and how much was earned. Bigger events are covered in the news media.

The first angel community and network was set up with the aid of the Finnish Independence Fund, Sitra. (Sitra is a state-owned but independently operated fund with the mission of supporting Finnish society, for example by investing in areas of national importance.) The network and activity grew and transformed, finally becoming a private association called Finnish Business Angels Network (FIBAN).

JAN D. OKER-BLOM is the Managing Director of the Finnish Business Angels Network, a nonprofit network. He worked as the Financing Adviser and the Corporate Account Manager at Aktia Bank Plc. Since founding ASAN Security Technologies, he has had a strong interest in entrepreneurship and innovative start-ups. He as founded Oker-Blom Ltd (a holding company), Pakuovelle.com (a car rental business) and Pikkujuttu Ltd (a renovating firm, pikkujuttu.com).

Today FIBAN is a privately funded nonprofit with over 450 members. The number of Finnish angels has been steadily growing and is expected to exceed 500 in 2015. FIBAN is one of the world's largest angel networks and arranges over 100 events annually. The average invested amount and total investment are not very large, but both are growing and still relevant in proportion to GDP. According to FIBAN surveys, the current total annual sum is around €50 million. This is fairly significant given the size of the country. FIBAN's focus is on both lowering the barrier to investment by promoting syndicates, as well as increasing the chance of success by providing education and training.

FINLAND'S ENTREPRENEURIAL ECOSYSTEM

Entrepreneurship is a key interest for Finland and there are many networks, groups and other forms of support for entrepreneurs. This extensive support system is reinforced by the fact that Finnish society is very receptive towards new enterprises. Especially promising is the number of highly skilled entrepreneurs. Finland has several incubators, most of which are sustained by universities or municipalities. These institutions help with additional financing beside the relatively low fees that early stage companies and start-ups pay. Their interest is in supporting home-grown companies to create jobs and ideas.

Finland also holds annual competitions, many of which are international and well-known. These include the "(young) entrepreneur of the year" and the start-up summer award, for one of the participating companies at the accelerator "start-up sauna." There are other notable accelerators as well. One special form is called "Vigo." These are private companies that are approved by the government to work with chosen start-ups, which usually have received public financial support. The hope is that "qualifying" certain private companies will provide a certain level of accreditation and lower the risk barrier for all parties involved. Science parks in Finland are mostly part-financed by municipalities, and focus on identifying promising technological innovations in their own area.

ANGEL GROUP STRUCTURES AND ORGANIZATIONS

FIBAN is a national angel network and the only relevant group in Finland. It operates through subgroups in different parts of Finland. Having a common association for the whole country ensures extensive, high-quality deal flow, concentrated lobbying power, comprehensive statistics, and enhanced networking and learning between angels. Public organizations such as Finnvera, Tekes and Sitra are close partners of FIBAN and offer substantial direct and indirect support. FIBAN also has a number of private corporate members. These companies offer services and advice to members, and pay an annual fee to FIBAN to support its operations.

Finland has a number of crowdfunding platforms. Given the important differences between crowdfunding and angel investment, there is only a very basic level of cooperation between angels and the platforms. FIBAN members invest an average of €25,000 per company in each round, while the typical crowdfunding sum is closer to €500.

POLICIES TO PROMOTE ANGEL INVESTING

The government and FIBAN share similar views on investment principles and cooperate extensively. Their objectives differ, however, partly because the public actors focus on later-stage companies, and partly because they prefer to invest indirectly though funds and not directly in specific start-ups. Anyone who invests in a designated start-up can deduct 50 percent of the investment from their capital gain income. This incentive is set to expire at the end of 2015, though there is hope that it will be prolonged as there was substantial discussions during the 2015 elections on the economic role of start-ups. FIBAN's policy has been to support measures that make it easier for entrepreneurs and private investors to operate, rather than ask for more tax breaks. The main public investor is Tekes. It invests approximately €20 million annually in early stage funds and supports start-ups with hundreds of millions in loans and grants. An extension of the angel tax incentive would be extremely beneficial. It is also hoped that Tekes will be able to actively invest in start-ups. In general, diminishing bureaucratic thresholds is more important than more tax breaks.

ANGEL INVESTMENT TRENDS

The general trend in Finland is positive and the amount of angel investing is expected to increase over the next few years. Angel investing will also become more lucrative and have a pronounced effect on Finland's economic growth.

Switzerland

Brigitte Baumann

OVERVIEW

Switzerland is a country with a vibrant entrepreneurial and investor community. It has a well-functioning entrepreneurial ecosystem and is one of the world leaders in innovation. Apart from a slight dip in 2008 due to the global financial crisis, the annual number of new ventures reported in the Swiss Start-up Monitor has risen each year since 2005.[1] Financing figures are also respectable, with 90 angel rounds worth CHF415.3 million taking place in 2013. This was up from 61 rounds worth CHF316 million in 2012.

In 2013, 20 start-ups accounted for CHF340 million (82 percent of the total) and in 2012 they accounted for CHF300 million (95 percent of the total). The number of financing rounds higher than CHF2 million has doubled from 15 in 2012 to 30 in 2013. The majority of financed companies were in the early stage (45 received CHF121.8 million), followed by late stage (30 received CHF290.9 million) and seed stage (15 received CHF2.6 million). Life science is the preferred sector with

BRIGITTE BAUMANN is a business angel and the founder and CEO of Go Beyond Investing, which offers training, coaching, practical investing sessions and syndication for angel investors. Its clients are individuals, groups and corporations and it is active in France, UK, Switzerland and Malta. She is a past president of the European Business Angels Network (EBAN). She received the European Business Angel of the Year in 2015.

biotech absorbing CHF185 million and medtech, CHF91 million. Information and communication technology was also popular (CHF92 million), as was cleantech which rose from CHF2 million in 2012 to CHF 30 million in 2013.[2]

With respect to geographic area, Zürich leads in number of financing rounds, sums invested and start-ups supported. It is followed by Vaud and Geneva. The main reason behind this is the location of Switzerland's two main Universities, ETH in Zürich (Eidgenössische Technische Hochschule Zürich) and EPFL in Lausanne (École Polytechnique Fédérale de Lausanne). In 2013, Zürich registered 35 rounds of investment, Vaud 18 and Geneva 9, 64 percent of which took place in German-speaking Switzerland. The respective sums were CHF114.2 million in Zürich, CHF89.7 million in Vaud and CHF64.8 million in Geneva. German-speaking Switzerland accounts for 60 percent of the total amount invested.[3]

ENTREPRENEURIAL ECOSYSTEM

Switzerland's high level of innovation is supported by an extensive entrepreneurial ecosystem. This includes accelerator programs, incubators, and the two aforementioned universities, ETH and EPFL. A particularly important role is played by these two universities. In fact, 80 percent of EPFL and 88 percent of ETH spin-offs are still active, and 7 percent of EPFL and 5 percent of ETH spin-offs have been acquired. Moreover, 7.2 percent of the registered patents were from EPFL spin-offs and 5.3 percent from ETH spin-offs.[4] In order to commercialize scientific research these universities provide infrastructure, offer a local entrepreneurial community, and promote entrepreneurial activities. For example, EPFL's Enable program offers internships to accelerate the transfer of EPFL inventions to industry and reduce the risk of start-up projects. It also helps raise student awareness about the innovation processes, technology transfer and entrepreneurship.[5]

EPFL's Innogrant program offers one year salary for EPFL innovators. It was launched in 2005 with the support of Lombard Odier and has financed more than 70 teams and 45+ start-ups. These start-ups subsequently received more than CHF100 million in additional grants and equity.[6] At ETH, the Innovation and Entrepreneurship

Lab (ieLab) aims to cultivate a climate of innovation, exploration and translation. Talented young students with a flair for entrepreneurship are supervised, supported, encouraged and challenged by experienced coaches (who are successful serial entrepreneurs themselves) on their way to realizing their entrepreneurial goals.[7] ETH also offers Pioneer Fellowships for individuals or groups of individuals who are independently developing highly innovative products or services to be exploited commercially and/or for the benefit of society.[8]

ACCELERATORS AND INCUBATORS

Startup Weekends are 54-hour events where entrepreneurs have the opportunity to present their projects and receive feedback on how to improve their business models. Advice is provided both by fellow entrepreneurs and by panels of experts. These events take place in Zürich, Bern, Geneva, and Neuchâtel, among other cities. Venture Kick works in collaboration with Swiss universities in the field of high-tech entrepreneurship. Its goal is to help potential entrepreneurs and give them the possibility to win up to CHF130,000 in pre-seed capital. It also provides start-ups with expert advice and access to a national network of investors.

INCUBATORS

Switzerland entrepreneurs have access to over 32 incubators in cities such as Zurich, Vaud, Fribourg, Lausanne, Geneva, and Valais. The most prominent are perhaps Blue Lion (www.bluelion.ch), Fongit (www.fongit.ch), Impact Hub (http://zurich.impacthub.net), Y-PARC—Swiss Technopole (http://www.y-parc.ch), Swiss Start-Up Factory (http://swissstartupfactory.com/incubator), and Technopark Allianz (http://www.technopark.ch). The Technopark Allianz is comprised of the technopark facilities in Aargau, Lugano, Lucerne, Schlieren, Winterthur and Zurich.

PRIVATE VENTURE COMMUNITY

Swisscom Ventures is the venture capital arm of the Swisscom Group, the leading telecommunications and IT Company in Switzerland. Since 2007 Swisscom has invested in over 35 companies, mainly in the digital media, IT and telecommunications sectors which are strategically relevant to its business. In addition to the financial support, Swisscom provides expertise, technical infrastructure and marketing channels.

In 2005, Zürcher Kantonalbank launched a start-up investment program called Pionier. Since then, it has invested in more than 165 early stage companies for a total of CHF100 million. The Bank is willing to invest up to CHF15 million in seed capital per year. Its preferred investment size is CHF0.3 million to CHF1 million per company, with follow-up investments possible. Companies interested in applying for Pionier have to show a reasonable business plan in line with the conditions defined by the bank and a prototype or proof of concept. ICT is their preferred industry, although they also accept life sciences, automation, sensors, materials, and cleantech companies.

The Swiss Private Equity and Corporate Finance Association (SECA) is the representative body for Switzerland's private equity, venture capital and corporate finance industries. SECA has the objective of promoting private equity and corporate finance activities in Switzerland. Members of SECA include equity investment companies, banks, corporate finance advisors, auditing companies, management consultants, lawyers and private investors.

Startupticker.ch is an online platform that aims to increase the visibility of young Swiss companies. The news portal communicates in English, German, French and Italian and provides information on company results, innovation launches, financing, exits, support services, events and award tenders.

ANGEL COMMUNITY

There are many longstanding angel networks/platforms in Switzerland. Go Beyond Investing (GBI) is a leading European and US angel platform/community that enables individuals to access angel investing as an asset class through its unique platform, tools, training and expert angels. GBI works with individual investors, family offices, professional groups and corporations. Its team is comprised of seasoned entrepreneurs and general managers who are now active business angels. GBI allows smaller investors to syndicate and therefore participate in any investment opportunity. It also provides investor training to learn investment best practices. The amount of investment per company ranges from CHF50,000 to CHF1 million, including follow-on rounds.[9]

Business Angels Switzerland (BAS) is an association providing young entrepreneurs with the opportunity to present their projects to seasoned investors and successful entrepreneurs, and obtain financing and/or coaching. Their 76 members are split in two sections: Zürich for Swiss-German individuals and Lausanne for Suisse Romande individuals. Entrepreneurs register on their website and a committee of experts decides which ones are invited to present at the monthly dinner meetings. Each investor decides individually if they want to invest and the start-ups must be willing to give shareholders board seats. Most investments are between CHF100,000 and CHF250,000.[10]

Start Angels is a non-profit association that gives angels access to investment opportunities in early stage Swiss companies. It was founded in 2000 and has 80 members experienced in different industries and positions. It acts as a platform and does not invest in start-ups itself. Start Angel members usually invest between CHF50,000 and CHF200,000. In the case of co-investments the total amount raised may amount to CHF1 million to CHF2 million.[11] B-to-V is a venture capital firm and investor network that invests in highly scalable tech companies. After successfully passing a screening process, companies are presented to the investor network through video meetings, one-on-one meetings or investor talks. Eighty percent of their investment is in Germany, Austria and Switzerland, with the remaining 20 percent in the rest of the world. After the initial financing, B-to-V provides companies with support during periods of follow-on financing, growth and exit.[12]

Verve Capital Partners is a Swiss company dedicated to the development and implementation of innovative financing concepts. In 2010 it launched Investiere, a European online start-up investment platform for private investors. It allows them to examine pre-selected investment proposals and invest in the start-ups of their choice through a standardized online investment process. The Investiere community is comprised of close to 1,000 investors, serial entrepreneurs, start-up enthusiasts, industry specialist, and academics, among others. The most common investment is between CHF25,000 and CHF250,000.[13]

GOVERNMENT PROGRAMS TO PROMOTE ANGEL INVESTING

The Commission for Technology and Innovation (CTI) is the federal innovation promotion agency responsible for encouraging science-based innovation in Switzerland by providing financing, professional advice and networks.[14] Its goal is to improve the competitiveness of Swiss business in general and SMEs in particular. CTI supports high tech companies through four programs that ease the transition from R&D to business development. CTI Entrepreneurship provided training and education modules for business founders on business ideas, concepts, creation and development. It is active at almost all universities, technical colleges and technoparks. CTI Label is a coaching program for business founders and young entrepreneurs. The coaching is based on a structured, four-phase process. Start-up companies are given an initial assessment of their business plan (phase one and two). Once accepted into the CTI Start-up program the company is assigned a professional business coach (phase three). CTI coaches have a proven track record in growing start-up companies and are able to draw on a wide network of business contacts. They support the company for up to two years and stay in regular contact with them. In parallel, workshops are offered to give companies a specific boost in fields such as intellectual property rights, financing, business modeling, and sales. The process culminates with the award of the CTI Startup label. This award can be a real asset when it comes to securing future financing from the market. CTI also provides "post label support" for another three years if needed and keeps the companies in its network. CTI Project Support R&D offers financial support for application-oriented research and development projects usually done in education institutions in partnership with the start-ups. Lastly, CTI Invest is a platform for business financing through angels and national and international venture capital firms. It was founded as a private association in May 2003 and association members include over 50 angels, venture capital firms and risk capital firms. Its members are drawn from both Switzerland and other countries.

PROGNOSIS

Switzerland is a good place for an angel investor because it has many of the critical components of a strong entrepreneurial/investor ecosystem: attractive conditions for entrepreneurs to start and grow a company;

simple and good tax conditions for angel investors; strong IP; well informed professional service providers; and supportive government policies and programs. Angel investing should develop further in the wake of two new movements. First, CTI has started to support programs to grow the number of angels by providing angel investor education and sharing best practices. Second, local corporations are getting more involved in the ecosystem. Both of these bode well for the growth of the Swiss angel community.

Endnotes

[1] Swiss Start-up Monitor Report 2013.

[2] Ibid.

[3] Ibid.

[4] Ibid.

[5] http://enable.epfl.ch/.

[6] http://vpiv.epfl.ch/innogrants.

[7] https://www.ethz.ch/en/industry-and-society/innovation-and-setting-up-companies/ielab.html.

[8] http://www.pioneerfellowships.ethz.ch.

[9] https://go-beyond.biz/.

[10] http://www.businessangels.ch/index.

[11] http://en.startangels.ch/.

[12] http://www.b-to-v.com/.

[13] https://www.investiere.ch/

[14] http://www.kti.admin.ch

Over the Horizon

The Editors

Chinese culture is 4,000 years old, the United States is more than 200 years old, venture capital as an organized segment of private equity is 60 years old, and angel investing in an organized form is barely 20 years old. Enormous, enduring economic value has been created by each of these disparate entities, wealth that has transformed lives and livelihoods. Yet we still know so little about which common denominators are responsible for success. Central questions remain unanswered. What enables some economies, or regions within economies, to suddenly create more firms, attract more capital and produce bursts of inventions? What combination of formal and informal practices sparks the innovation that so many governments seek? Is it possible for one nation to transplant successful entrepreneurship from another?

Angel investors who play pivotal roles at make-or-break moments in the life of an enterprise are an invaluable resource to begin the process of answering those questions. This is why we were intrigued to see whether we could examine angel investing not only from the perspective of the private sector and public sector, but also in both developed and developing economies. We put out a call for thought leaders, and we were pleased that 26 angels and professionals in the fields of investing and entrepreneurship accepted our offer to paint a picture of activities in their respective home countries.

In addition to the questions above, we asked them to venture answers to somewhat more difficult questions. How often are angel investors within your country investing across borders? And, how much do we know about the evolution of cross-border angel investing?

What we discovered in the process of publishing *Angels without Borders* has been illuminating but perhaps not surprising, as it has been repeated so often in other spheres. Ideas travel first and fastest. Technologies and techniques are usually next. Then come pioneering individuals. And last comes capital. Today there is clearly a growing common lexicon among angel investors, regardless of their location. Angel investors, even in developing nations, are clearly borrowing the techniques that their venture capital peers developed in the 1990s and early 2000s. Transnational platforms such as EBAN, ABAN, ABAF, GBAN and the like are flowering and bringing talented individuals together. Deal syndication and facilitation of exits across economies and cultures is just now visible. On balance, however, angel investing is still largely local. The old rough rule of thumb about 90 percent of angel investing being local still holds true at the national level, and at the international level.

One of the most compelling discoveries we found in the course of editing this book was the skyrocketing demand for angels. Angel investors are being sought out and cultivated in every nation we surveyed. Their nations want them to perform the functions that angels are uniquely equipped and qualified to do: serve as sophisticated, hands-on investors who are willing to patiently mentor start-ups from infancy onward to the world of venture capital and, ultimately, the realm of institutional investors, all while accepting the likelihood of significant failure rates. It is little wonder, then, that mission-driven investors and crowdfunders also want to collaborate now with angel investors. Where else could one find such a rare combination of capital, knowledge and personal commitment?

In light of these developments, let us dare to provide some predictions about the field in the coming years:

- Organized groups of angels from multiple countries targeting investments in multiple countries will flourish.
- Increasingly a geographically diverse portfolio will be seen as a plus.

- Ever larger pools of co-investment funds will be raised to enable passive investors to participate in deals created by far-flung angels, angel clubs or angel networks.
- Nonprofit groups like GBAN will provide the educational framework to accelerate cross-border deal creation.
- Emerging angel segments of untested economies will continue to learn from teams based in more experienced nations, such as New Zealand from Scotland.
- Last, affinity groups—whether university alumni, impact investors, women-led funds, or key subsectors such as health care—will be some of the first to establish trust across borders and will be a cornerstone of the global angel movement.

None of this will be self-fulfilling. Let us not take our eyes off the big picture and the work to be done. We still need better support for the entire entrepreneurial ecosystem of which angels are a small but important part. Every one of our chapter contributors wrote of the need for improved public policies, legal systems and entrepreneurial cultures to improve the yields from organized angel investing activity. Even in the most sophisticated economies, angel investors still assume huge risks and are obliged to perform extensive due diligence in tax policy, political infrastructure, or societal factors. Economies that are only now organizing their angel activities should learn from their predecessors' mistakes and define success in their own terms.

Finally, on a somewhat personal note, we want to acknowledge that this book was itself created by a microcosm of this bubbling, ever-growing ecosystem. We could not have provided this perspective without our dozens of chapter contributors, our fellow editors and Singapore publisher—a team spanning almost 30 countries and 20 languages. The group was truly diverse in culture and gender. Our editors helped to create a window into global angel activity that otherwise would never have been born. We can't wait to see what is ahead for angel investing!

Printed in the United States
By Bookmasters